Al Dente

Al Dente

Madness, Beauty and the Food of Rome

DAVID WINNER

**SIMON &
SCHUSTER**

London · New York · Sydney · Toronto · New Delhi

A CBS COMPANY

First published in Great Britain by Simon & Schuster UK Ltd, 2012
This paperback edition published by Simon & Schuster UK Ltd, 2013
A CBS Company

1 3 5 7 9 10 8 6 4 2

Simon & Schuster UK Ltd
1st Floor
222 Gray's Inn Road
London
WC1X 8HB

www.simonandschuster.co.uk

Simon & Schuster Australia, Sydney
Simon & Schuster India, New Delhi

A CIP catalogue for this book is available
from the British Library.

ISBN: 978-1-84739-442-2
ISBN: 978-0-85720-881-1 (ebook)

Typeset by Hewer Text UK Ltd, Edinburgh
Printed in the UK by CPI Group (UK) Ltd, Croydon CR0 4YY

For Mum and Dad

'Italian cuisine is delicious, and the Roman most of all.'

Giulio Andreotti, *Il Divo*

Contents

Vatican

Piazza del Popolo

Pantheon

Duodenum

Ileum

Al Dente

Cecum

Colon

Cloaca Maxima

Colosseum

Introduction

There were only eight million stories in *The Naked City*. Rome has so many more.

Wander its graffiti-ravaged, gorgeous streets, wait for a sweaty bus, watch any movie made here, and there's a faint chance of vertigo. The problem is that there's just too much Rome, extending limitlessly in every direction – especially backwards. Glowing and crumbling, sublime and sinister, this lodestone of our collective imagination cannot easily be comprehended in a single lifetime. No book can hope to squeeze it all in. The best one can do is to get a taste of the place. Hence this little volume.

It's a book about Rome and food. Yet it is not exactly a book about Roman food. Rather than write a restaurant guide, a recipe collection or an academic study, I hit on something else.

The idea came to me when my friend Boris took me to the kingdom of tiramisu (described in Chapter XIV). I'd lived in Rome for a couple of years by this time but it had never before struck me that the Roman way of food is profoundly different from ours. Romans think about and discuss the subject all the time. Yet they are not foodies in the English sense of being gourmets or conspicuous consumers. Rather, every aspect of life is – and always has been – pickled in alimentation.

1

Disturbances in the food world proved even more fascinating. The mirror to Rome's history of indulgence and pleasures lies in its no-less potent traditions of hunger, poverty and asceticism.

Since all things are connected to all other things, I found that looking at the city this way opened strange and intriguing vistas. Viewed in the correct historical perspective, a plastic cup of cold water can give us a glimpse of the cosmos. A mushroom can be made of concrete. Vegetables become erotic. A pizza restaurant provides an encounter with the Pope's personal executioner.

The end result is a portrait of the city, but a very partial and particular one. It's my view of Rome. So there's lots of history, and strange saints, and films and Jews and politics and paintings. I won't tell you anything about pasta *all'amatriciana*, but if you want to pick up information about snails or doves I think I can help.

What follows, then, is a series of linked explorations of Roman food, hunger, history and culture. Digestion turned into digression. Alimentation and alienation were more closely connected than I ever imagined. Food became my route, my passage through Rome. I hope it gives you something to chew on.

David Winner
Rome, August 2011

I: The Water

The thin November sun is fading as we push through crowds in front of the Trevi Fountain. Every day, travellers from around the world gather here to enact the solemn and significant ritual of taking silly pictures of each other. Because this is a Sunday, the tiny piazza is even more packed than usual.

'My goodness!' The square is dominated by a sheer wall of curly, creamy marble. Beneath pilasters and sculpted gods and horses, vast volumes of luminous water sparkle, splash and dance into the wide curved pool. The ideal way to approach the space is, of course, alone, at night, as Anita Ekberg did in La Dolce Vita. 'Marcello! Come here . . .!' But Michele Del Re, professor of criminal law, gives barely a glance to either the movie landmark or the showy fountains. He is headed for a more obscure treasure: a modest drinking fountain almost hidden in an alcove to the back and right. Among his many accomplishments the dark-eyed Del Re is an authority on Buddhism, the life of Casanova, links between crime and Satanism . . . and the waters of Rome.

For this water is not like water elsewhere. It first bubbled from an ancient spring named after a pagan maiden and was brought here by the right-hand man of the emperor

Augustus. The water here may, in fact, be the most remark-able on the planet. Into it is distilled the essence of the city's soul, its ancient laws, culture and philosophy. To sip this stuff will be to taste the essence of Western civilization itself.

Just as well I've brought along a little plastic cup.

One of the Bangladeshi street traders working the crowd points a plastic gun at us and fires gaudy bubbles of deter-gent and trapped air. For just a few euros we could own this remarkable device! Erm, no, I don't think we need one of those. Now our way is blocked by a group of Japanese women taking turns to pose in front of Neptune, God of the Sea. Giggling Roman teenagers, backs to the edge of the water, hurl coins over their shoulders, for luck.

Finally the professor and I reach our destination, the little drinking fountain ignored by everyone else. I take from my bag the cup I've brought for the occasion from Spizzico's pizza restaurant. I lean in and try to catch water from the fountain's two strange jets. The flow is so strong it just splashes straight out of the cup and all over me. Eventually I collect enough and carefully hand the cup to the professor. He is a small, dark man, dapper in a velvet-collared hunt-ing jacket. His large expressive eyes twinkle. He steadies himself, sips the water much as a wine taster might savour a Mouton-Rothschild. He smiles the enigmatic smile I've seen often on the face of his daughter.

'Well?' I ask.

'Well what?' he says.

'How does it *taste*?'

'Ahh. It tastes . . . of the *cosmos*!'

When I first came to live in Rome I found it a bleak and arid place. I'd lived in Amsterdam for four years and the transition was traumatic. The Dutch capital has water, water everywhere with hundreds of canals and air so moist the light glows. Rome seemed bathed mainly in heat, noise and traffic. Objectively, I noted, its huge quantities of marble, gold and dusty architecture somehow added up to 'beautiful'. Mostly, though, Rome just made me anxious.

The problem was in me. I suffer from a kind of psychic hydrophilia, an obsessive need to see or feel the presence of water, preferably in large quantities. In its absence, my soul aches; I know no peace. In London the feeling can get so bad I sometimes drive, in the middle of the night, to Little Venice or Whitestone Pond just to sit and stare at the reflection of street lights in the tiny waves. Even in my old Amsterdam apartment I used to squeeze up tight to the window just to see a microscopic patch of canal at the end of the street.

Rome has no canals. And its one great public water space, the River Tiber, can be downright nasty. In my first week, against advice, I visited the riverbank at Ostiense, expecting a café or two, sleepy river views, trees, cheery locals on bicycles. What I got was graffiti, garbage, the smell of urine . . . and an odd-looking dog with short legs and a long tail running towards me on the towpath: a rat, with a body about a foot long.

The Tiber may be one of the most famous rivers in the world. But, thanks to a history associating it with inundation and disease, Romans despise it and treat it as a criminal. Imprisoned by massive containment walls inside the city, the Tiber is trapped thirty metres below street level and has all the charm and status of a swirling sewer.

Thus it took me a while to adjust to and appreciate the fact that Rome is every bit as watery a city as Amsterdam – perhaps even more so. It's just that Rome's aquatic soul reveals itself in unexpected ways. Its water doesn't flow in great channels or hang around, dark and listless. Rather, it is deployed in tiny, potent, sparkling bursts. Rome derives delight from a wholly man-made water-form: the fountain.

In little piazzas across the city, water leaps, spurts and gushes from the mouths of stone beasts. It drips, cascades and prances in and out of marble basins and polished granite seashells. Even the city's churches and basilicas are awash: there's 'holy water' in baptismal fonts and in the little marble *acquasantiere* at every entrance. At Christmas, by custom, every Roman crib is decorated with running water. Each street in the metropolis has its little spout dispensing cool spring water all year round, 24/7, entirely for free. Romans insist the water from these *nasoni* (so-named because the taps look like big noses) is the best in the world for drinking. In the piazzas of the city centre stand hundreds of baroque marble fountains, each one 'a poem in water and stone'.

And why this panoply? Because of the ancient Romans, of course.

We think of the Pantheon or Colosseum as the structures that best exemplify ancient Rome. But they're not. The true essence of old Rome, its pulsing heart, its throbbing lymphatic system, was its astounding network of aqueducts. Indeed, the ancient city was even more watery than the modern one; its entire civilization and culture were drenched with reverence for the stuff. Romans considered water the foundation of all things. It held sway over earth and fire, 'challenged possession of the very heavens' and lay at the core of Roman laws, beliefs and sense of identity. Especially crucial was the idea of water as *res communes* – a common thing, shared freely. In the early Republic, the punishment for murder was not death but something worse: the criminal was banned from receiving water.

After all, water is the source of all life. As General Ripper told Mandrake: 'Seven tenths of this earth's surface is water. Why . . . seventy per cent of *you* is water.'

Rome, of course, was not the first ancient civilization to treat water with respect and intelligence. The Minoans had flushing toilets by 1700 BC. The first aqueduct in history was built by the Assyrians fully 400 years before Rome had the idea. But Romans took water technology to an unprecedented level, building aqueducts and other waterworks throughout their empire on a scale and with a vision unmatched until the nineteenth century. And at the very heart of this empire, in Rome itself, they made a water culture unlike any in history, extravagantly mixing the sacral and the scatological, combining pomp with purity.

For Rome's lowliest plebs there were hundreds of fountains decorated with statues and columns dispensing water for drinking, washing and cooking. Water served religious functions, made the city's gardens bloom, flushed its public latrines and filled the vast 'water theatres' in which emperors bloodily re-enacted naval battles with thousands of men fighting to the death. Most important of all was the system of public baths. These noisy, vibrant pleasure palaces, decked with gold, marble and mosaics, serviced by armies of slaves and equipped with ever-burning furnaces, lubricated the city's social, psychic, medical and sexual life. People organized their lives at baths, fought at the baths, were sent by doctors to be cured at the baths, met prostitutes at the baths, got robbed at the baths. Sometimes they even just bathed there. The entire population was addicted. By the early third century, when Emperor Caracalla built his staggeringly opulent (and still-standing) complex in the south of the city, baths had devoured vast tracts and were drinking most of the aqueduct supply.

The aqueducts kept this water-world going, bringing fresh supplies surging ceaselessly from lakes and springs up to fifty kilometres away to every part of the city. Mostly, aqueduct water flowed underground in channels cut by hand through living rock. Sometimes, it was borne aloft on fabulous curving arcades, some of which survive today in Aqueducts Park near the Cinecittà studios. Ancient contemporaries were astounded by it all. 'So great is the amount of water brought by the aqueducts that veritable rivers run through the city,' said the Greek writer Strabo. And Frontinus, one-time governor of Britain, later head of Rome's water system and author of by far the most important book on the subject, *De Aquaeducto Urbis Romae*, declared the aqueducts greater than the Pyramids of Egypt.

In total eleven great aqueducts were built by various consuls and emperors over 500 years, as well as dozens of smaller channels. (The modern city survives on six.) Inevitably the system failed to survive the collapse of Roman power. During a siege in 537 a Goth king called Vitiges tore open the main aqueducts. Subsequently Rome's population plummeted, the baths died, a cluttered new mediaeval city later grew up on the bend of the Tiber, and the countryside south of Rome, swamped by water from the stricken aqueducts, turned malarial. Eventually, though, the waters of Rome returned. Frontinus' book turned up in an abbey in 1429 and inspired the popes to recreate the spirit if not every detail of the Roman system. Sixtus V cannibalized some of the old aqueducts to create his new one, the Acqua Felice. Until the high-capacity Acqua Peschiera was finished in

1980, most of Rome's water system essentially followed the routes and principles of the Caesars. There was one crucial difference, though. Where the emperors consolidated their power and delighted the people by building baths, the popes pulled off much the same trick by commissioning artists like Bernini to create amazing fountains.

Water was many things to the Romans, but it was never mundane. In his book *The Natural History* the writer Pliny the Elder, who died in the volcanic eruption that destroyed Pompeii, described waters with phenomenal properties: waters to cure sterility or insanity, to kill or burn, to aid memory or produce forgetfulness. There was water to cause laughter and weeping, foretell the future, even to cure love.

Perhaps that's why I'm here today. Years ago I was keen on the professor's daughter. She spoke often about her illustrious dad, but I got to meet him only last summer at a sweltering summer dinner at his book-lined house at the foot of Monte Mario. We ate in the garden, arms and faces smeared with citronella to ward off mosquitoes. We had a priest, a political journalist and about a thousand cicadas for company and, late in the evening, Michele began to share some thoughts on his latest research into esoteric aspects of Rome's water system.

Why, he'd been wondering, did so many ancient cultures believe that water carried the essence of 'the feminine principle'? How had this idea soaked through all subsequent thought and language? As he talked, he drew a sequence of letters, pictograms and hieroglyphs from various languages, including Chinese, ancient Egyptian and even the mysterious script of the vanished Etruscans. He showed us how each character was a symbolic wave, the sequence becoming ever more stylized until it culminated in the Latin letter 'M'.

'See how similar these characters are? In each language, this shape represents water, and in each case it is also part of the most important word in the language: "mother". In Latin, we have *mater*. In Italian it is *mamma*. Now look at these in English . . .' On his paper he wrote two more words: *memory* and *mummy*. 'See how many *waves* are here. These words are almost *made* of water!' We talked until late that night, and he offered to guide me to the heart of Rome's watery mysteries. Some weeks later it was clear that a plan had emerged. Michele had decided to introduce me to the oldest virgin in the city.

Thus, early this morning, I found myself standing with him on a Renaissance balcony gazing down onto one of the least-known but most sublime sights of Rome: the sunken garden of the Villa Giulia. Calm and almost infinitely beautiful, it's also a place where cross-currents of the past seem to swirl suddenly into a riptide and gently drag you way out of your depth. For the last century, the villa has housed the world's greatest collection of Etruscan artefacts. That's several hundred evocative years of prehistory for starters. But there's more, for this is where antiquity and modernity meet and fuse in a mist of unlikely sensuality.

The villa was built by Pope Julius III, the last of a line of great Renaissance popes. Legendary aesthete and patron of the arts, he had scandalized the city by making his seventeen-year-old boyfriend a cardinal. In 1550, wanting something nice for his lovely new home, Julius commanded a small hole to be cut in the fabled and recently rediscovered Aqua Virgo, by then known by its Italian name, Acqua Vergine. It was like cutting a hole in time itself.

When it was built back in 19 BC, the Virgo had been Rome's fourth and newest aqueduct. Constructed and paid for by Marcus Agrippa, second-most powerful man in the world after his friend the Emperor Augustus, it was named after the young girl who revealed its source waters to some thirsty soldiers. Later the Virgo would be endlessly celebrated for its taste, but Agrippa wanted its water for his fancy new baths complex on the Field of Mars (or Campo Marzio), built right next door to one of his other new ventures, a mega-temple called the Pantheon. Even then, the Virgo was an engineering marvel. For most of its twenty-one kilometres it ran underground. Powered by gravity, water in the channel dropped precisely thirty-two centimetres per kilometre – just enough to keep it flowing at perfect speed. The structure was also destined to be the only aqueduct in the city to survive everything that history would throw at it. It came virtually unscathed through the Fall and multiple destructions of Rome, through the Dark Ages, even through the systematic mediaeval plunder of classical sites for building materials.

. . . And now the old girl was poised for a comeback. Pope Julius decided to welcome her to the edge of Rome with a *nymphaeum*, a water shrine in the ancient manner, yet more spectacular than any antiquity had seen. The Florentine architect Bartolomeo Ammanati was commissioned and duly delivered a cool erotic masterpiece: the Fontana dell'Acqua Vergine. Old water now gurgled through marble grottoes to a pond full of lilies and goldfish guarded by bare-breasted nymphs. Here, the Pope spent long summer days eating picnics under the gaze of Neptune and river gods.

Today the *nymphaeum* looks wonderful. But the symbolism is making my head spin. Why, at the height of the

Counter Reformation, with all Europe ripped by war over competing interpretations of Christianity . . . Why, in such a context, would a pope, even a pope partial to the shagging of teenage boys, dabble so shamelessly with the paganism of antiquity? Michele has an answer: during the Renaissance, knowledge of the ancient became culturally crucial. And Julius was nothing if not a deeply cultured pope. 'This place is one of the important places where the old Greek and Roman tradition re-emerges. They started to re-use the old gods.' Even so, he's tickled by the sheer cheery idolatry of the place: 'Look at all the stuff about Neptune! And look at the *style* of this place! Remember: a *nymphaeum* is a home of the nymphs! That makes it even more pagan!'

This is just the first stop on Michele's ambitious mystery tour. He plans to reveal the secrets of Rome's water by showing me *all* the fabulous fountains now driven by Virgo water. We will end, where the aqueduct now ends (and where this chapter began) at the Trevi – the most famous of them all.

Academic books on Rome's water can be desperately dry and encrusted with arcane detail on masonry and piping techniques, cubic capacities, *castella* and *fistula* stamps. As befits a man who travels the world studying religious ritual, Michele is much more fun and tirelessly enthusiastic, his thoughts turning effortlessly to universal questions of spirituality and belief. 'Every stone in Rome has a story,' he declares, and he seems to know most of them.

He explains: 'The central idea of the Romans was "*aquas disjunco, populus conjunct*" – "divide the waters to unite the people". It was very marvellous, and it explains why the enemies of Rome did not resist longer than they did. Every Roman emperor would enact this principle. When they arrived in a little town, say, in Africa, the first thing they did was build an aqueduct for the town. The water was a *bene comune*, something for all of the people. Even slaves had the right to the air and to the water. It is an extremely modern concept. Only now do we say again that water is a common good.'

We head through the Villa Borghese, all golden, dripping dead leaves and crunchy gravel, to marvel at the Virgo-fuelled fountains of the Piazza del Popolo ('the most perfect square of the world, like a symphony by Beethoven!'). Here, everything – the fountains, the statues, even the trident-shaped layout of the roads leading out of the square between legendary twin churches – *everything* is dedicated to Neptune, a god with whom Romans were not, tradition-ally, on good terms. 'Oh yes, and over there, under that walnut tree, is where the Devil lives.' What? 'Oh yes! He is imprisoned under the roots of the tree . . . according to the legend!'

As we walk on towards more treasures, Michele reminds me that Rome was founded on hills *near* its river rather than *on* it. Much flowed from this. Although Tiber water was fit to drink, the local volcanic landscape had plenty of accessible natural springs and wells and the earliest Romans preferred water from these sources. The habit persisted, as did the first associations with spiritual-ity and health. In the Roman mind and language, rivers and the sea were male, but springs, each of which had its own personality, were feminine and nurturing. To be bathed in their waters was to be purified, and this puri-fication always implied symbolic rebirth (the idea later melded easily with Jewish rituals of purification to create Christian baptism).

We head on via the dry Fountain of the Cannonball (fired in a whimsical moment by Queen Christina of Sweden, apparently) and reach the Barcaccia, Bernini's gorgeous boat-shaped fountain at the Spanish Steps. It's just under the window of the room where the poet John Keats, thinking Rome to be a supremely healthy city, came to die of consumption. Now, Michele is keen to show me equally magnificent fountains in the Piazza Colonna, the Piazza Navona, the Via del Babuino, the square beside the Pantheon ... But I protest. I already know all these fountains. And I know they're all magnificent! And now I know where their water comes from, too ... So why not let's go and actually drink some of the stuff? He looks disappointed, but only for a moment. 'You won't be disappointed,' he says. 'Vergine water is fantastic!'

This has been a core belief among Romans for centuries. The emperor Nero preferred his water to be first boiled, then poured into a glass and cooled in snow, but he was mad. Most Romans liked their water *running*. This idea persists. For most of the twentieth century, Roman housewives instinctively preferred water to drip from their kitchen taps, as if something terrible would happen in the heart of their home if the tap stopped. Roman pride in the ancient waters still sells. Not much except the name links the popular modern bottled brand called Claudia ('the water of the Gods') with the most important of the ancient aqueducts, the Aqua Claudia, built by the emperor Claudius. The aqueduct delivered water from the *east*; the water in the bottles comes from *north*. But who cares? According to the label, this water 'has always been appreciated by whoever knows how to enjoy life. Its unmistakable taste has tickled the palate and the spirit of the Romans for centuries'.

Then there's Egeria, named after the water nymph who lived by a spring south of the city and gave Rome its first legal code. According to legend, Numa Pompilius, Rome's second king, fell in love with her. She then taught him to be wise and guided him in every detail in his lawmaking. The king died, as mortals do, but Egeria lived on, adapting to each new age. In Republican Rome she was associated with fecundity and childbirth. Later, as Rome fell under Greek cultural influence, she became a Muse. An ancient *nymphaeum* in her name exists in the Caffarella Park and she dwells now in green plastic bottles, manifesting in both *naturale* (still) and *frizzante* (fizzy) guises. Apparently she's terrific for digestion.

To the Ancient Roman palate, the best drinking water was 'cool and wholesome': transparent, clean, odourless, and unflavoured. Latin writers debated the merits and potential health benefits of 'light' water. Groundwater, from springs or brought by aqueduct, was preferred to water from rivers. Water stored in cisterns was known to spoil, and stagnant surface water was simply beneath contempt. Pliny reckoned the two aqueducts with the nicest waters were the Aqua Marcia, finished in 140 BC, and the Virgo. Water from the Virgo was cool, soft and pure. Pliny described it as 'the most celebrated water throughout the whole world, and the one to which our city gives the palm for coolness and salubrity'. Restored in the nineteenth century as the Acqua Pia Antica Marcia, it now flows into the city in two channels running side by side, the Old and the New. Since the sixteenth century Romans have called it 'Trevi Water' and all the best people drank it. In the days of the Grand Tour English visitors insisted on making tea with Trevi Water; Michelangelo kept five jars of the stuff in his cellar.

And ... Here we are, at last, right beside the Trevi Fountain. It's turning chilly, but this water tastes of the cosmos!

Now it's my turn to sip. I close my eyes, put the cup to my lips. And it's ... Well, it's, um ... A bit cold, obviously – which is quite nice. And, er ... smooth, as in not fizzy. And it's a bit, well ... *tasteless*, actually. I'm not sure how to put this. 'When you say "cosmos", do you mean the big thing with planets, or the New York football team from the 1970s?' Michele gives me his mock not-angry-just-*very*-disappointed look then smiles: 'When we drink water, it is always a union with the cosmic presence of the water. It gives us a different but essential knowledge, not only with our brain but also our body. To drink water is to know again from our ego to the world. We don't just connect we *participate*. We enter the world, and the cosmos, which is born from the water.'

No Roman – not Marcus Agrippa, nor any of the popes or Michelangelo, or even the Emperor Claudius himself – could have put it more nicely.

II: The Feast

'You're grotesque. Grotesque and disgusting! Why do you eat if you're not hungry? It's ridiculous!

La Grande Bouffe

The seed for the most scabrous, disturbing but oddly beautiful film ever made by Romans about food was planted in an eatery far, far away. One Sunday in the early seventies the anarchic film-maker Marco Ferreri, mischievous genius and fearless fatty, found himself, as he often did, in Paris with a group of friends, including the actor Ugo Tognazzi. They decided on lunch at Prunier near the Arc de Triomphe and enjoyed a generously portioned meal that lasted well into the afternoon. When the time came to leave, most of the men were so stuffed they could barely move, but Ferreri had a more pressing worry: 'What are we going to eat *tonight*?' Someone suggested pasta, he agreed and they all staggered back to a friend's apartment where Tognazzi, a renowned chef as well as one of Italy's best-loved romantic-comedy performers, started cooking immediately. They carried on eating late into the night. Next day, Ferreri woke in a state of excitement. 'What do you think about making a movie about what we did yesterday?' he asked. 'We already wrote the script! Four people lock themselves up somewhere to eat. They eat and fuck to death! It's called *La Grande Bouffe*!' He rushed to his producer's that afternoon. By evening the contract was signed.

Of all Rome's post-war cinematic geniuses, the darkly subversive Ferreri is the most neglected but the most intriguing on the subject of food. An unhappy child, he grew up in Milan and got a job in a drinks factory where he was allowed to make short promotional films. In the late forties, as the post-war film boom got under way, he moved to Rome and hung out with other aspiring writers, actors and directors at the Trattoria Otello on Via della Croce (it's still going strong). Friends of the time remembered him as a Milanese boy with an 'Ancient Roman mask'. In photographs he resembles a bizarre combination of cherub, gargoyle and emperor, with mesmeric eyes set in a plump face framed by a Solzhenitsyn beard. He rarely discussed his childhood except in terms of a troubled relationship with his mother (who was also large) and amused his friends by eating huge quantities of spaghetti, meat and cakes followed by equally large helpings of salad ('so as not to get fat'). He had, said one acquaintance, 'blue crying eyes and a bitter smile ready to turn into a complaint about an overcooked steak or a salad not properly dressed'.

Ferreri tried acting and production and made plenty of friends. But he never quite fitted into a Roman film world still dominated by the spirit of neo-realism. Realism didn't interest Ferreri; he preferred the fantastical and darkly allegorical. By the late fifties, when he briefly edited a film-theory magazine, Rome's economy and mood were shifting and the city stood on the brink of its filmic golden age. American money was flooding into the 'Hollywood on the Tiber' at Cinecittà. The 'sword 'n' sandal' boom was under way and Fellini and Antonioni were limbering up for their medium-altering masterpieces *La Dolce Vita* and *L'Avventura*. Rome was a heady place to be a young film-maker. So Ferreri left town. His move from the city of 'the sweet life' to the Spain of Franco and Fascism proved surprisingly liberating. Ferreri's imagination meshed with ancient Spanish traditions of the grotesque and fantastical and, in Barcelona, he hooked up with Rafael Azcona, a Buñuelist scriptwriter, who became a lifelong friend. Azcona and Ferreri would work together on seventeen films, including *La Grande Bouffe*. They made three small movies together in Spain before Ferreri returned to Rome in 1961 to direct the 'adultery' section of a portmanteau film called *Italians in Love*.

Now Ferreri was properly on his way. Over the next few years he made increasingly wild black comedies satirizing bourgeois society and hinting at his more anarchic and primal obsessions. Most of his films revolve around food, sex and death. His view of relationships between men and women is bleak, and he believes civilization is at the point of collapse. One Italian critic praised him for his 'humour, poetry, cruelty and love'. Another denounced his 'insolence, repugnance and misogyny'.

Either way, few directors ever deployed such peculiar recurring motifs. Dogs, for example, often appear in Ferreri movies, representing the animal side of humanity and usually linked with death. The seaside is a place of murder and escape. Ferreri often shows us the dome of St Peter's, sometimes in ruins. He also alludes to Ancient Rome, generally as an emblem of decay, excess and false memory. As we shall see, this notion of overeating as an evocation of imperial Rome would be a subtext in *La Grande Bouffe*. This was spelled out more explicitly in *Bye Bye Monkey*, where the apocalyptic climax takes place in a kitschy 'Waxwork Museum of Ancient Rome'. The owner fraudulently claims to be saving civilization from decadence and ruin. He sexually exploits the young while reciting speeches from Shakespeare's *Julius Caesar*, and models himself on the emperor Nero. After an upsetting scene involving rats and a pet monkey, the entire worthless edifice is burned to the ground.

Ferreri was also in the habit of playing one film against another. In *La Grande Bouffe*, for example, four men die while one woman survives. In the earlier *The Harem* it was the other way around. The central character is a young architect called Margherita (like the Neapolitan queen and the simple pizza which bears her name). Margherita is the epitome of a liberated Italian New Woman of the sixties. Beautiful and strong, she avoids committing herself to any of the four men in her life, but eventually they turn on her. First they force her to make them a meal, then they insult her cooking skills and throw spaghetti in her face. Finally, they kill her by pushing her off a cliff. (According to Carroll Baker, who played her, this was originally planned as a comedy but Ferreri lost his nerve and played it straight.)

Meanwhile, Ferreri was building relationships with the world-class actors who would appear in *La Grande Bouffe*. The key performer was chocolate-voiced Ugo Tognazzi, a close friend with whom he first worked in 1963. Previously, Tognazzi was known as the suave, warm-hearted star of light romantic comedies and TV variety shows. For *Queen Bee*, Ferreri made him a middle-aged bachelor, working in sight of the Vatican, who marries an innocent-seeming girl from a respectable family. She proceeds to emasculate and eventually kill him with sex. The following year, in *Ape Woman*, Ferreri cast Tognazzi again, this time as a bully who exploits an unusually hairy woman by putting her in a freak show, causes her death, then falls in love with her corpse. In *The Audience* (1972) Tognazzi plays a policeman who helps destroy an innocent fool who wants to meet the Pope. Tognazzi does not only steal the man's wife: he even takes over his kitchen, too.

In the mid-sixties the great Marcello Mastroianni joined the troupe. 'Ferreri is a director who leaves space for the actor,' Mastroianni later wrote in his autobiography, *I Remember, Yes, I Remember*. 'For me he has a great quality: he says little. My relationship with him is made of very long silences, which are absolutely refreshing. But we understand each other in these silences. I like his vision of the world, of things, of people, always seeing further than one's nose. He's original. I like him very much also as a friend. He's affectionate.' In *The Man with Five Balls*, the first of their five films together, Mastroianni plays a businessman with an absurd obsession: trying to figure out the point at which balloons burst. When his wife leaves him he starts sharing his meals with his St Bernard dog. One evening he realizes he will never solve his balloon problem, so he jumps through the window to his death and lands by chance on the car of passing Ugo Tognazzi. Tognazzi is very upset about this – because his car is ruined. Upstairs, the dog finishes Mastroianni's dinner. In *Liza* Mastroianni lives alone on an island with a dog until Catherine Deneuve turns up on a yacht. Deneuve first kills the dog then becomes the dog. She wears its collar, sits in a corner and begs for scraps of food. Neither man nor woman can escape this horrible relationship, so they starve to death. Back in the big city, Mastroianni's abandoned wife and daughter assuage their pain by gorging themselves.

Ferreri's critical breakthrough came in 1969, with *Dillinger is Dead*, thanks in part to an astonishing freewheeling performance by another great actor, Michel Piccoli, as the terminally bored owner of a gas-mask factory in Rome's Fascist-built suburb, EUR. Piccoli comes home to find his wife – Anita Pallenberg – in bed with a migraine. He brings her pills and a hot-water bottle then spends a whimsical night cooking, eating, watching home movies and seducing the maid (by the simple ploy of feeding her slices of water melon). In the kitchen he finds an old revolver, which he cleans with olive oil, paints red with white polka dots and uses to mime suicide. At dawn he goes to the bedroom, covers Pallenberg with pillows and calmly shoots her three times in the head. He then drives from Rome to the sea and gets a job as a cook on a yacht bound for Tahiti. The film, made in the wake of the 1968 'revolution', caused a scandal. According to Piccoli, who is on screen continually, improvising with almost no dialogue, it was about the desperation of a solitary man who has 'made it' but 'is caught between despair, suicide, insomnia and dream'.

Ferreri could act a bit himself, too, and often made cameo appearances in friends' films and his own. In *Pigsty*, Pasolini's deeply weird parable of Fascism, Ferreri appears as an industrialist. Probably his strangest performance was as a corpse (a victim of a mysterious global plague) in his own film *Seed of Man*. Like *Bye Bye Monkey*, this film features a museum to a vanished civilization – but this time it's ours. Exhibits include a fridge, a television, a parmesan cheese and a pile of Cirio tinned tomatoes. This, by the way, is the first film in which Ferreri dabbled with cannibalism. A wife kills her husband's lover on a beach then serves one of the legs, cooked very rare. 'This is good meat,' says the husband. 'What is it?' 'Just enjoy,' says the wife, and gives him a kiss. (In the later *Meat*, a man in another beach house kills his lover, puts her in the fridge and eats her one slice at a time, and in *How Good the Whites Are* a group of European aid-workers bringing charity to the Sahel get eaten by locals, though only after a night of wild sex.)

By the early seventies, as film-writer R. T. Witcombe said, Ferreri had become obsessed with the idea that modern society was 'in its death-throes, gorging, consuming itself to extinction'. This was to be the principal theme of *La Grande Bouffe*. But the film also reflects Ferreri's own problematic relationship with food. Some time before shooting started he spent several weeks in a Swiss overeating clinic. He also visited a clinic in Brittany that specialized in extreme-slimming diets based on vegetables and infusions. Such treatments never worked, though, because Ferreri always made sure to eat lots of sweets, cream and chocolate cakes.

Thus we come at last to *La Grande Bouffe* (known in Italian as *La Grande Abuffata* and in English as *Blow Out*). This extraor-dinary film follows four successful middle-aged friends as they get together for a 'gastronomic seminar' in a suburban Paris villa. It's often considered a French movie but its heart is pure old Rome. The villa looks like the one on the hill in *Psycho*, but what's most striking is the daring displayed by Ferreri's actors. It's hard to picture modern stars being as fearless or as free as Mastroianni, Tognazzi, Piccoli and Philippe Noiret (appearing in his first Ferreri film, and later loved for his performances for other directors in *Cinema*

Paradiso and *Il Postino*). Each man plays a character named after himself. Marcello is an airline pilot, Ugo a chef, Michel a TV executive, Philippe a breast-obsessed diabetic judge. They plan to eat themselves to death, but they never say why.

On their first day together terrifying quantities of food arrive in two large vans. One, refrigerated, is full of prime meat. The other overflows with vegetables, fruit, groceries and fish. We see at least half a dozen whole pigs and hear an inventory: ten dozen guinea-hens 'fed on grain and juniper', suckling pigs, three dozen young roosters, twenty dozen chickens, ten salt-marsh lambs, 'a fierce wild boar ready for all the subtlest marinades', 'two superb soft-eyed deer', flesh redolent of the perfume of the forest. There are oysters, too, and blood pudding, and sausages, and chocolate, and fine wines, and champagne, and cheeses, and much else besides. The garden pond and a glass tank in the kitchen are both fully stocked with live fish. Geese and pheasant wander around the house and the decaying ornamental garden. Hens get drunk on Armagnac. There's plenty of prime beef as well. 'You'll see how much fun it is to cut up,' says Ugo. Michel does a sort of pagan dance, holding aloft a cow's head and reciting the soliloquy from *Hamlet*. 'The feast begins . . .' says a grim-looking Marcello.

And so it does. Amid the faintly rotting splendour of the villa artfully stuffed with paintings and chintzy bric-a-brac, the men begin to chew, chomp, suck and drink continuously. Some of the time they sit at the dinner table or in the kitchen. Other times they recline on gold cushions like Roman emperors. There's light relief when Ugo does an uncanny impersonation of Marlon Brando in *The Godfather*. Michel puts on a leotard to perform ballet exercises at the barre, though after a few days this becomes impossible. There's plenty of sex, too, and naked women decorate the food. But three prostitutes the men hire soon leave in disgust, vomiting (a healthy response) and escaping. 'You're grotesque,' says one of the girls. 'Grotesque and disgusting! Why do you eat if you're not hungry? It's ridiculous!'

Much of the food is French, but Ugo pointedly makes a pizza, and a spectacular tagliatelle, and speaks in Italian to a pig he is spit-roasting. Marcello brings in a tortellini with cream mushrooms. (This reflected off-screen friendship: Ferreri, Tognazzi and Mastroianni often got together in Paris to eat 'Italian-style', usually with Tognazzi cooking.) When Michel, bloated with gas, takes to his bed, Ugo whips up a gigantic 'medicinal' chestnut purée and chides him in a parody of a doting mother: 'If you don't eat you won't die.' Michel, in fact, is pretty obsessed with chestnuts – a reference, presumably, to the legendary 'Ballet of the Chestnuts' (also known as the 'Borgia Orgy') which took place at the Vatican in 1501. This involved a search for chestnuts by naked prostitutes and cash prizes for the cardinals who had the most sex.

Back in the villa, the men's physical condition swiftly deteriorates. Marcello goes to the bathroom to 'freshen up' and inadvertently triggers a fountain of shit that explodes from the toilet bowl. The sight of him screaming and covered in the stuff particularly shocked Italian filmgoers. 'It's the universal deluge,' says Michel. 'The smell – we'll never be rid of it,' says Ugo mournfully.

Only one person in the house, an innocent-looking schoolteacher called Andréa (French actress Andréa Ferréol), is destined to survive this debauchery. She arrives for dinner on the second night and never leaves. Revealing prodigious appetites of her own, she is soon serenely out-eating and out-fucking all the men in the house. Ferréol was uneasy about the part but accepted because she didn't want to miss doing a film with some of Europe's biggest stars. Disturbingly, before filming, Ferreri asked her to fatten for the part. Every time she thought she'd eaten enough, Ferreri wanted more. None of the other actors put on weight. At first Andréa seems to be a sainted whore of a kind fairly common in Italian cinema. But it's not long before she reveals a darker aspect. When she and Philippe go to slaughter some turkeys in the garden, she seems disappointed to learn he has never, as a judge, sent anyone to the guillotine. She picks up his sword and, like some latter-day Mastro Titta, chops off a turkey's head. Now she becomes an angel of death, coaxing, seducing, goading and guiding the men to oblivion.

The deaths, when they finally come, are among the oddest in cinema. Fetishist Marcello, an impotent sex maniac, freezes in the seat of his beloved antique blue Bugatti, one of the few places he can get an erection. (Later we notice a dog has taken his place in the car seat.) Michel, troubled by increasingly painful and debilitating build-up of intestinal gases, eventually farts to death. There are no funerals, though. Philippe and Ugo set their friends' corpses upright in a big fridge and press on. The garden begins to fill with stray dogs. Ugo's demise is the most outrageous. As chef of the group, he's done most of the cooking. Now he produces his final masterpiece: a gigantic duck and chicken pâté in the shape of the dome of St Peter's. This, he insists is a work of poetry. 'It's shit poetry,' says Philippe, who refuses to eat it. Ugo therefore eats the whole thing on his own. By nightfall he can barely sit upright. Sweating, he reclines on a gold cushion on the kitchen table while Philippe feeds him the last pieces of the dome and Andréa, eyes filled with tears, masturbates him to a terminal climax. Ugo's orgasm and death are simultaneous. Next day, it's the turn of Philippe, a diabetic with a breast-fixation, for whom Andréa makes a 'very sweet and very good' tit-shaped blancmange. He dies in Andréa's arms as another white van full of prime meat arrives. Andréa gently pushes away his corpse and tells the delivery men to leave the meat in garden, which is now overrun by howling dogs.

Had all this been shot flamboyantly by an Argento or a Fellini, *La Grande Bouffe* would probably be so gross as to be unwatchable. But Ferreri underplays everything. His shooting style is elegant and relaxed, helped no end by Philippe Sarde's seductive, melancholy score, which Michel picks out on a piano. Mastroianni later said the atmosphere on set was like being at 'a feast or a joyful funeral'. Tognazzi recalled that he enjoyed the smell of food at first but the pleasure was soon replaced by a sense of desolation. 'The moment came when all these fragrances turned to be annoying and then nauseating.' Ferreri, he explained, 'let the cake rot by itself', filming his story chronologically, and killing off characters in the order in which his actors had to go to their next jobs. Yet each fictional death produced real anguish. 'It wasn't about acting; we lived the loneliness,' said Tognazzi. 'When it was my turn, Noiret was shocked. "Don't die," he told me. "I'm scared!"' For Piccoli, however, the experience was a delight: 'At the time Ferreri was considered a political danger, a mental danger, a sexual danger. You never heard about four men who got together to kill themselves by eating! We had fun in being the grotesque puppets of grief, in order to die in climaxing; to die with an animality, not to die of mental despair . . . Of course we had read the script, but as soon as the shoot began nobody looked at it again. We were inventing incessantly, while remaining very attentive to Ferreri, but he too was paying attention to our pranks. Ferreri had a very deep imagination. He was a man of freedom of creation and he understood that we entered into his game with a lot of pleasure.'

The film was a worldwide art-house smash hit but critics couldn't agree on a verdict. Was it a sick affront to public decency, a nihilistic joke or a satire on the bourgeoisie? The film never explains why the men want to die and nor, in subsequent interviews, did Ferreri. All he would say was that it was a 'physiological' film about 'the only tragic reality, the body'. In Tognazzi's view it was about consumerism, loss of faith and the modern existential crisis. Piccoli observed: 'Meat, food, and sex were always very prominent in Ferreri's cinema; they become rituals for killing time.'

La Grande Bouffe was the highpoint of Ferreri's career. His later films – *Tales of Ordinary Madness, Diary of a Vice* and the rest – were widely assumed to be mere attempts to shock. Critics became increasingly hostile, audiences stayed away and Ferreri died of a heart attack in 1996. More recently, though, there has been a reappraisal. A hagiographic documentary, *Marco Ferreri: The Director Who Saw the Future*, appeared in Italy in 2007, as did a book, *Marco Ferreri: A Milanese in Rome*, which included a glowing foreword by the Mayor of Rome. A forthcoming study by a feminist professor at Sapienza University may be less complimentary.

Meanwhile another critic, Maurizio Viano, had made an interesting discovery about *La Grande Bouffe*: the apparently randomly placed props in the film, especially paintings on the wall of the villa, were in fact clues suggesting, among other things, a link to the ancient 'humoural' system of the ancient Greek-Roman physician Galen. Galen worked in second century Rome and his work influenced medicine until the Renaissance. Viano explains: '[*La Grande Bouffe*] uses iconological characteristics sanctioned by centuries of woodcuts, engravings, drawings and paintings. The four temperaments originate in the four bodily fluids thought to circulate in the human body. They also correspond to the four elements: melancholic, black bile, earth; choleric, yellow bile, fire; sanguine, blood, air; and phlegmatic, phlegm, water [...] In perfect keeping with classical-mediaeval thought, [*La Grande Bouffe*] ranks the sanguine on top and the melancholic at the bottom.' Michel, for example, represents air. His 'flatulence is a textual necessity and not gratuitous provocation'. Marcello, represents fire (he loves engines) and is linked to bile and faeces.

Going a little further back, it seems pretty clear the film not only refers to but re-enacts debauches of imperial Rome. Specifically, it evokes the era when, as food historian Patrick Faas puts it, Rome – not unlike the Western materialist society Ferreri disliked in the 1970s – became the 'stomach of the world'.

Imperial Rome gorged itself on the produce of empire and slaughtered and ate so much of North Africa's wildlife that many species became extinct. The gold cushions and covers in *La Grande Bouffe* recall the third-century Emperor Elagabalus (also known as Heliogabalus) who 'covered his couches with golden coverlets' and 'abandoned himself to the grossest pleasures' [Gibbon]. In the crowded field of debauched Ancient Romans Elagabalus stands out. Just fourteen years old when he ascended the throne, he displayed an astonishing appetite for food and sex. Even when everyone in the city aspired to gastronomic excess, Elagabalus took the *biscotto*. He thought nothing of blowing three million sesterces on a single meal and ate twenty-two meat courses at a sitting (each course naturally followed by a quick time-out to 'dally' with women). Because exoticism was prized above all, Elagabalus ate camel heels, nightingale tongues, flamingo brains and pheasant heads and once served the heads of several hundred ostriches. Even his animals ate luxuriously: goose livers for the dogs, rare grapes for horses, parrots for his pet lions. Like Mastroianni's character in *La Grande Bouffe*, the emperor's appetite for food was inseparable from his obsessive sexuality, yet, as Gibbon tells us, 'the extremity of his activities were insufficient to satisfy the impotence of his passions'. Marcello in *La Grande Bouffe* sniffs panties and wears them on his head before he can have sex with the whores; Elagabalus dressed in drag to lecture the whores of Rome 'on various kinds of postures and debaucheries'. Marcello is turned on by his little blue Bugatti. Elagabalus had gold-encrusted chariots pulled by lions, tigers and elephants, and rode around naked in a wheelbarrow dragged by teams of beautiful naked women. For trips out of Rome, the young emperor travelled in a 600-wagon convoy. (One wagon for him and the rest for his 'lusty partners in depravity'.) Obviously, as in *La Grande Bouffe*, fun on this scale couldn't last. Elagabalus was murdered in a toilet by his guards who then stuffed the body into a sewer and threw it in the Tiber.

Elagabalus spent more than anyone, but his tastes were by no means unique. Alarming combinations of food, sex and death were pretty much routine. Juvenal, in one of his satires, derided those 'whose sole reason for living lies in their palate' and spent more than they could afford on the fanciest foods. Even a widely admired emperor like Claudius (builder of aqueducts, conqueror of Britain, mild-mannered hero of *I, Claudius*) regularly laid on banquets for hundreds of guests and was 'ready to eat and drink at any time or in any place'. He 'set no bounds to his libidinous intercourse with women' and enjoyed watching tortures and executions. His predecessor Tiberius once insisted on being served by naked waitresses. Caligula, Domitian and Nero were all famed for blow-outs that involved too much food, exotic sex and, often, death. Plautianus, the *consiglieri* to the emperor Septimius Severus, 'became the most sensual of men; for he would gorge himself at banquets and vomit as he ate'. His boss also 'prided himself especially on his largesse' and, for the wedding of his son Caracalla, threw a banquet featuring 'the customary cooked viands but also uncooked meat and sundry animals still alive'.

Even more intriguingly, the 'fierce wild boar' and 'suckling pigs' of *La Grande Bouffe* refer directly to the 'wild boar of immense size' and 'little suckling pigs made from pastry' of the feast in *Satyricon* by Petronius. This ancient satirical novel, written at the time of Nero, mocks the vulgarity of imperial Rome – and was a favourite of Ugo Tognazzi. The best-known section of the book describes a preposterous banquet given by a former slave called Trimalchio. This involves many different types of meat, sausages, blood-puddings, whole roast pigs, geese, chickens and fish. Trimalchio's feast, too, is heavy with the scent of death, not least because he forces his guests to attend his own (mock) funeral. The narrator comments: 'We, by this time nauseated, were ready to vomit.' In 1968, when Tognazzi heard Fellini was planning to make a film of *Satyricon*, he begged to be allowed to play Trimalchio. Fellini turned him down but Tognazzi did the part anyway, wearing outrageous make-up and an orange wig in a third-rate spoiler rushed out to reach the cinemas first. It was a Pyrrhic victory. Fellini sued, and the makers of the film were prosecuted for allowing an underage boy to appear in the fairly graphic sex scenes.

Tognazzi, best known in the English-speaking world for his performance as one of the gay nightclub owners in *La Cage aux Folles*, was a major cultural figure in Rome. He had a restless, intellectual side and often flirted with scandal. He also directed five minor films, some laden with sex. In 1978, the year of Aldo Moro's kidnap and murder, Tognazzi was reported arrested as a leader of the terrorist Red Brigades. Pictures of him being dragged from his home by police were widely circulated and believed to be authentic. In fact it was a stunt for the satirical magazine *Il Male*, and Tognazzi had eagerly cooperated. In 1983, mindful perhaps of the fun Michel Piccoli had in *La Grande Bouffe*, he played (*con brio*, as they say) the lead in *Il Petomane*, the true story of French 'fartiste' Joseph Pujol, who entertained audiences before the First World War by farting in tune to music.

Tognazzi's true passion, as he often said, was for food. In one of his autobiographical cookbooks, *L'abbuffone* (a word derived from *La Grande Abbuffata* and meaning something like 'The Feaster' or 'The Blow-Outer'), Tognazzi boasts that he knows the chefs of all the best restaurants in Europe and has cooking in his blood. 'Of course, my blood has red and white blood cells, but I think also a good percentage of tomato sauce. I'm addicted to the stove.' He often refused to appear in films unless there was a kitchen scene for him to show his cooking skills. 'I feel myself come alive when I'm in front of a pan. To my ears, lightly frying oil is the best music. I would use the fragrance of a meat sauce as aftershave . . . Proust recalled the past through any kind of object. In the same way I recall the old times through food. For example, boiled hen reminds me my grandmother.'

As we shall see in the next chapter, the culture of bulimic excess in Rome was wrecked in the end by the economic collapse of the empire and by the anorexic impulses of Christian asceticism. Eventually, though, the pendulum swung back again. The Dark Ages faded, the old books were rediscovered, and sensuality found its way back to the power centres of Rome. In 1984 Tognazzi alluded to all this in a remarkable book called *Aphrodite and Cookery*. Illustrated by erotic cartoonist Guido Crepax, it is a combination of recipes and Platonic symposium. (Ferreri later borrowed the idea for *The Banquet*, a re-enactment of Plato's *Symposium* for French TV.)

For his book, Tognazzi cooked a slap-up meal and invited along a bunch of Roman intellectuals to discuss the relationship between sexuality and alimentation. The intellectuals agreed to take part on condition of anonymity. Naturally, as Tognazzi recounts, the subject of the Borgias came up. In popular legend, Rodrigo Borgia, later Pope Alexander VI, is seen as a fantastically bad guy, along with his scary son Cesare and deadly daughter Lucrezia. At Tognazzi's symposium, however, the 'historian' speaks of the Borgia Pope with undisguised admiration, not least because of the Ballet of the Chestnuts: 'Fifty wonderful, beautiful courtesans were completely naked, picking chestnuts on their hands and knees. And these chestnuts were thrown to them by the men of the party, so the party gets hot and, at the end, rich prizes were offered to the men who had proved the greatest virility with the fifty courtesans. It was an authentic orgy which well recalls the atmosphere of the age!' Far from being a scandal, the historian went on, it was one of the highlights of the Renaissance, an era notable for its 'strenuous search for beauty and a rediscovery of classical values'. Instead of being condemned, he declared, 'Papa Borgia' should be praised for his 'high level of curiosity about sexual matters'. During the Renaissance 'humanity was reborn' and the courts and power brokers of Italy competed with each other to create wealth and beauty. It was an era of universal genius, incomparable art and tolerance. Geniuses such as Leonardo, Francesco Sforza and Isabella Gonzaga, who happened to have been born illegitimate and might have been shunned in less tolerant ages, were fully, thrillingly accepted into society. And all this brilliance was underpinned by the kind of sensuality represented by the Borgia Pope. Warming to his theme, the historian went on to praise the libertinism that spread across Europe during the Enlightenment. 'If we follow Casanova in his memoirs, we have a picture of a world in the grip of a sexual frenzy. Sexual relationships between three or four people. Orgies between aristocrats and workers, and nuns and servants!' By now most of the guests at the symposium were being swept along by his enthusiasm. Tognazzi reports: 'The liberty of spirit and reason, the exultation of this empirical analysis, all seemed to find an echo around the table and the historian opened his arms in a theatrical gesture, as if to thank his audience.' General conversation resumed and the diners started eating again. Only the anthropologist seemed unconvinced. He scratched his beard and asked: 'Are you telling us the important thing about the Enlightenment was that it . . . led to *orgies*?' The historian, no doubt, had a perfectly good answer to this, but he couldn't speak. His mouth was full.

III: The Fast

'Let her meals always leave her hungry'

Saint Jerome

He was a giant of the formative age of Christianity, a historian, biographer, translator and a friend of the Pope. And in the year 385 the man we know as Saint Jerome was run out of Rome by a food-and-sex scandal. As a young man Jerome was educated in the city but he'd been away, developing himself as a scholar and theologian. He had a reputation as a champion of austerity, but also as a vain and vituperative man whose intense friendships tended to end bitterly. (When his best friend died suddenly during a theological argument conducted by letter Jerome called him a 'multiple-headed Hydra that has ceased hissing'.) After his student days in Rome, Jerome travelled widely and wrote a biography of Paul of Thebes, the hermit who lived in the desert on nothing but dates and half loaves of bread delivered by a raven. Jerome also translated the works of Origen (the theologian said to have castrated himself in the service of God, though he probably didn't). For three years Jerome tried hermiting too, blackening his skin in the Syrian sun and fasting until his body was a bag of bones, never quite escaping the torments of lust. Back in Antioch he had himself ordained as a bishop. In Constantinople he studied under Gregory of Nazianzus. When Jerome finally returned to Rome in 381 Pope Damasus made him his secretary and persuaded him to begin his great work of translating the Hebrew and Greek scriptures into Latin. The result was the Vulgate Bible, the most important book of mediaeval Europe.

On the Aventine Hill, the Pope introduced Jerome to a circle of wealthy aristocratic ladies for whom he became a sort of Rasputin in reverse. Whereas the twentieth-century monk dominated the Empress of all the Russias in order to indulge his prodigious appetites for food and sex, Jerome psychologically dominated his circle in order to promote the strictest asceticism. It was now seventy years since Constantine had made the once-persecuted cult of Christianity the state religion and moved the imperial capital to Byzantium, rather leaving Rome high and dry. The city had lost much of its grandeur and now the remnants of its aristocracy were Christianizing. Jerome noted with satisfaction the change stealing over the city: 'the gilded capitol falls into disrepair, dust and cobwebs cover all Rome's temples [. . .] the city shakes on its foundations, and a stream of people hurries, past half-fallen shrines, to the tombs of the martyrs'. But even prominent Christians regarded Jerome's fanaticism with suspicion. He in turn dubbed them 'sham' Christians, denounced the city's clergy and stuck ever more firmly to his circle of admirers, which included Paula, a rich Christian widow with five children. Under Jerome's influence, Paula's religious devotions became ever more rigorous. She ate the simplest food, prayed constantly and slept on the floor of her mansion.

Jerome began to take a keen interest in the spiritual welfare of her daughters, too.

Rome was poised at one of its hinge moments with its old civilization about to be obliterated by a new force. Jerome was a player in this process, and helped to shape new attitudes to food and the body that were the diametric opposite of those the city had known. Where classical Graeco-Roman thinking set man at the centre of the world and treated the body with respect, Christianity's leading thinkers promulgated a new concept: the human body was inherently sinful, an object whose needs were to be feared and curbed. The normal functioning of the body was reclassified as moral crime. Jerome's views can be seen in one of his most famous letters, to one of Paula's older daughters, the teenager Eustochium. Rich food, he told her, should be avoided because it encouraged lust. Food had led to the Fall of Man because Adam 'obeyed his belly and not God'. Likewise, wine should be avoided 'like poison' for it was 'the first weapon used by demons against the young'. Many of the other holy men helping to shape the punishing new Christian asceticism of the time practised and preached fasting as part of a wider spiritual discipline. But Jerome viewed it solely as an antidote to the thing he feared most: sex. He considered virginity the ideal human state and viewed marriage as acceptable only because it created virgins. (He was also one of the founders of the idea that Mary, mother of Jesus, was a perpetual virgin, insisting that she and Joseph had not been wife and husband and that Jesus had cousins rather than siblings. To back up these views and, as it turned out, cement them into Christian culture, he mistranslated the prophecy in Isaiah (Isaiah 7:14) 'behold a virgin [Hebrew *alma*] shall conceive and bear a son'. As Miri

Rubin explains in *Mother of God*, the word *alma* didn't mean 'virgin' but 'young woman'.)

Jerome believed that food should be eaten as little as possible because this was the best way to suppress the sexual impulse. In his letter, to terrify and inspire young Eustochium, Jerome described in detail his experience as a hermit when 'tears and groans were every day my portion'. He said: 'Of my food and drink I say nothing: for, even in sickness, the solitaries have nothing but cold water, and to eat one's food cooked is looked upon as self-indulgence [. . .] I had no companions but scorpions and wild beasts, I often found myself amid bevies of girls. My face was pale and my frame chilled with fasting; yet my mind was burning with desire, and the fires of lust kept bubbling up before me when my flesh was as good as dead.' If the dangers of lust were bad for him, how much worse must they be for a vigorous young girl like Eustochium? 'If such are the temptations of men whose bodies are emaciated with fasting so that they have only evil thoughts to withstand, how must it fare with a girl who clings to the enjoyment of luxuries?' Jerome sternly warned Eustochium to pledge herself to chastity, pray constantly and keep the company only of other hungry female virgins.

In another letter, to Paula's daughter-in-law Laeta, who had asked for advice on how to raise her own daughter, Jerome urges: 'Let her food be herbs and wheaten bread with now and then one or two small fishes [. . .] let her meals always leave her hungry and able on the moment to begin reading or chanting [. . .] let her feel frightened when she is left to herself [. . .] Let her not converse with people of the world'. Jerome was firmly opposed to old pagan notions of hygiene: 'He who has bathed in Christ does not need a second bath.' For a fully developed virgin, 'deliberate squalor' was to be encouraged and bathing strictly avoided. A virgin 'should blush and feel overcome at the idea of seeing herself undressed. By vigils and fasts she mortifies her body and brings it into subjection. By a cold chastity she seeks to put out the flame of lust and to quench the hot desires of youth. And by a deliberate squalor she makes haste to spoil her natural good looks. Why, then, should she add fuel to a sleeping fire by taking baths?' Or, as his disciple Paula would later say: 'A clean body and clean clothes betoken an unclean mind.'

It was the death of Eustochium's older sister Blaesilla that led to the end of his sojourn in Rome. Blaesilla, who was twenty, had been a happy, normal, vivacious married young woman. When her husband died suddenly, Jerome persuaded her to become a devout Christian. Stop mourning your husband, he told her, and mourn the loss of your virginity instead. He inspired her to pray, fast and take the all-important step of renouncing remarriage. Then Blaesilla fell ill with a serious 'burning' fever, which was good, said Jerome, because it would help her to move away from her 'over-great attention to that body which the worms must shortly devour'. So severe was the fever that it temporarily stopped Blaesilla eating. When she recovered, Jerome advised her to continue to fast so as 'not to stimulate desire by bestowing care upon the flesh'. Desire was indeed not stimulated. Blaesilla now 'tottered with weakness, her face was pale and quivering, her slender neck scarcely upheld her head'. The approach of death 'made her gasp and shiver' and finally Christ 'raised her up'. In less than four months under Jerome's supervision Blaesilla had gone from healthy young woman to dead nun. When her mother fainted from grief at the funeral, Jerome rebuked her, saying her daughter was now 'alive unto Christ' and any Christian 'must rejoice that it is so'. In life Blaesilla had 'savoured somewhat of carelessness'; in death she sat 'at meat with the Lord'. Paula appears to have accepted this line of reasoning.

In 384 Jerome's patron and protector Pope Damasus died. Now Jerome's enemies in Rome, including the council of Roman clergy which had been appalled by his behaviour in the Blaesilla affair and suspected that his relationship with Paula was sexual, ordered Jerome to leave the city. Paula and Eustochium followed him. After touring the holy places of the Holy Land, they all ended up in Bethlehem together. There, with Paula's money, they advanced the cause of the emerging monastic movement by setting up monasteries for women, and one for men. Jerome finished translating the Bible and lived until the year 420. All three are now considered saints. Along with Augustine, Ambrose and Pope Gregory I, Jerome continues to be revered by Catholics as one of the four original Doctors of the Church.

An imaginative insight into Jerome's strange relationship with Paula comes in *The Raindrop's Gospel*, a 'novel in verse' published in 2010 by the feminist poet (and one-time Fellow of the American Academy in Rome) Maurya Simon. She honours Jerome as the 'Father of Punctuation' but sees him as a tragic 'character at war with himself' whose religious writings and public persona were at war with his private desires. In the poem his attraction to Paula is both blatantly sexual *and* spiritual. He first notices her among the 'doughy dowagers and diplomats' widows' and is drawn by her lips ('pomegranate red, slightly puckering / around the liturgy vowels and consonants'). Later, he suffers erotic dreams about her, picturing her naked in her bath. This vision so disturbing that one of his first thoughts on waking is that baths should be banned. As the poem progresses, his erotic reveries about Paula push Jerome to the edge of madness. He tears his chest and stabs his flesh with a crucifix. Paula, meanwhile, adores Jerome as a moral guide and a man with a rich baritone voice. While her friends 'revel in gluttony' Paula feels herself 'richly clothed in faith'. Simon is careful to offer a balanced view of Jerome's take on food. In Rome as a student, we see him at a banquet feasting on luxurious food:

> The tender flesh of quail and crane
> A dolphin's heart marinated in honey,
> simmered in opium, so as to enhance the senses.
> Platters of steaming sturgeon, wild rice
> studded with olives and flowing from gourds.
> Great plenitude reflected from golden goblets.

But none of it provides spiritual nourishment: 'I have eaten / still I'm hollowed by hunger.' His twisted, thwarted sexuality and his anguished spirituality are inseparable long before he heads into the desert ('Daily, the world tempts my flesh – / nightly I succumb') and he thinks constantly about sex in terms of food. There are Nubian beauties with 'their genitals swollen like guava' and Hebrew whores with 'breasts succulent as Persian melons'. He is in prison but doesn't want to be free. *Desire is quenched by desire*. The poet is notably sympathetic to Paula and Eustochium. Yet lines she puts into the mouth of Paula's younger daughter, Rufina, speak for a different sensibility. The daughter condemns Jerome as a 'blighted man' responsible for Blaesilla's death,

Eustochium's 'marriage to Christ' and Paula's useless martyring of herself and her wealth to a 'ranting zealot'. Rufina prefers scepticism to faith and would rather martyr herself to pleasure. She tells Jerome: 'I will *never* never join your virgins.'

Jerome's philosophy was intimately linked to Rome's fate and to the momentous religious and political revolutions taking place during his lifetime. The popular image of Christianity at the time of the fall of Rome tends to be of the church in a benign and rescuing role. The city and the western empire succumb to barbarian hordes because of inherent weaknesses. As imperial political, economic and military strength withers, the old pagan culture simply runs out of steam and becomes torpid and irrelevant. In this terrifying time of violence and moral collapse it is Christianity which picks up the pieces and fills the post-imperial vacuum with love and coherence. Eventually the Church, with its vibrant, confident vision of the world, rescues Rome as a city. Later, it does the same for all of Europe as well. In the last decade or so, historians of early Christianity have proposed a different interpretation. The most challenging of these, Charles Freeman, suggests that in the fourth and fifth centuries the old Graeco-Roman culture didn't fall. It was pushed.

In *The Closing of the Western Mind: The Rise of Faith and the Fall of Reason* (2002), Freeman traces the philosophical and political revolution which saw Christianity move from persecution to acceptance and on to domination. Emperor Constantine's initial aim had been to co-opt the religion to make his empire stronger. His Edict of Toleration in 313 promised that 'no one whatsoever should be denied freedom to devote himself either to the cult of the Christians or to such religion as he deems best for himself'. Yet he ended up inaugurating a new politics – the politics of imperial Christian theology. The churches began to grow wealthy and the image of Jesus became that of an imperial, warrior king.

Constantine hoped that by making Christianity the religion of empire he would bring unity. The problem was that there was not one Christianity, with a settled system of beliefs, but many competing and often mutually hostile sects. Arians, Gnostics, Manicheans, Ebionites and others offered wildly different versions and there were countless local and regional variations. To resolve tensions and bring clarity, Constantine organized a council, at Nicea in 425, which attempted to provide a definitive answer to the essentially unknowable question of nature of the Godhead. Was Jesus the same substance as God, or was he created later and therefore subordinate? This was what Arius and most early Christians thought, but, at Nicea, they were outmanoeuvred and beaten. Arius was declared a heretic and the many Christians who disagreed with the new formula were written off as 'demented and insane heretics'. Nevertheless, the council's rulings were widely ignored and in the decades that followed the old culture tolerance survived in large part as a succession of councils knocked the issue back and forth. The turning point came with emperor Theodosius and his Council of Constantinople – an event whose significance Freeman examines in a book entitled *AD 381*. It was Theodosius, he says, who decisively broke the old habits of toleration and introduced the new concept of religious totalitarianism. Theodosius was a tough-minded soldier desperate to stop the empire fragmenting. Fatefully, he believed that the way to do this was through coercion under a single religious formula.

At Constantinople, Theodosius summoned a council of bishops (none from Rome or speaking Latin) and ordered them to endorse his new policy. Soon the state began enforcing new laws against dissidents, with the Manicheans the first to be banned. By the 390s all forms of pagan belief had been condemned. Heretics were now suppressed and pagan temples destroyed. The list of banned Christian heresies expanded inexorably. This went hand in hand with the crushing of the old philosophy. St Paul had said, 'I will destroy the wisdom of the wise', and so it came to pass. The philosophical schools were closed, the great libraries burned. It was 'the extinction of serious mathematical and scientific thinking in Europe for a thousand years'. Once the principle that the state could control religious belief had been established, the law pushed far beyond Christianity. In 385 the empire executed its first heretic. By the 430s heretic-burning had become normal. By 500 staying alive depended on being the right kind of Christian. The last Olympic Games took place in 393. One of the last of the great pagan philosophers, the mathematician Hypatia, was torn to pieces and her body burned by a mob of monks acting on behalf of one of the most vigorous defenders of the new faith, Saint Cyril of Alexandria. 'The Greek intellectual tradition was suppressed and did not simply fade away,' says Freeman. The last recorded astronomical observation in the Ancient Greek world was one by Proclus in AD 475; it would be more than a thousand years – until the publication of Copernicus's *De revolutionibis* in 1543 – before these studies began to move forward again. When the empire fell in the West, argues Freeman, church history was rewritten and the crucial role of Theodosius was hidden: 'Few Christians ever realize that their freedom to discuss their own religion was, in effect, destroyed by a Roman emperor [. . .] The history of Europe would have been very different if [the] formula that God enjoys being worshipped in a diversity of ways had passed into the Western tradition after the fall of the empire.'

Critics have nibbled at Freeman's theory – charging, for instance, that he underestimates the degree to which pre-Christian Greek and Roman culture was in decline and was itself irrational. In the later *A New History of Early Christianity* Freeman concedes that Christianity had plenty of good points. It met many human needs, brought much comfort, provided a framework in which society could survive in time of breakdown, developed ethics, inspired important social movements and great art. But he repeats: 'While in some ways Christianity has broadened perspectives, in others it has narrowed them [. . .] imperial Christianity created an ethos in which free discussion was next to impossible. The subjugation of philosophical thought went hand in hand with a denigration of the natural world.'

What followed was described by Petrarch as the Dark Ages. Literacy rates collapsed and Europe entered a thousand-year Age of Stupid which began to abate only when Thomas Aquinas in the thirteenth century insisted that reason was, after all, a gift from God and integrated Aristotle into Catholic thought. Now faith and reason could be to some degree reunited. Aquinas said the one sustained the other. A century or so later, a Tuscan law student (Petrarch himself), bored beyond endurance by the lack of intelligent conversation among his contemporaries, sought out the long-lost writings of classical Greece and Rome, came to think of the ancient writers as his friends, and ushered in the age of Humanism and the Renaissance.

Meanwhile, back in the fourth century, another new Christian phenomenon had arisen, which would change Rome forever: the political bishop. The American Christian scholar Philip Jenkins has likened the fanaticism of such men to that of modern Islamist gangsters. 'The level of Christian violence in that early era is amazing. You have bishops and patriarchs commanding armed mobs of holy men and monks, who they turn out against rivals, very much like Muslim mullahs or ayatollahs in Iraq or Lebanon today. They issue anathemas that throw rivals out of the community of faith, like modern *fatwa*s. Mobs murder rivals over theological issues, they behead them and carry their heads around the street.' Some bishops were less extreme. Ambrose of Milan assisted the process of smashing the old temples and declared that 'all pagan gods are devils'. In 388 he opened the theological way for Christian violence against Jews. A synagogue had been burned by a mob incited by a bishop in Mesopotamia and the emperor had ordered the perpetrators be punished and the synagogue rebuilt. But Ambrose insisted the 'glory of God' was involved and the rule of law must be set aside. No one would be punished because a synagogue was 'a home of unbelief, a house of impiety, a receptacle of folly which God himself has condemned'.

Pope Damasus, protector of St Jerome, owed his own position as Bishop of Rome to violence. When his predecessor died, another candidate, Ursinus, declared himself Pope. Fighting broke out and supporters of Ursinus took refuge in the Liberian Basilica (now Santa Maria Maggiore). Unable to force the door, Damasus's fighters climbed to the roof, tore a hole and rained down heavy tiles on those inside, killing 137. This secured Damasus's position, though he took the precaution of hiring gladiators as bodyguards. Jenkins likens the Alexandrian bishops to the Sopranos crime family. The zenith of their power came with the Second Council of Ephesus in 449 when their monks beat the Patriarch of Constantinople to death and broke the fingers of anyone attempting to write to the outside world. The event was so corrupt and violent it became known as the 'Gangster Council'. In Gibbon's description, 'The monks, who rushed with tumultuous fury from the desert, distinguished themselves by their zeal and diligence [. . .] In almost every province of the Roman world, an army of fanatics, without authority and without discipline, invaded the peaceful inhabitants; and the ruin of the fairest structures of antiquity still displays the ravages of those barbarians who alone had time and inclination to execute such laborious destruction.'

Damasus enhanced Rome's status as a centre of Christianity and pushed the papacy towards the form we know today. Previously, in Christian terms, Rome was in the shadow of Jerusalem, Antioch, Alexandria and Constantinople. But Damasus initiated a major rebranding by insisting, anachronistically and on the basis of the slenderest evidence, that St Peter had been the first Pope and that Rome was therefore the 'Apostolic See' with all popes linked to Peter by 'apostolic succession'. Damasus also promoted the cult of martyrs, persecuted Arians and persuaded a new emperor to exempt all popes from secular law, thereby neatly sidestepping the charge of murder that had hung over him since the Ursinus business.

In his book *Jesus Wars: How Four Patriarchs, Three Queens, and Two Emperors Decided What Christians Would Believe for the Next 1,500 Years* Jenkins shows how intractable theological problems were decided on grounds of political ambition and expediency. In the fifth century a new problem arose: to what degree was Jesus human and divine? On one side of the argument Monophysites believed Christ had one nature (his humanity absorbed by his deity); this put them in heated dispute with Nestorians, who said Christ had two natures (human and divine). Battle swayed this way and that. The Monophysites imposed their view at the Second Council of Ephesus. Two years later, The Council of Chalcedon reversed this. Now Christ officially had two natures and anyone who thought differently was in big trouble. At every stage things could have gone differently. Political machinations or raw luck often determined what orthodoxy became. In one case, says Jenkins, the world turned on the misstep of a horse, which threw and killed the champion of Monophysitism, Emperor Theodosius II. His death paved the way for his sister Aelia Pulcheria to impose her views. Her husband Marcian organized the Council of Chalcedon to destroy the power of the Monophysites in the West and thereby preserve what we now call Catholicism. Without that horse, Rome would have remained on the Christian margins and Alexandria would have become the capital of Christianity. That might have led to a united, Eastern Christianity, unencumbered by conflict with Catholic Rome, resisting the Muslim invasions of the seventh, eighth and later centuries. Without that horse the world would now be a very different place.

To get back to the actual world of Jerome and his views on sex and food, was there a connection between the newly authoritarian and powerful church and avant-garde Christian thinkers who became hostile to the body? How did the self-inflicted torture of starvation come to be seen as spiritual 'perfection'? Why, as Harvard academic Veronika Grimm puts it, did Christian propaganda of the era so violently reject the healthy human body with its basic biological needs? Most of all, how did a search for purity end up as a general fear of food?

It would be hard to blame Jesus, his circle or even those who followed immediately afterwards for any of this. Austere and tormented though St Paul had been, he had nothing against food – though later food-phobic ascetics misquoted him to claim that he did. His lines about the enemies of Christ whose 'god is their stomach [. . .] Their mind is on earthly things' are not a condemnation of food per se but of gluttony. For Paul, sharing bread and wine was an essential aspect of the Christian life. The Eucharist was originally part of a full communal meal which sustained body and soul. Paul did bequeath to Christianity a neurosis about sex, as well as the idea that the body was a 'temple' defiled by it. But he accepted it within marriage: 'it is better to marry than to burn'.

In her book *From Feasting to Fasting: the Evolution of a Sin* Grimm detects a clue in the fact that the push towards extreme asceticism came *after* Christianity triumphed as state religion. Freeman makes a similar point: Christianity became more pessimistic when it came in from the cold. This was also the era of the building of the first opulent churches (an innovation shocking to some Christians derived from paganism and often using the buildings of the old gods), a display of new church wealth and status that may have produced a reaction. Grimm suggests that harsh asceticism may have derived from a form of spiritual one-upman-ship. As the line between political and religious authority blurred, so leading-edge Christians looked to maintain their moral edge. St Paul paved the way by seeing sex as something suspect. Now rejection of sex became a demonstration of 'holiness'. The politicians had turned Christianity into a mass-membership religion for everyone. For the most devout this was a threat. The sudden invasion by 'unworthy, even downright poisonous elements' endangered the purity of the Christian ideal society.

The authors of Christianity's new views on sex and food came after the first century. Clement of Alexandria, born about eighty years after Paul's death, said that eating, drinking and marrying were all permitted – but only so long as they brought no pleasure. Wine was the 'drug of madness', which stimulated 'wild impulses and festering lusts' in the young. Because moist bodies were thought more prone to lust, Clement, in the heat of Alexandria, advised adults to drink nothing at all during lunch. Even water might be spiritually hazardous. Another innovation for which we can thank Clement is the idea that even the most intimate aspects of private life are governed by Christ. Everything pertaining to the body was open to scrutiny. From now on, says Grimm, 'the church increasingly asserted its right to control the core of an individual's private life, with the psychological, social and economic consequences that such control entailed'.

Another key figure was Tertullian, so-called 'father of Latin Christianity', who lived in the late second and early third centuries. Misogynist and obsessive, Tertullian was a furious denouncer of heretics, invented the term 'Trinity' and had a unique line in arguments. He is best known for saying: 'And the Son of God died: it is wholly credible because it is ridiculous. And, buried, he rose, again: it is certain because it is impossible.' Tertullian viewed fasting as a way of atoning for sin and urged penitents to 'nourish prayers with fast, to groan, to weep, and to bellow day and night'. His biggest contribution to food phobia came in a treatise called *Apologeticus* in which he claims Christians touch God by being 'parched with fasting, pinched with every austerity, abstaining from all food that sustains life, wallowing in sackcloth and ashes'. Tertullian derided a rival Christian sect: 'with you "love" shows its fervour in saucepans, "faith" its warmth in kitchens, "hope" its anchorage in waiters'; and his treatise 'On Fasting' is the earliest extensive Christian treatment of the subject. Fasting, he asserts, pleases God as an excellent sign of self-abasement. With Athanasius's book on desert hermit St Antony a century later the new, self-punishing Christian ideal was set. (Ascetic ideals and practices are still in place, though less talked about. In 2009 it was revealed by one of the Polish nuns who used to look after him that Pope John Paul II had regularly whipped himself while he was in Rome. 'We were in the next room and we would hear the sound of the blows,' Sister Tobiana Sobodka told a Vatican commission investigating the late Pope's suitability for sainthood.)

Men like Athanasius and Jerome inspired the monastic movement, but later voices such as Basil of Caesarea and Augustine moderated the calls for starvation and self-torture. They felt Christians ought not to eat and drink beyond what is necessary for health. Augustine said the body should be treated like a slave: only its basic needs should be met. Basil urged 'denial of the pleasant things'. In practice, monks came to eat sensible diets that sustained health and strength. In the East, John Chrysostom advocated asceticism for monks, but spoke realistically to ordinary people: 'Enjoy your baths, your good table, your meat, your wine in moderation – enjoy everything, in fact, but keep away from sin.' Nevertheless, an abiding and bleak anti-sensuality remained to permeate Christian thought, along with a suspicion of food. Augustine, the most important of all Catholic theologians, worried constantly about lust and condemned the 'ominous' enjoyment of eating. Augustine was scarcely less morbidly obsessed with sex than Tertullian and Jerome were. He invented the concept of original sin, derived from Adam's Fall, and the cruel concept of limbo (where went un-baptized dead babies, otherwise innocent but tainted by the 'original sin'). Augustine was preoccupied with sinfulness, especially his own, and thought of God as an entity who shows love by punishing. Augustine's vision is bleak: mankind is mostly doomed because sinfulness is passed on through sex. Not even baptism or good works might save more than a fraction of humanity. Earthly exist-ence was something to be viewed almost with contempt: 'the Christian's eye must always be trained on eternal life. The more he loves what is immortal, the more vehemently he will hate what is transitory.' Augustine's language is less violent than his friend Jerome, but he is, in the words of the German theologian Uta Ranke-Heinemann, 'the man who fused Christianity together with hatred of sex and pleasure into a systematic unity'.

In *The Confessions* Augustine declares that, while eating is necessary, pleasure in eating will turn man's mind from higher things. In fact, food may be taken as remedies against the 'fevers' of hunger and thirst: 'I look upon food as medi-cine.' In other words, the normal processes of the body are sick. In *The Usefulness of Fasting* Augustine takes this one stage further: 'Your flesh is below you; above you is your God.' The personality is split, the body becomes an external object to be trained and mortified. Such breaking up of the human personality, says Grimm, has cast a long shadow over Western mentality. 'The annals of psychiatry up to our days testify to the efforts that have gone into trying to put the pieces together again.'

IV: The Snails

'No real happiness exists', wrote Rome's leading food guru of the twentieth century, 'where no attention is given to such an essential part of our life as food.' Ada Boni was a warm and formidable upper-middle-class lady said to have invented her first dish at the age of ten. Her family were famous goldsmiths and her uncle Adolfo Giaquinto was a famous chef. Between 1915 and 1959 Ada edited her influential cookery magazine, *Preziosa* (*Precious*). Her best-seller *Talisman of Happiness*, first published in 1929 with 882 recipes (later expanded by other hands to more than 2,000), is reckoned almost as important a text for modern Italian gastronomy as Artusi's *Science in the Kitchen*. For decades Boni's book was what Italian brides were most likely to receive as a wedding gift. Elegant, gifted and popular, she broadcast on radio and was rarely seen outdoors in summer without her white parasol. She gave cookery lessons to other upper-crust ladies at her family home in the Palazzo Odescalchi and declared that cooking was 'the most cheerful of the arts and, at the same time, the most joyous of the sciences'. As the *Talisman* spelled out, she was no feminist: 'Many of you, dear ladies and girls, know how to play the piano well or to sing with exquisite grace; many others have very exalted titles for upper-level studies, know the modern languages, are pleasant writers or fine painters; still others are experts at tennis or golf, or confidently guide the steering wheel of a luxurious automobile. But, alas, certainly not all of you, if you examined your consciences even a little, could claim to know how to cook two soft-boiled eggs to perfection.' She was also a gifted researcher, and a proud sixth-generation Roman. Her 1930 book *La cucina romana: piatti tipici e ricette dimenticate di una cucina genuina e ricca di fantasia* (*Roman Cuisine: typical dishes and forgotten recipes of a genuine cuisine rich in fantasy*) was a labour of love, recording a style of cooking that was disappearing under the pressures of modernity and which might otherwise have been forgotten. Below, from that book, which was never translated into English, is her charming description of traditional Vineyard Snails:

There is a traditional Roman feast in June, the Eve of St John's. Over the years it has lost a great part of its characteristic vivacity. However, it continues to represent the destination towards which good-natured parties from all parts of Rome converge. Amid the scent of carnations and of spikelet, among a thousand of multicoloured lights and strolling street concerts of guitars and mandolins, these parties long to perpetuate the popular rite. And, as you know, these things end up always the same way, the Roman people assault the *osterie* [inns], the little *trattorie* [eating houses] and the many improvised stalls to eat the traditional dish of which we here give the absolute authentic recipe handed down in Roman families.

The characteristic cry of the snail pedlar who owns a certain quantity of raw snails, preferably picked from vineyards, is *'de vigna le lumache!'* ('snails from the vineyard!'). They keep the snails in a big container (usually a wicker basket) and cover it, making sure air can circulate inside. For the recipients inside the basket they put some soft pieces of bread, which have first been dipped in water and then squeezed, and some grapevine leaves.

Leave the snails for a couple of days. After that, pour the snails into a big basin full of water with a pinch of salt and a cup of vinegar. Start by mixing the snails with your hands: through this first washing they will produce plentiful amounts of foam. Wash them for a long time, changing the water a couple of times and adding salt and vinegar, until they no longer make any foam. Then rinse them again carefully in fresh water, changing the water a few times. At this point put the snails in a little cauldron on a weak fire. As the water becomes warm, the snails will start to pull their heads out of their shells. This is the right moment to turn up the fire so that the little creatures can pass to a better life without going back inside their little house. When the water reaches boiling point, leave the snails boiling for about ten minutes. Then take them out with a large perforated spoon and wash them again for the last time in a large basin of cold water. Now take a large earthenware frying pan. With regard to earthenware it is useful to point out that Roman cuisine has a preference for using earthenware receptacles, frying pans and pots, which in Rome are called *di coccio*. Put some oil and a few cloves of garlic in the pan. When the garlic is lightly fried take it away. Add three or four anchovies which have been washed, boned and cut into pieces. Squash the anchovies with a wooden spoon and, when they are melted, add a quantity of tomatoes proportionate to the quantity of snails. Remember that tomato sauce has to be plentiful in this dish. Tomatoes need to be peeled, devoid of seeds and cut into pieces. When the sauce thickens dress it with salt, plenty of pepper and a pinch of mint leaves (the kind of wild meadow mint known in Rome as *mentuccia*). Generally, the sauce should be quite spicy, adding a few pieces of red chilli. If the sauce is too thick, add a little water. Put the snails in the pan and leave them to absorb the flavour for about half an hour on a moderate flame.

V: The Fish Juice

'The debate about fish sauce is ongoing and remains
controversial'

Grocock & Grainger (editors), *Apicius*, 2006

It was the smelliest stuff in the empire, the most gastronomically prized, and no one alive knows quite how it tasted. Fermented fish juice – *garum* or *liquamen* – was as ubiquitous in Ancient Roman food as soy is in the cuisine of Japan. Or fat to burgers. Or salt to Vlaamse Frites. Or salty anchovies to salty-anchovy-flavoured pizzas. One of the most sought-after and expensive *garum* brands came from Carthage and was made by drowning mackerels in the liquids of other mackerels, then letting them decompose, then skimming the good stuff off the top of the resulting mess. This delicious product was known as *garum sociorum*; cost, 1,000 sesterces a go. 'Hardly any other liquid commands such prices, apart from perfume,' said Pliny the Elder.

We know *garum* must have tasted both pungently fishy and exceedingly salty. Experts say the nearest modern equivalent is probably the salty Vietnamese fish sauce Nuoc Nam. At great expense and effort I have now acquired a bottle of Nuoc Nam and can report that it is fishy and salty, though probably not as much as *garum*. *Garum* for gourmets was also said to be clear, dark and vinegar-coloured. So is this. But the Roman stuff was likely made to various degrees of quality, consistency and smelliness. And tasted different. So, I'm the proud owner of a bottle of Vietnamese fish juice – but none the wiser.

No one knows for sure if *garum* was made from whole fishes, from fish intestines, from fish blood, or a combination of the above plus other stuff, like skin, brains, spices and herbs. Was one fish species used? Or a mixture? The manufacturing process is likewise shrouded in mystery. Were the mixtures of fish flesh, blood, guts and so forth left to rot and ferment in the sun for months? (It happened at some sites, which smelled so horribly they were set as far away from human habitation as possible; production inside Rome was banned.) Alternatively, was the liquid (or paste) from fish (or fish bits) acquired by a salting process? Very good questions. The residues were also used, but had different names, were cheaper, and didn't taste the same.

Whatever the answers, we can say that Roman cuisine was probably at all times and in all circumstances fish-flavoured. In the only recipe book to survive from the imperial era, *De Re Coquinaria*, we find it in almost every dish. The book, published in the fourth century under the name of a first-century foodie called Marcus Gavius Apicius, features fish essence with pretty much everything: with red meat, with white meat, with vegetables, with fruit . . . with fish. Name any food eaten anywhere in the empire and the chances are that Ancient Romans thought it tasted better with salty, pungent fish juice.

VI: The Peach

Most of the time fruit is just fruit. Occasionally, it is something else. A striking example lurks in the undergrowth of the frieze of the fabulous frescoes at the Villa Farnesina in Trastevere, built by the banker Agostino Chigi, who in the early sixteenth century was probably the richest man in Europe. Chigi managed to persuade the greatest artist of the day, Raphael, to decorate part of his *palazzo* with panels depicting the story of Cupid and Psyche. Raphael handed the lush borders around this instant masterpiece to his pupil, Giovanni da Udine, and he gave us a cornucopia of ripe, firm, lifting, young, juicy, tender, succulent (you can see where this is going, can't you?) fruit and vegetables. Amid festoons of flowers and leaves we see a great profusion of melons, gourds, carrots, apples, grapes, pomegranates, figs, peaches, cucumbers, cabbages, corns, peaches, gourds, peaches, apples, peaches and peaches. At one end of the room is a trumpet-carrying, gold-caped but otherwise naked Mercury. Born aloft on his winged heels, this messenger of the gods wears a helmet and a surprised expression. With one hand he gestures towards a shocking intrusion into the vegetarian scene: an unmistakeable packet of meat and two veg. The thrusty-looking giant gourd and its attendant aubergines plainly represent a penis and testicles. Nearby is an equally vivid curly cluster of black grapes, overripe and being penetrated by another gourd. And, over there, a juicy split melon is being entered by a cucumber. Or is it a melon? Or another gourd? With all this fucking fruit around it's hard to tell.

Scholars tell us that this work, painted in 1517, inaugurated something of a High Renaissance craze for bawdy depictions of orchard-and-garden produce. Pretty soon the metaphor had become commonplace. 'Compositions framed with garlands of tumescent fruits and vegetables', says art historian John Varriano, 'could be found in the most respectable locations, sometimes even in chapels and churches.' The delight taken in this conceit was shaped by traditions of humour and quack medicine. Popular at the time was the 'doctrine of signatures', based on the work of the occultist Paracelsus, which held that objects resembling each other might exert influence upon each other. From this came the notion that parts of the body could be treated by using objects resembling them. Meanwhile, sixteenth-century Italy was drenched in a culture of metaphor. This was reflected in, among other things, a thriving market for 'learned erotica' suffused with food imagery. In Rome, which had a higher proportion of males in its population than any other European city, sexual puns were more widespread than anywhere else and the idea of fruit became the 'perfect metaphor for the culture of post-Reformation Rome, a culture whose quest for religious and political orthodoxy frequently led to further uncertainties' and where humour alone offered an acceptable outlet for transgressive desire.

The craze would last about a hundred years. Portraits by Milanese artist Giuseppe Arcimboldo had faces made entirely of fruit and vegetables. Specialists of a more overtly erotic genre included Vincenzo Campi, who painted arrays of plants and animals, much of it highly suggestive, and Niccolò Frangipani, whose best-known picture, *Allegory of Autumn*, depicts a drunken young man asleep beside a pile of rude fruit. Crouching beside him is a leering satyr, representing the man's dream, who holds a big sausage with one hand and sticks a finger in a slit melon with the other. This sort of metaphor was also hugely popular among artists and intellectuals, especially in the private literary 'academies', which were like intellectual drinking fraternities or secret societies. Here, says another scholar, Adrienne von Lates, 'amateur and professional poets regaled one another with recitations of bawdy poetry that exploited the sexual symbolism inherent in pagan rites of initiation and Dionysiac harvest sacrifices'. The mighty artist Bronzino wrote burlesque erotic poetry which was widely circulated. Michelangelo wrote similar stuff, though he insisted his poems were 'only good for tambourines and wrapping, for innkeepers, latrines, and brothels'. In Siena, Antonio Vignali founded the *Accademia degli Intronati* (Academy of the Stunned) and wrote an anticlerical, homoerotic, politically satirical hagiography of penises called *La Cazzaria* (*The Book of the Prick*). The most important academies were in Rome. The *Accademia degli Insensati* (Academy of the Senseless Ones) became something of a fan club of the new greatest artist in town – Caravaggio. Members, including one of the painter's early employers, composed songs and poems about his paintings. Caravaggio had friends in another academy, too – the *Umoristi*. Members included sons of the powerful Colonna family and the young Maffeo Barberini (a friend of Caravaggio's patron), whose portrait was painted by Caravaggio. (Barberini went on, as Pope Urban VIII, to support the arts and destroy Galileo.) In Milan, Caravaggio's family patron ran a literary academy called the *Inquieti*. One of these 'restless ones' was Lomazzo, a painter who was both friend to Caravaggio's teacher and leading light of yet another academy, a drunken country-side Bacchus-worshipping group that celebrated the erotic delights of harvest time. Back in Rome, notables of the papal court staged bawdy poetry contests under the auspices of the *accademia* of Vintners and took on phallic pseudo-nyms such as 'Mister Radish', 'Mister Carrot' and 'Mister Big-Branch'. They too celebrated harvest time but a more typical night out involved a big supper in Rome and the reciting of poems in praise of the fig (symbolizing female genitals) and melon (female bottom). There are parallels between the imagery in one of Caravaggio's well-known early pictures, *Self Portrait as Bacchus* (the *Bacchino Malato*), and a homoerotic poem by Vintners founder member Francesco Berni in praise of velvet-skinned peaches (boys' bottoms): 'Oh fruit blessed above all others / good before, in the middle and after the / meal, but good before and perfect behind.'

In his Bacchus picture Caravaggio paints himself as muscular but faintly greenish-skinned. Wearing an off-the-shoulder white toga, he turns his head to gaze at the viewer like a coy but rather ill pin-up. On the stone table at which he sits rests a bunch of black grapes and two peaches placed, according to Von Lates, 'on the edge of the table as if they are being offered to the viewer. The fleshy peaches are also posed in a highly suggestive manner, recalling human buttocks observed in both the upright and reclining posi-tions.' The peaches recall the phrase *dare le pesche*, translated in an Italian–English dictionary of 1611 as 'to yield one's bum, or consent to unnatural sinne'.

Another of Caravaggio's other early pictures, *Still Life with Fruit on a Stone Ledge*, seems much more blatant: a veritable fruit-and-veg orgy whose meaning, says Peter Robb in his book *M: The Man Who Became Caravaggio*, 'not even the sourest counter-reformation prude could have missed'. The picture shows a fruit basket stuffed with plums, grapes, peaches, a pear and an apple. The apple has a dark wormhole; the peaches and apple bear 'a more striking than usual resemblance to pale human buttocks'. There's a couple of ripe pomegranates (one 'slashed open to show the glowing moist red seeds') and some 'very ripe figs, soft skin abraded and one of them too, split open in its ripeness to display its mass of reddish purple flesh and tinier seeds'. These small fruits are 'jostled aside by the rotundities of a mass of big melons, marrows and pumpkins'. One pumpkin is 'slashed open like the pomegranate to show a crescent-shaped gash of its voluptuous moist interior. So was the watermelon, revealing its pink flesh and slippery black seeds.' Behind are what Robb calls marrows but are actually gourds, 'long, uncut and remarkable'. These are the key players in a 'tumultuously physical free-for-all of *vegetable love*, as one long curved marrow thrust itself diagonally across the slab toward the moist gash of a pumpkin. Behind it, another smoothly elongated marrow was rearing even more suggestively into the viewer's face, its end caught in a brilliant play of *chiaroscuro* contrast, looming into the picture in the centre of the falling shaft of light, coming right at you through the fruit as unmistakeably the head of an engorged penis.'

Another of the artist's recent biographers, John T. Spike, sees in this picture religious as well as erotic meaning:

A profuse harvest of late summer fruits, squashes, and melons, fills its surface, dramatically illuminated from above. The allusion is [...] to Amos's likening of the imminent judgment to the end of the summer season. The fruits and cucurbits are for the most part disposed in pairs, one intact and the other split open. The spilling of seed – of pomegranates, in particular – is a Christian symbol of Resurrection. The wicker basket at left contains the grapes and vine leaves of the Eucharist alongside the apples and peaches of original sin. The wormholes and other blemishes on these luscious fruits are Caravaggio's symbol of the transience of human life.

He, too, acknowledges the erotic visual puns:

The serpentine forms of the bottle gourds seem explicitly phallic [...] seem to slither and writhe like eyeless serpents. The bristling figs take up this masculine motif, while the lush interiors of the squash, and the sliced pink watermelon readily suggest thinly disguised representations of the female sex. To anyone thinking along these lines, the pair of peaches staked on top of the basket bear an uncanny resemblance to dimpled derrières.

Then again, sometimes fruit and veg can also be ... Well, fruit and veg. American horticulturalist Jules Janick is not convinced by such overheated metaphorical talk. 'It appears to me that Caravaggio was simply displaying his pride of painterly skill, and his sheer love of the shapes and lushness of his horticultural subject.' In a brilliant essay he argues that, while these fruit and vegetable paintings may or may not reveal much about sex or faith, they certainly tell us quite a bit about horticulture in late Renaissance Rome. 'The fruits of 1600 surely looked as luscious as the fruits 400 years later, giving the lie to the often-quoted suggestion that modern breeders have improved the appearance of fruits to the detriment of their quality, although quality is hard to determine from the picture. They underscore the rich diversity of fruits available [and] demonstrate that diseases and pests were a problem then as they are now.'

Discovering Caravaggio's super-realist fruit images was a revelation for Janick, like finding a cache of 400-year-old colour photographs. Others have explored Caravaggio's tempestuous life and art. Many have noted how his realism, his method of painting direct from life, transformed art, opened the door for Rembrandt and Vermeer and made possible the modern way of seeing. Professor Janick spotted a hitherto neglected aspect of his genius: Caravaggio, chronicler of Italian cultivars between 1592 and 1603. For example, Caravaggio's pears, of various sizes and colours, appear in six paintings. These include the soft-fleshed *pyrus communis* mentioned in *The Odyssey*. This pear was a 'gift of the gods' in the gardens of Alcinöus and dried slices of it have even been found in Ice Age cave dwellings. Caravaggio's paintings 'suggest substantial genetic diversity in melons' of his time. He also shows us cantaloupes, which get their name from Cantalupo, the papal country villa in the Sabine Hills where they were first brought by missionaries. The pumpkins are interesting too: this was a species only relatively recently arrived in Europe from America. Some of Caravaggio's apples, well known in Ancient Rome, look remarkably modern. His quinces, too, look like the fruit of today, though quinces, being acidic and used mostly in preserves, are less popular now. The *Lute Player* features a single cucumber, a fruit Tiberius liked so much he had it grown in a *specularium*, an early greenhouse.

Furthermore, Caravaggio shows us diseases and other defects. In the *Bacchus* there's a half-rotted quince, a red apple with a wormhole, another with rot ('likely a form of botrysphaeria'). The discoloration of a grape leaf suggests potassium deficiency. Another leaf, on the crown worn by Bacchus, seem to have 'crown gall, induced by *Agrobacterium tumefaciens*'. The *Supper at Emmaus* depicts the risen Christ at a meal consisting of bread, a chicken, white wine, water, and fruit that looks as if it has just been bought at the market. This provides a wealth of information. For a start, although the biblical supper takes place at Easter, the fruits are autumnal. They also reveal the problems of an organic production system that would have benefitted from a few modern insecticides and fungicides. Fungal spots discolour the grape leaves. There's something wrong with all the apples: scab lesions caused by a fungus, wormholes, black rot. The pomegranate has spots. The looseness of the cluster of black grapes is evidence of poor pollination. And behind the fruit bowl is a very dead chicken. Its legs, sticking bolt upright, indicate the onset of rigor mortis.

Caravaggio was drunken, violent and criminal. He committed a murder and preferred the company of the city's bad boys and girls – thieves, prostitutes, thugs and *bravi*. It must also be admitted that Caravaggio on occasion took food more seriously than was strictly necessary. Dialogue preserved in Rome's criminal court records makes him sound like Joe Pesci in *Goodfellas*. When a waiter brings him artichokes cooked in butter instead of oil, Caravaggio snarls: 'It seems to me, you fucking prick, that you think you're serving some two-bit crook.' He then attacks the waiter and stabs him in the face. On another occasion, the artist and his mates threaten a rival artist: 'We'll fry your balls in oil.' He contemptuously refers to an employer, Monsignor Pandolfo Pucci, as 'Monsignor Insalata' because salad was all he gave him to eat. It was 'appetizer, entree and dessert [. . .] accompaniment and toothpick'.

Thanks to his genius, though, and perhaps also to the now-marketable combination in his life and work of sex and violence, Caravaggio's star has never been higher. A slew of books about him has been published. A big exhibition of his work at the Quirinale in 2010 marking the 400th anniversary of his death was sold out for months. I've started to feel fairly close to him myself because I recently came across his astonishing St Matthew pictures in the Contarelli Chapel at the church of San Luigi dei Francesi, near Piazza Navona. I'm a bit of a church addict and can visit up to a dozen a day, but had never realized he was in there. There's a more than vivid contrast between his paintings and the baroque clutter of angels and gold and marble piled around the rest of the church like wedding cakes heaped one on top of another. Seeing Caravaggio's three pictures from the life of Matthew was like being struck across the soul with a baseball bat.

And now the great man has, rather surprisingly, turned up in person. Sort of. Scientists in Ravenna announced that some old bones found in Tuscany are '85 per cent likely' to be those of Caravaggio, who may have died of lead poisoning rather than, as was previously thought, murder, or the exhaustion of life in exile. On TV the bones were treated with the reverence of those of a mediaeval saint.

I am suddenly seized by the idea of recreating one of his pictures. If I buy the right fruits I can restage the thing with my little digital camera. But which picture? One candidate is the slightly mysterious *Basket of Fruit* (1599), said by some to have inaugurated pure still-life painting. But that picture features just five types of fruit (grapes, apples, figs, a pear and a quince) and that doesn't seem sufficiently ambitious. Nor is there much of a Rome angle. Caravaggio painted it here but the picture hangs in Milan. The *Sick Bacchus*, meanwhile, boringly features only grapes and peaches, and I certainly don't fancy that chicken from *Emmaus*. By contrast, *Still Life on a Stone Ledge* does have nice figs, peaches and such, and I like the story of how Caravaggio achieved his stunning chiaroscuro effects: he cut a hole in his landlady's ceiling. But I don't actually like melon (not even pornographic melon) and where am I going to find serpentine, penis-like giant gourds in Rome on a Monday?

After long reflection I decide to go early and plentiful. I'll try to recreate *Boy with Fruit Basket*, painted between 1593 and 1594. It was painted in Rome. It hangs in the Galleria Borghese. And my girlfriend Valeria is up for playing the part of the boy holding the basket, young Mario Minniti, who went on to become a painter in his own right. The image was good enough for Caravaggio. It's been interesting enough for Derek Jarman and Simon Schama to recreate it for films about Caravaggio. And it will keep Valeria's family fruited for days.

Thus to the venerable fruit-and-veg market at Campo de' Fiori. The place has some history of its own. Julius Caesar was assassinated nearby, outside the old Theatre of Pompey. In Caravaggio's day, the Campo was a horse-and-cattle market. It was also where books and heretics were burned. In 1553, a huge pyre was made of Hebrew books seized from Jewish homes. In 1600, flames consumed the great philosopher and former monk Giordano Bruno, burned alive by the church for heresy. Bruno had come to doubt the tenets of Catholicism. He had also advanced a theory of atoms, argued that the Earth orbited the sun and believed the universe contained an infinite number of sun-like stars. He had to go and it's entirely possible that Caravaggio witnessed the burning. There's nothing to commemorate Caravaggio in the square, but a brooding, cowled statue of Bruno dominates the place. It was put up in 1889 by a group of anticlericals who considered him one of the great martyrs for free speech. People gather here each February to honour him. The modern Campo's cafés and bars have made it a night-time hot spot for the young. When visiting soccer fans gather here before European matches, AS Roma fans make a sport of trying to stab them in the buttocks, another jolly tradition dating back to Caravaggio's time. But by day, as it has been since 1869, it's still the fruit market.

It's going to be hot, so we've come early. My friend Anna, four months pregnant, is wearing a white hat and we have a shopping list derived from Professor Janick. We require the following late-sixteenth-century items:

one peach
four clusters of grapes (two black, one red, one white)
one ripe pomegranate (to be split)
four figs (two black, two light)
two medlars
three apples
two branches with small pears attached
two virescent grape leaves (one with fungal spots;
    another with a white insect-egg mass)
peach leaves with spots
two sprigs with reddish foliage (perhaps mint)

We can probably forget about finding leaves damaged in the correct manner; it's the sort of thing modern fruit-sellers go out of their way to hide. And we probably won't find varieties of precisely the right colouring either. So we'll go for fruit types. And if any can't be found here, we'll go to a supermarket and if we have to buy fruit in plastic packaging so much the better. We'll arrange them in the basket that way to prove that 400 years have indeed passed.

First: a peach! We meet Marcella, cheerful and dark-haired, who has been working her stall for thirty years, since the age of sixteen. As I explain why we need a single peach, Marcella feeds little pieces of bread to her friend, a sparrow called Cirillo, who darts back and forth between her hand and the stall canopy. Cirillo watches us with jerky head movements and trusting eyes. Marcella wears a black T-shirt emblazoned with 'I ♥ Roma' and a picture of the Colosseum. 'It used to be so different here, with completely different people. The square was full of butchers and bakers, not pubs and cafés. And we used to have wooden tables, and now they're all metal. It's a lot of tourists now, but we still have some of the old local customers. The produce has changed a bit as well, but the main thing is people buy in smaller quantities now.' The peach (plus leaves without spots) costs four euros. 'In the spirit of Rome of the 1590s, will you take a couple of scudi?'

For the pears we select a stall on the right side of the square manned by Raf, a twenty-seven-year-old Bangladeshi wearing an orangey-pink T-shirt. I explain our project, but obviously not very well.

'I don't have any. You need to go to an art shop,' says Raf.

'No, we want fruit *in the painting*.'

'Oh yes, I can do that. I have pineapples, bananas, kiwi . . .'

'But those aren't in the painting. I'm not sure Caravaggio ever saw a pineapple, or a banana, or a kiwi. Have you got any pears?'

Raf does have pears. He fled his village in northern Bangladesh ten years ago, looking for a better life in Europe, and lives near Termini. 'I have many brothers and sisters but I'm here on my own and my family is in Bangladesh. For me, Rome is good. Life is better here.'

Next up: the pomegranate. This amuses the girl at the stall near the Farnese cinema no end. She has fragile-looking teeth, a cigarette dangling from her lip and a generously proportioned laugh. 'Pomegranates? Come back in November! Pomegranates are not in season.' Medlars then? 'Ha! That's for spring.' Grapes? 'Well, you can get them from Sicily now, but we don't have any. We only sell stuff we grow ourselves. With us it's what's in season.' As she turns to serve an old lady and her Filipina maid, her sister joins us. Her name is Sandra Bottoni, and here are some of the things she tells us. The stall is a family operation. Her dad, Giacomo, known as Giacomino, started it more than thirty years ago and the business currently involves Sandra, Sandra's husband, Sandra's sister, and Giacomino. They all live in Velletri, south of Rome, and grow their own fruit and vegetables and sell only freshly picked produce. Intriguingly, they do this in accordance with ancient principles regarding the cycles of the moon. Local lore holds that planting and sowing should take place when the moon waxes. 'There are very old ideas and we try to sustain that culture,' says Sandra. This and the local volcanic soil ensure that their vegetables taste like no one else's. A regular customer, just back from Japan, stops by for a half melon. As Sandra cuts it for her she explains why she's been coming here for years. 'The supermarket doesn't give quality, but here it's very high. And I love Sandra's father. Giacomino really is the best man in the piazza!' According to Sandra, shopping habits have changed. Families used to buy two or three kilos of peaches at a time. Now individuals buy just three or four pieces of fruit. 'People used to buy once or twice a week in big quantities. Then the euro, the supermarkets, the shopping centres changed everything. Young people now don't understand the culture and tradition of the market. They're in a hurry. It affects us, of course. But the quality of food in the market is higher and people who understand that keep coming to us.' For the Caravaggio I buy the apples (which turn out indeed to be terrific). Anna does her whole weekly shop.

We chat amiably with Zaira from Romania and a man who sells dried pasta sauces, but the morning is beginning to burn towards noon and Anna is tiring. So we hurry through the last four items, getting most of them from the 'Maria' stall on the other side of the square, beside the Bruno statue. Here they get all their produce from the big market at Lunghezza near Tivoli. Do you have any out-of-season fruits? 'We have everything!' says Alessandro, whose mum is called Maria, as was her mum, hence the name of the business which started in the 1920s selling wild herbs to local restaurants. Alessandro has figs from Sicily, pomegranates from Israel, red grapes from Chile, white ones from Sicily, and staggeringly fragrant mint from the Roman countryside. 'I've been here since I was a baby,' he says. He lives now in Ostia, but well remembers when the centre of Rome was full of poor people. 'An apartment round here with five rooms would have a different family in each room. Then came the boom in the sixties. Now the same apartment with five rooms has just one person in it. Or, at most, one family.'

We still need medlars, though. And we get them from Sonia, an English Literature graduate, who runs a stall with her mum on the far side of the square. The medlars, from Spain, are pretty old but we're lucky to get them. Sonia studied English at La Sapienza, then in Boston, in London and at the University of Manchester. She did a teacher-training course in Grenoble as well but she came back to work with her mum. Why? 'It's the family business, and if you don't know somebody you can't get anything. It was like that when I was younger and it's like that now.' Her mum is wearing an AS Roma shirt, and an odd necklace of dried chillies. She looks at us, smiles, clenches her fist and shouts: 'Roma! Roma!'

Back at the flat comes the tricky business of actually recreating the painting. The whole family joins in. I suggest using the blue plastic washing-up bowl instead of a wicker basket in order to convey postmodern irony. Valeria snorts her derision and goes looking for a sixteenth-century-style wicker basket. There's one in the dining room. Liberato (Valeria's dad) gets bored and wanders off to watch TV. Nadia (her mum) meanwhile is studying the painting and working out which bits of fruit must go where. She and Valeria start arranging fruit as if it's a jigsaw puzzle. The pomegranate is split open. We have to cheat with the foliage, using bougainvillea leaves from the balcony. Liberato pops in to see how it's going. Finally the basket is finished! If you were picky, you'd notice details: where Caravaggio's pears are red ours are bright green. We don't have black figs and that pomegranate really should be smaller. But it's not bad, and our basket is definitely better than Derek Jarman's basket. He filled his with melons, lemons and tangerines! Amateur! All that remains is to take the picture. I've been playing around and realized I can't reproduce the background light and shade. So we'll have to do the post-modern-ironic thing after all. Valeria in her toga, looking rather good as a sixteenth-century rent boy, complains about the heavy basket. Gamely, she stands on the balcony. The light is fading fast but in the background you can just make out the church, and the neighbours' apartment building and the plane heading for Ciampino and the field where they're building the new sports centre. Oh this is all right. This is great! They should hang this in a museum!

VII: The Rats

'It's a cliché that all Italians love food. That's only the image for foreigners.'

Dario Argento

The world's greatest maker of horror films, Dario Argento, has shown us plenty of scary things in his forty-year career. In one sumptuous, blood-drenched masterpiece after another, he summoned demons, maggots, rainstorms, rats, ravens, razors and homicidal maniacs from the depths of his imagination and set them before us in the form of opulent, operatic nightmares with titles like *Inferno*, *Trauma* and *Sleepless.* His movies are famous for the disturbing and perverse ways in which people die: diced by falling stained-glass windows, stabbed with dressmakers' scissors, skewered by modernist sculpture, run over by trains, strangled with their own intestines, slashed to death by a crazed chimpanzee. So what do you imagine is the thing Argento hates most?

Cheese.

He'll tell you why himself in a minute, but first let's be clear what we're dealing with. We're dealing with artistic genius of an exalted and peculiarly Roman kind. Argento is one of the last of the golden generation of the post-war film-makers whose work constitutes the city's most important eruption of creativity since the age of Bernini and Borromini. If you hadn't heard of Argento until a few seconds ago (and a surprising number of benighted souls haven't) it's probably because he's worked almost exclusively in genres disdained by the respectable: thrillers and supernatural horror. Nevertheless, the so-called 'Italian Hitchcock' is unmistakeably a giant. He more or less invented modern splatter and, like his hero Antonioni, contributed a good deal to the uniquely Roman cinema of dreams. His fans span the globe. Juno, the pregnant American teenager of *Juno*, is a big Argento fan. So is Quentin Tarantino. Fellow horror maestros George Romero and John Carpenter are close friends and acknowledge a deep debt. The Japanese novelist Banana Yoshimoto has described how she was saved from suicide by watching *Suspiria*; she never realized anything could be so beautiful.

In his heyday in the 1970s and 1980s, Argento was Italy's most popular film-maker and earned so much money he bought a Greek island. In the nineties, tastes changed and Italian movies became embalmed in saccharine. Dario sold his island. He kept making movies, though, and even his oft-derided later work has a kick to it. He's never been much interested in dialogue or linear story structure. He's not even particularly good with actors, regarding most of them as 'false'. But his films glow and provoke because he remains faithful to his gothic, brutal, painterly visions and creates dense, dazzling, swift-moving slices of pure cinema. His movies are journeys to the id, free-floating dreamscapes, disorientingly presented within the conventions of horror and the detective story. They are drenched in references to alchemy, the occult and every painter from Botticelli and Caravaggio to Mondrian and Escher. Dario has been accused of sadism and misogyny. *Tenebrae* was foolishly banned in Britain in the 1980s as a 'video nasty'. His response is that he's searching for images that are poetic and profound rather than shocking. It's also true that the more times one sees them, the more impressive his films become, revealing unexpected layers of beauty and meaning. Maitland McDonagh, author of the best book about him, *Broken Mirrors, Broken Minds*, calls his films 'the most baroque, most stylish, most inventively violent, most dreamlike, most nightmarish and most haunting' Italy has produced. Not only does Argento's work look like nothing else, it also sounds unique. This is because, in the mid-seventies, Argento ditched the great Ennio Morricone for a previously obscure Roman rock band called Goblin. The band and its resident genius, Claudio Simonetti, went on to create for him a series of pounding, mesmeric soundtracks. Horror-film music was never the same again.

Rome is fond of the man universally known as 'Dario'. His biographer Alan Jones reported that when Argento filmed on the city's streets, crowds gathered to watch, proclaim their approval and shout things like 'Dario! Who's the killer?' He was born and bred in the city, and they see him as one of their own. His work reflects something essential: Rome's beauty and its dark side.

One of the city's odder shops is the little boutique of horrors Dario owns on Via dei Gracchi in Prati. It's called Profondo Rosso (Deep Red) and is a shrine for goths, ghouls and his fans from around the world. Signs in the window advertise fresh mice and cockroaches. The shelves are lined with horror DVDs and rubber masks of terrifying screen characters such as Frankenstein's monster, the Creature from the Black Lagoon and Silvio Berlusconi. In the basement museum, arranged like a dungeon and filled with props from Dario's movies, his voice assures visitors they are perfectly safe because the demons who live there have only just finished eating the last visitors. It's as scary as a much-loved teddy bear, but I was hoping to meet Dario here. I thought perhaps we could do an interview beside the gruesome child from *Phenomena*, or sit together beside the naked woman atop the cursed tomb from *The Church*.

Disappointingly, Dario proposes instead that I come to his apartment near the Portuguese embassy in Parioli. Finding the place is tricky because his flat number isn't listed at the main door. My heart leaps. A Dario game! But no, the building supervisor simply erased the number by mistake. Valeria and I ascend in a clanking old elevator like the one that killed the killer in *Profondo Rosso* and, at the top, Dario greets us wearing a comfy sweater and brown corduroys. Looking nothing whatever like the gaunt, lank-haired madman of his publicity pictures, he is small, charming and friendly. He ushers us into a large room, one end of which is sparsely furnished except for a huge plasma screen. On the wooden table lie piles of papers and a box of DVDs of *Inferno*. Nearer the door is a long white couch and a fine marble coffee table on which sits a menorah and a black cat, just like the cat who tormented Harvey Keitel in *The Black Cat*. (Dario's devotion to cats, especially black ones, rivals that of any of Rome's *gattare*, the old ladies who feed the feral moggies of the city's monuments. Dario feels for them because they were persecuted in mediaeval times when they were thought to be witches.) As we talk about his career, and his upsetting relationship with food, Dario gesticulates colourfully and even makes sound effects to accompany his anecdotes. He doesn't offer coffee, though, and he doesn't eat a thing. This is because there are many foods his body cannot tolerate. 'I'm coeliac so I have problems with food,' he explains. 'I am intolerant to lactose, any kind of bread, pizza, and many other things. Butter, cheese, milk. They all make me ill. I eat only because I need to, though sometimes food is a pleasure, like Japanese food. I like sushi, sashimi. And when I was in Bali I found I liked *nasi goreng*. But I don't like eating, and I don't like to see food around, especially on the set. When I make a film I don't eat at all.'

This is, of course, why in Dario's films people eat horrible things or nothing. In *The Bird with the Crystal Plumage* an artist recluse keeps a colony of plump tabby cats. You can probably guess why. (The hero heaves when he realizes he's unwittingly eaten one.) *Cat O' Nine Tails* features breast-shaped cartons of poisoned milk. The beer in *Sleepless* is toxic. In *Profondo Rosso* the coffee machine emits only noise and scalding steam. The only food consumed is a sandwich eaten open-mouthed by a repellent cop, and the only drink drunk is a cup of tea a professor spills seconds before he is murdered. In *Trauma* Asia (pronounced Ah-Zia) Argento, Dario's daughter and star of most of his later films, plays an anorexic who, when forced to eat, takes two bites ('*Happy* now?') then runs to vomit. *Inferno* is a volcano of alimentary vileness. A cat munches a twitching mouse, a green lizard chews a white butterfly, hundreds of rats swarm from a sewer to devour an antiquarian bookseller.

The sheer mania of Argento's food anxiety is even more evident in *Suspiria*, about a young American student called Suzy who enrols at a dance school in Germany run by witches. On her first day she gets hexed by a fat Russian cook (later seen chopping raw meat with a hatchet) and collapses. Water is then forced into Suzy's mouth from a cut-glass decanter and a creepy doctor puts her on a diet of slimy food and vile wine to 'build the blood'. A brief beer-drinking scene seems innocuous enough until you realize it is set in Hitler's favourite *Bier Keller*. In a phobic final pièce de résistance Dario takes symbolic revenge on all the food that ever made him ill. Suzy realizes she is being poisoned, so she pours the wine down the sink (where it congeals hideously), and chucks dinner into the toilet (where it splashes yukkily). She then sets off to destroy the witches' coven. Never in the history of cinema has food looked less appetizing. 'It's really disgusting!' says Dario gleefully. '*The most disgusting ever!* I put in some special colour, a mixture of blue and yellow so the food becomes the colour of cheese. Because cheese is the thing I hate most.' Because it's poisonous to you? '*YES!* In that scene, she throws some fish away and as it falls into the toilet and splashes it looks like *shit* with the drops – *ppshhh*! The drops which are coloured! It is revolting! *Revolting!* Like a *vomit!*'

I wonder if Dario's difficulties with food distanced him from other Italian film-makers, and from most Italians. 'No! It's a cliché that all Italians love food. That's only the image for foreigners. Not everybody is like this, especially film directors. I don't know why, but most directors don't like food. So the image of Italy is wrong! I don't even drink coffee. I don't like it.' But surely people like Fellini were renowned for their eating habits. 'Fellini didn't like food.' Eh? 'I know the image is different, but Fellini liked *restaurants*, not food. He was very sociable. But, like me, he was not a big eater. My sister worked as his assistant on *Juliet of the Spirits* and she told me he really didn't like to eat so much.' I thought Fellini's entire relationship with Mastroianni was based on their shared love of food? 'No. It was *Mastroianni* who loved eating. And the food he liked the most was *polpette*, meatballs. And of course Sergio Leone also loved food. I worked with him to write *Once Upon a Time in the West* and he was a big eater. It was also the cause of his death. First he was too fat, then he dieted too much, too fast. And you know the great obsession in his life? Marlene Dietrich. He believed Marlene Dietrich was bad luck. Whenever he heard the name "Marlene Dietrich" he'd go: *"Grrr-oowww-phhwahhh-nno!"* I never knew why, but just mention one of her films to him and it would be, *"Noooo! Aachhhhggghhh nooo!"* Always! It's true. Then, strange destiny. On the night he died, there was a Dietrich film on television. Sergio and his wife were watching together. At the end of the film, the wife goes, "Eh, Sergio, wake up," and he was dead.'

I ask about Luchino Visconti. 'Ahh! Visconti! A count. An aristocrat. Always *molto elegante* and very little portions. A very charming person and he ate just perfectly, everything balanced and tiny because very rich, important people eat very little. Did you know that? Like Giovanni Agnelli of Fiat. I was invited to his house when I was in Turin making *Profondo Rosso* and he ate the same way. Tiny portions. Tiny! Also Dino De Laurentiis. Just tiny pieces of meat like this [thumb and forefinger together] and a small salad like this [same gesture] and finish. No pasta. And live long!' How about Pier Paolo Pasolini? 'Not nice. Absolutely not. He was very brutal, very arrogant every time we tried to talk with him. He only liked poor people. To me it was: "But you are the son of the bourgeoisie, so you are disgusting." He looked at me like a piece of shit. Great films. Marvellous films! But as a person he was different.' Ugo Tognazzi?

'A *real* gourmet! One time I had a project with him and, when I went to his villa in Velletri, he cooked all the time. Food was so important to him and I found it very interesting. He would show me: "This is *duck*! Ah, *wonderful duck*! And this is *this*, and this is *that* . . ." Enchanted by cooking, very passionate.' A sexual thing? 'No, no, I don't think it was sexual, because he also had lots of sexual . . . He was a sexual man. He was famous for this. One time I was in the same hotel with him. We were making different films and I was on another floor, but my director of photography was on the same floor as him, and the next day he tells me: "I couldn't sleep because Ugo was all the night making noise with three women." Ugo liked his food, but he also liked women.'

Dario grew up after the Second World War, a sensitive and imaginative child in a big house at Piazza del Popolo. His father, Salvatore, was a film producer. His mother, Elda Luxarda, was a Brazilian-born model and actress. Dario has described his childhood as normal but a nurse stimulated his morbid imagination by telling him scary bedtime stories. In his teens he discovered the stories of Edgar Allan Poe, with whom he is still obsessed. Other frequently cited influences include the Brothers Grimm, Alfred Hitchcock and the films of Murnau and Fritz Lang. A no less important teacher and inspiration was the fabric and spirit of Rome itself, its churches, art and architecture.

In Rome, the weight of the past is overwhelming. In Elizabeth Bowen's phrase, 'What has accumulated in this place acts on everyone day and night, like an extra climate.' So it is in Dario's stories, where the crimes of his killers are invariably explained by past trauma, personal or historical. Few other storytellers have made the past so omnipresent.

Dario's scripts rarely refer to this directly, but in *Mother of Tears*, the last in his 'Three Mothers' trilogy about witches, a psychic makes the idea explicit. In Rome, he says, ghosts and spirits rise continuously from the city's 'layers of cemeteries'. Dario began to sense this when young: 'I absorbed the city when I was a child. It was like a big meadow, a playground for me. Like cowboys, me and my friends went everywhere. I discovered strange churches and strange places. Especially churches. We were a small group, a few teenagers. We were very interested in the church of the Anglicans on Babuino. We found it very mysterious, but the priest was so gentle with us. Also the marvellous one in Via Nazionale with the Pre-Raphaelite windows. I have so many favourite places in Rome. You know Santa Maria del Popolo, with the two big, marvellous Caravaggio paintings? This was my church, the church of my family, and the paintings are marvellous! And the architecture is marvellous! And on the floor were marble bas-reliefs of the graves of saints. You could walk on their faces because they were sticking out from the floor. I found it interesting to walk on the faces and the bodies of saints and warriors.'

His schooling nearby at the hands of Nazarene priests was ghastly enough to turn him atheist. 'Most of the people from my school became complete atheists because these priests were terrible. Not physically cruel. There were no beatings. But all the time surveillance, interrogations. Every morning, very early, we had to go to Mass. We went, but we hated it. School was until five o'clock – and in winter five is dark, so, when we left, we had to go down this long corridor past big paintings of the old saints looking very severe. Huge paintings! Huge statues! All very frightening. I came back to the religion when my father died [during the making of *Opera*], but until then I was an atheist.'

As a teenager Dario wrote for film journals and, when he finished school, didn't go to college but became a reviewer for Rome's evening paper *Paese Sera*. 'I was a follower of the *Cahiers du cinéma* and I liked the dark movies of America, the noirs, Jacques Tourneur, *Catwoman*, *The Seventh Victim*. The films I loved were the ones the critics didn't like and it got controversial with my newspaper. Every week the director would tell me. "Dario, someone has complained . . ." Every week! He'd say: "Why do you write these stupid things?" And I'd say: "I *like* Westerns. For me they are marvellous!" I made a stand, on purpose, to provoke. I'd say: "These films are beautiful, marvellous, *beautiful*! All these things. And they would say, "But this newspaper is Communist and Ford is a Fascist," or, "Howard Hawks is a Fascist." And I would say: "No, I don't think he is a Fascist; he is *a great director*!"'

In the late sixties Dario landed his first proper gig in film, co-writing with Bernardo Bertolucci *Once Upon a Time in the West* for Sergio Leone. Dario was paid just $400 for six months' work, but the film is now regarded as the finest Western ever made. Not bad for starters. Soon he was directing his own scripts, and working with Leone's favourite composer, Ennio Morricone, on three stylish, deliciously named 'animal' films, none of which is about animals: *The Bird with the Crystal Plumage*, *Cat O'Nine Tails* and *Four Flies on Grey Velvet*. These were terrific-looking but relatively conventional thrillers in the Italian tradition of *giallo* (yellow-paged pulp thrillers popular in the thirties and forties). Dario later dismissed them as 'a bit boring'. But no one is ever likely to say that of his breakthrough film, *Profondo Rosso*, a madly inventive murder mystery from 1975 notable for its haunted house (borrowed from some nuns), Goblin's first score and the presence of the English actor David Hemmings, who was cast because he had starred in Antonioni's *Blow-Up*, a film to which *Profondo Rosso* refers constantly. More important was the female lead, a clever and already famous scream queen called Daria Nicolodi with whom Dario now began the stormy central relationship of his life.

The couple never married but she became his lover, muse, co-writer, and, later, mother of Asia. Daria inspired Dario's most creative period, stimulating his interest in the occult and providing the story on which *Suspiria* was based. (Her Jewish grandmother Ivona Müller was a white witch who once spent time at a German school full of very dark ones.) One early crisis came when Dario refused to cast Daria as Suzy in *Suspiria* and gave the part to American actress Jessica Harper. Over the next decade attentive fans followed Daria/o's troubled relationship through the ever-more bizarre fates suffered by the characters she played in his movies. In *Profondo Rosso*, at the height of their bliss, Daria glows on screen and is merely stabbed, not even fatally. In *Inferno* (1980) she plays a sympathetic, neurotic minor character murderously attacked by cats. In *Tenebrae* (1982), a particularly bloody thriller inspired by Dario's encounter with an unhinged fan, Daria survives but ends the film screaming non-stop for a full thirty seconds. In *Phenomena*, a tale of mass murder and telepathic insects, she gets razored to death by a monkey. By 1987 the couple's relationship had hit the buffers, and in *Opera* Daria gets shot through the eye. But it may not have been personal: most of Dario's films are family affairs. His father and brother served as his producers. On screen, dreadful things happen to nearly all his actors, including his daughters. Fiore, the oldest, was beheaded in *Phenomena*. Asia, now one of Italy's most compelling screen performers, has been variously raped, seduced, rescued, blessed with the power of invisibility and traumatized by the sight of her mum decapitating her dad and walking off with his head.

One of Dario's least appreciated but most interesting premises is in *The Stendhal Syndrome*: the power of great art to cause great damage. The film is based on a book by psychiatrist Graziella Margherini about illnesses triggered by profound beauty. The condition takes its name from Stendhal's description of the palpitations, panic and sense of imminent collapse after his visit to one of the most beautiful churches in Florence. Symptoms of modern-art sensitives include fainting, panic attacks, hallucinations and split-personalities. In Dario's take on this, Asia plays a detective struck down by paintings at the Uffizi Gallery. She is then kidnapped and raped by a serial killer and ends up turning into a killer herself. Typical Dario, in other words: examine a highbrow subject through the devices and conventions of gory populism. The film gave him a chance, he says, to explore the fascinating process by which 'you look at a painting and your soul changes'. Most critics hated the film, but Dario defends it. 'It is a very good film. Yes! I can say that. I'm a critic! I'm objective! It's rich with paintings and Freud and craziness and many important things.' The syndrome occurs more commonly in Florence than Rome but it can strike anywhere. In an earlier version of Dario's project, Bridget Fonda played the detective and was struck down by a Hieronymus Bosch painting in Arizona. Dario points out that the wounds and blood of the *Christ* of Grünewald have apparently driven lots of people crazy, including, perhaps, Mel Gibson, whose *Passion of the Christ* was influenced by it. 'I saw that painting too, and it is terrible. And in Orvieto we have *The Last Judgement*. Many people go crazy in front of that also.' Dario suffered a dose of beauty sickness when he was a teenager too. 'I was with my family at the Parthenon in Athens and I became crazy. I became dizzy and felt terrible pain in my stomach. I was very sick. My father said it was the Greek food, which he thought was too heavy for me. But it wasn't that. It was the place.'

Argento films have always carried a powerful sense of the Catholic. In *Suspiria* witches perform a black mass. Subliminal bursts of church-organ music give the score of *Profondo Rosso* an ecclesiastic edge. The library in *Inferno* looks more like a gothic cathedral than most gothic cathedrals. But only in 1988, with *La Chiesa* (*The Church*), a film Dario wrote and produced but allowed protégé Michele Soavi to direct, did he shoot in a real church. 'In Italy no one will hire you a church for filming. And not in Germany, or France or Switzerland. Then a friend of mine said, "Go to Hungary," which was still Communist at that time. We went and they said: "You want to shoot in the church? OK you can shoot in the church." So every morning a priest came to deconsecrate the church. He desecrated it for us! And each night he came back to make it holy again. It was wonderful!' The film opens with a massacre by proto-Nazi Teutonic Knights wearing black crosses. One of their victims is a demon, but most are simple civilians. To cover their crime, the knights hide the burial pit (clearly signalled as a Nazi-style massacre) with a church. Flash forward to the twentieth century, and the pent-up furies of the victims rise to destroy the damned house of worship. But I'm confused.

Are the massacre victims meant to be Jews? Are they demons? Or innocent? Or innocent demons? Are there two types of demons? 'Exactly! Yes! They are different demons. The Christians are different demons.'

I'm still confused, but this leads to the interesting matter of the faint Jewish presence in his films – and to a surprising discovery. His former partner Daria, whose mother was Jewish, has said that much of the decor in *Suspiria* was Jewish; though (apart from some kabbalistic Hebrew lettering glimpsed in a single corridor) it's hard to see. In *Profondo Rosso*, however, Helga Ulmann, the blonde German psychic who gets murdered, sits at a Star-of-David-shaped table, has a giant menorah on her wall, and gets a Jewish funeral. When I ask Dario about this his answer surprises me: Helga is Jewish because Dario is himself a bit Jewish. 'I am Marrano [a Sephardic Jew forced to convert to Catholicism in the heyday of the Inquisition]. Yes! "Argento" means "Silver" in English, like Silverbaum, so I have a very Jewish name. My family was from Sicily and in the 1400s they had to decide to become Christian or to leave. So they stayed as Christians. Most of the Jews went away, some stayed. Then came the Inquisition, which was very heavy, like in Spain. My family converted but only to save their lives. They would say: "Oh yes, we go to church," but they became atheists.' The family came to Rome at the beginning of the twentieth century. I'm still intrigued about how Helga, who doesn't look Jewish and doesn't have a Jewish name, is Jewish. 'Some people are Jewish who don't look Jewish. And you have Jewish people called Müller. It's a German name but Jewish too. Helga is Jewish because she's a heroine. She is very beautiful, she has a pure spirit and is played by Macha Méril, a wonderful actress with a great spirit who was the lead in some of the most famous films of Godard. My scenographer [production designer] Giuseppe Bassan was Jewish, and we spoke about this, then we decided to put in all these symbols.'

Another oddity of Dario's movies is that even if he shoots them in Turin, which he loves, or Budapest, or New York or Minneapolis or even the 'Swiss Transylvania', most of his locations end up looking a bit like Rome. In *Inferno* New York's Riverside Drive and Central Park seem to have been transplanted to the banks of Tiber. In one of *Suspiria*'s best scenes – the murder of Daniel, the blind piano-player – Dario turned a famous Munich location into a nightmarish vision of Ancient Rome. The sequence starts in the Hofbräuhaus, where the Nazi Party was founded, then switches to the Königsplatz, a neo-classical space created in the nineteenth century, which was later altered to provide a setting for Nazi rallies. To this blighted location, visited by Mussolini in 1938, Dario adds an extra layer by lighting it to look like one of Giorgio de Chirico's metaphysical architecture paintings. (De Chirico, whose work explored Italy's relationship with its artistic and architectural past, died in Rome a year later.) The scene is unusually strong. We first see Daniel and his guide dog leave the beer hall, pass policemen, and venture alone into the vast, empty granite-paved square which is dominated by neo-classical temples. Birds flutter, shadows scamper and a stone eagle seems to shriek. Goblin's music becomes a series of nerve-shredding screams, drumbeats and bass chords. Evil spirits, ancient and modern, have awakened. As the music dies away and the audience relax, Daniel's guide dog jumps up and rips out his throat.

The location, says Dario, was chosen for its Nazi connections and the way it evokes Mussolini's Rome. 'This is Nazi architecture, similar to what you find in Turin and some parts of Rome. For me this architecture is a little bit evil. Like EUR, where I shot all of *Tenebrae*. It is uncomfortable to be there. It's a place that feels very modern but it is "old modern", from the 1940s. And it's from 2,000 years ago as well, because Hitler and Mussolini were obsessed with Roman architecture.' Argento's Fascist uncle played a part in shaping these thoughts. 'When I was very young, about five years old, my uncle came to Rome from Milan. He was in the same camp with Ezra Pound, a Fascist. For my uncle, Mussolini was a genius. So one day he says to all the nephews, to me, my brother and his sons: "Come with me; I want to show you something." So we go in the car and drive and drive. The street finishes, and we walk and walk across fields. At a certain moment we see EUR. This is just after the war and, because it was Fascist, EUR had been abandoned. I mean *completely* abandoned. It was something unbelievable for me to see these big marble buildings! These enormous buildings where nobody lived. *Nobody!* So we go to the big church, the *huge* church. It is abandoned too! We go inside and birds are flying around – *Psheww! Pshwewwww!* – like this! *So many birds!* Everything is abandoned. The fields around, *abandoned*! Wonderful farms, *abandoned*! It was one of the impressions of my life. I was just five and something like that goes very deep at that age. It was like discovering an abandoned city, like Machu Picchu or Angkor Wat. And because I was small, the buildings seemed even bigger! I thought: "*Ahhh my God! What is this?!*" (The abandoned church inspired the great scene in *Opera* where a flock of vengeful ravens swirl around an opera house during a performance of Verdi's *Macbeth*. The film is even more famous for way the killer forces his victim to watch his murders by taping needles under her eyelids.

The idea came from Dario's irritation with people in his audiences who close their eyes during his screen murders: 'I film these images because I want people to see them and not avoid the positive confrontation of their fears by looking away.'

Approaching his seventies, Dario now spends much of his time attending fan conventions around the world – he's just got back from Seoul – and he still inspires remarkable devotion. In London an admirer persuaded Dario to autograph his arm, then had the signature tattooed to make it permanent. Despite largely hostile reviews to his last film, *Giallo*, he's busy researching a new project, which will have something to do with a French monster called Gilles de Rais – 'the most evil person in history'. He explains: 'He was a very contradictory person. In the beginning he was the assistant of Joan of Arc. He was in every battle with her. Then, after she was killed, he turns against the religion and becomes the devil. In six years he killed more than a thousand young guys and young women. Then terrible torture and, at the end, hanging and burning. He was the most evil person in the world, but the film is not about this.' A romantic comedy, perhaps? A musical? 'It won't be directly about him.'

Meanwhile, Dario is appalled by the prospect of a remake of *Suspiria*. 'I don't know when and I don't know why. They didn't send me a script. I know nothing and I'm not involved in any way. I heard about it in the newspaper. I'll get very little money for it because the owners were 20th Century Fox. Voices tell me – I hear rumours – that Jessica Harper is the real producer. She's the wife of the chief of 20th Century Fox and she liked *Suspiria* because it was the best film she did, and now she wants to relive her glory. It's completely pointless, but they do it for the money and for the ambition of Jessica Harper to come back.' He reflects briefly on the changes that broke the post-war Italian cinema: 'We had about twenty-five to thirty years that were marvellous, then Italian films died for many reasons. There was TV and video, but mainly it was economic reasons. Our films became just comedy and romance. Absolutely boring, really. But we have a few new talents now, like Paolo Sorrentino. And *Gomorrah* is a wonderful film.'

He describes himself as 'lonely' and 'solitary' these days and doesn't go out as much as he used to. Even so, the ghosts of Rome retain their power to surprise. A couple of years ago he set the finale of *The Mother of Tears* in catacombs. Given that the script involved naked witches, acts of cannibalism and a perverse re-enactment of the spearing of Christ on the cross, the Vatican refused to let him film in any of their catacombs. The Jewish catacombs near Mussolini's former mansion, Villa Torlonia, were out of the question too because they were too dangerous to enter. Then Dario got lucky. 'We discovered a very noble old woman who has a big villa in Via Appia Antica which has private catacombs. We couldn't believe it. They are enormous! Kilometres and kilometres and no one has ever seen them! We were the first people to go inside. You just want to get lost in there but it is dangerous because the air is terrible. We filmed with flames and oil and when we went outside we were spitting black. We asked the prop man, "Please put bits of skull and bones around," and found we had real skulls and jaw bones. Bits of skeletons were coming up everywhere and we were walking on them. It was marvellous to shoot in this place with so much soul. We felt we were going to the deepest level of Rome. Old Rome starts about fifty metres down and you see how the new Metro [the C line] has destroyed many famous villas. The authorities don't say anything about this. They keep it a secret, but, really, they destroyed a lot. But there are many other villas. I think it's better for it all to stay underground. Leave it. Just *leave it*! Rome will bubble up by itself.'

VIII: The Doves

In 1975, Ugo Tognazzi, the great Roman actor, writer, producer, gourmet and lover, published his first book of recipes, punningly entitled *Il Rigettario*. Ricettario, with a 'c', would have been *Recipe Book*. The 'g' makes it the noun of *rigettare*, meaning 'reject' or 'vomit'. Tognazzi explained that his menus were 'inspired by what I call the "philosophy of rejection": rejection of everything that is in food and culinary art – with all due respect to the Great Experts, the Venerable Solons – conventional, fixed, coded. In this book you will find menus that are gargantuan, Trimalcio-esque, Franciscan, from the country.'

Here's one of his bold, unconventional recipes, for a casserole:

Ingredients for 10/12 people
8 doves (or pigeons or quails)
4 spoonfuls of butter
4 spoonfuls of oil
about 200 grams of Parma ham
sage
juice of 2 lemons
2 liqueur glasses of brandy

It is not possible to prepare a jugged hare for a dozen companions without offering the alternative of a less violent dish. This is the reason for the doves, which can also be pigeons (but maybe they're the same thing) or quails.

I prepare the doves. I pierce them with raw parma ham (sweet, to be clear, not mountain ham, which is very salty). I add a few little leaves of sage and sprinkle the doves, inside and out, with salt, then I leave them browning slowly with oil and butter in a saucepan and sprinkle them every now and then with a bit of broth.

I squeeze a couple of lemons which I sprinkle over the doves. I turn up the heat.

In a separate little saucepan, I put two liqueur glasses of brandy. I warm it, light and pour it over the doves, which are ready on a coarse plate.

IX: The Crumbs

You can catch a glimpse of Italy's female patron saint every day of the year in the little park beside the Castel Sant'Angelo. Austere and frail, one soft shoulder thrust defiantly into a cold wind, Catherine of Siena can be seen heading towards the Vatican. In one slender hand she clutches her trademark symbol of purity and virginity, a white lily. With the other she gently holds her cloak closed. Her nose is sharp, her lips pursed, her gaze otherworldly. The flapping folds of her marble habit resemble those in Bernini's sensual depiction of St Teresa of Avila across town. But unlike the Teresa of that statue, this stony Catherine doesn't appear to be in the throes of orgasmic bliss. She just looks very, very hungry. Which is perfectly understandable.

The white marble statue is the most visible part of a curious monument by the Sicilian sculptor Francesco Messina, better known for his dying green bronze horse at the Rai studios in north Rome and the black Pope Pius XII in St Peter's. It's easy to miss Catherine, for she is hidden in a stand of trees set back from street. It's even easier to fail to notice the scenes from her saintly life carved on the tomb-like slab beside her. The most striking of these depicts Catherine on bended knee, preparing to catch the head of a nice-looking young man who is about to be decapitated.

Relatively little known in the English-speaking world, mediaeval, mystical Catherine is one of the superstars of Catholicism, a theological giant to rank alongside the likes of Thomas Aquinas and Augustine. Her brief, strange career as a holy woman and political powerhouse in the late fourteenth century was marked by contradictions. She worked for peace between Christians but campaigned for 'sweet holy crusade against the wicked unbelieving dogs' of Islam. She was illiterate but a great writer (she dictated to secretaries). She was frail but levitated up stairs. She healed a big rift in the Church and triggered an even bigger rift in the Church. She was impressively kind and generous to strangers. She was mercilessly cruel to herself. Members of her own family sometimes found her actions upsettingly perverse and detractors considered her a fraud, possibly even a witch. Yet she offered moral guidance to the powerful, and fired off letters to warlords, kings, queens and popes. Catherine has been many contradictory things to many contradictory people: spiritual role model, poster girl for peace and love, champion of aggression, symbol of democracy, icon of strict hierarchy, Italy's answer to Joan of Arc, her country's best-known internationalist. Multitasking as only the very top saints can, she's also been *patrona* of nurses, the sick, firefighters, pious people who are mocked for being pious, and anyone tempted by sex.

Pretty much the only thing Catherine can never be is patron saint of a balanced diet. This is because her relationship with food was gruesome. She shoved twigs down her throat to make herself vomit, supped pus, dreamed of drinking blood and starved herself to death at the age of thirty-three. And all in a good cause.

Catherine started young, attempting her first fast when she was just six years old, in response to a visit from Christ who came to her in a vision, dressed as a bishop. According to Catherine's later friend, confessor and biographer Raymond of Capua, she soon afterwards developed a dislike for meat, gave up childish games and devoted herself instead to prayer and meditation. On one occasion, inspired by heroic tales of such 'desert fathers' as the pillar-dwelling Simeon Stylites, she spent a day as a hermit, hiding in a cave with just a piece of bread for nourishment, and praying for Jesus to show himself again. Instead, she levitated. She took this to be the work of the devil, and ran home. Around this time, together with a few other girls her own age, she formed a little group for secret sessions of prayer and self-whipping using specially knotted ropes. Following another divine visitation, this time by the Virgin Mary, Catherine pledged herself to perpetual virginity. Later, in protest at the idea of getting married, she cut off all her hair and married Christ instead, taking his holy foreskin as her wedding ring.

As Catherine grew older her holiness became ever more extreme. For three years from the age of sixteen she refused to speak to anyone in her family. She also drastically reduced her food intake, wore rough wool clothes and tied an iron chain around her waist so tightly it cut into her skin. She slept half an hour every other night. To expiate her sins (and the sins of the living and the sins of the dead) she flogged herself for four and a half hours daily with an iron chain until blood flowed. She refused to eat meat, hot food or wine and subsisted instead on small amounts of bread, cold water, raw vegetables and the Eucharist, with which she was obsessed. Catherine's body weight soon halved and she became depressed and tearful. When her mother, fearing her daughter would die, forced her to bathe at the local hot spring and sleep in a soft bed, the ever-resourceful Catherine found a way to use the sulphurous waters to scald herself, and secretly took sharp sticks to bed and stabbed herself though the night. Catherine came to believe she was being attacked by evil spirits and demanded to join a Dominican lay order called The Sisters of Penance. When she was turned down because of her youth and her mother's objections Catherine responded by developing a disfiguring pox and declared that she would not recover until she was allowed to join. She got her way.

At nineteen, Christ visited Catherine once more to tell her to go into the world and do good works. She promptly abandoned her isolation and flung herself into feeding and caring for the sick and the poor, developing a 'compulsion to serve others by suffering' and performing healing and food-multiplication miracles. When plague tore through her city, Catherine and her followers – known as Caterinati – tended the sick and buried the dead. She is credited with numerous healings, too, including that of Raymond who, dying of plague, prayed with Catherine, ate food she prepared, went to sleep and woke up feeling well. Another turning point came when Catherine dressed the pus-filled sores of a woman with terminal breast cancer. Determined to overcome her feelings of nausea and repulsion, she carefully gathered the pus into a ladle and drank it all. 'Never in my life have I tasted any food and drink sweeter or more exquisite,' she wrote. By way of reward, Jesus came to her again that night, more intimate now than ever, and told Catherine to drink blood from the wound in his side, which, of course, she did. (Catherine's letters are full of weaning imagery, and mediaeval culture often pictured Christ as female, with the wound in the side as breast, sometimes even vulva, and his blood as milk.)

This episode of blood-drinking curtailed Catherine's diet still further. 'Divine grace' now infused her stomach so she no longer needed normal food. Indeed, she could no longer eat at all without pain, though she did drink water and sometimes chewed bitter herbs before spitting them out. Generally, she was tired and listless, but when it came to performing charitable acts she became energetic, even hyperactive. Critics claimed she must be either eating in secret or getting some kind of demonic assistance, a charge she rebutted by ostentatiously eating a few mouthfuls a day, which caused even more suffering. 'Her stomach could digest nothing and her body heat consumed no energy,' Raymond tells us.

> Therefore anything she ingested needed to exit by the same way it entered otherwise it caused her acute pain and swelling of her entire body. The holy virgin swallowed nothing of the herbs and things she chewed; nevertheless because it was impossible to avoid some crumb of food or descending into her stomach and because she willingly drank fresh water to quench the thirst, she was constrained every day to vomit what she had eaten. To do this she regularly and with great pain inserted stalks of fennel and other plants into her stomach, otherwise being unable to vomit. Because of her disparagers and particularly those who were scandalized by her fasting, she maintained this lifestyle until her death.

Where normal food caused distress, Catherine developed an

overwhelming desire for the Eucharist, craving it constantly. She could detect un-consecrated hosts, and revered priests for their ability to preside over the 'miracle' of the sacrament. After reception, her mouth was said to fill with blood. Indeed, it is probable that no one in Church history has been more obsessed with blood. Catherine's letters are full of urgings to 'drown' and 'bathe' in the stuff. 'Become drunk with his blood, and sate yourselves with blood and clothe yourselves with blood,' she advises. And: 'I will have blood, and in blood have I satisfied and shall satisfy my soul.' In Catherine's view, blood is the ultimate super-food, a bridge between God and humanity. Blood is not just a substitute for food, it *is* all other foods blended into one. 'The blood is become beverage to all who will, and the flesh, food; and in no other way whatsoever could our appetite have been satisfied,' she explains. The baby Jesus is 'the little cask' whose body was 'tapped' when circumcised. As an adult crucified and 'emptied' (of blood) on the cross, Jesus becomes a celestial version of the food hall at Harrods: 'At the end of this grand stairway of the opened side you shall find an entire shop of scented spices [. . .] Hasten, then [. . .] that you may have the place where you can find [. . .] the table where you may take your delight, and the meat with which you may be sated: for he has become our table, our meat, our servitor [. . .]' In a letter to a monk called Jeronimo, Catherine depicts the Holy Trinity as a restaurant:

Jesus is the roast lamb cooked on the cross, the Holy Spirit is the waiter, and God the dining table: 'Oh tender Lamb, roasted over the fire of divine charity on the spit of the most holy cross! Oh sweetest of foods, filled with joy and happiness and consolation! You lack nothing, because for those who serve you in truth you are made table and food and waiter. We see well that the Father is a table for us, and a bed where the soul can rest. And we see the Word, his only-begotten Son, who has given himself to us as food with such burning love. And who has brought him to us? The waiter, the Holy Spirit – and because of his boundless love he is not satisfied to have anyone else wait on us but wants to serve as waiter himself.

Frances Stonor Saunders, in her book *Hawkwood*, suggests that Catherine's self-starvation and sexual repression may have contributed to a 'full-blown neurosis' but warns that it is impossible to psychoanalyse her retrospectively. Nevertheless, American mediaevalist Rudolph Bell's book *Holy Anorexia* argues that Catherine's relationship with food can be understood as an early case study of the illness we now call anorexia nervosa. Casting a late-twentieth century eye over her well-documented life, he located triggers for her behaviour in her family background. What began as religiously inspired fasting gradually escaped Catherine's control. 'As with present-day anorexics, she could be very active physically, slept very little, and claimed that she gladly would eat but had no appetite.' If she did eat 'it was only to enter into an eating/vomiting cycle such as is common among acute, long-term anorexics'. None of Catherine's friends, confessors, or enemies were able to change her ways or cure her anorexia.

Catherine was born to well-off parents just before the particularly ghastly plague year of 1348. Twenty-third in a family of twenty-five children, she was her mother's favourite, and the only child weaned by her mother. Her sickly twin,

Giovanna, by contrast, was sent out to a wet nurse and died. Giovanna's name was then passed on to the next (and last) daughter who was born soon afterwards. Catherine's father was a prominent and successful wool-dyer but in a time of famine, war and plague, tragedy was never far away. Bell links Catherine's abhorrence of food to a series of bereavements. Her early piety, he says, was merely 'tentative'. In a city traumatized by mass death and social upheaval, her imitation of adult religious practices was merely 'misplaced enthusiasm'. Catherine was playing a game. Even her childhood vow of perpetual virginity was normal for the time. Indeed, the most striking thing about Catherine's childhood, even as described by people who thought her a saint, is how ordinary she seems. Yes, she fasted and inflicted pain on herself, but 'not to excess by the standards of this age of heroic asceticism'. Apart from a budding desire for solitude and sense of guilt for the sins of others, Catherine seems to have been 'an obedient, happy, outgoing child'.

It was family tragedy that triggered her food trauma. Catherine was particularly close to a married older sister called Bonaventura who seems to have been a model of both moderation and sanctity. Bonaventura persuaded Catherine that sex and marriage might not be so bad, yet was also pious enough to go on hunger strike to stop her husband's 'immoral' behaviour. Catherine was impressed. Under Bonaventura's influence, Catherine even allowed herself to dress up a little and make herself pretty. Then Bonaventura died in childbirth, swiftly followed by the death of Giovanna, the youngest sister, named after Catherine's dead twin. Catherine seems to have blamed herself for both tragedies. It only added to her anxieties when her mother raised the possibility of Catherine marrying dead Bonaventura's husband. Now her self-starvation and mortifications started in earnest. Bell speculates on likely psychological triggers: 'Catherine lived when others had died and she believed that her graces in this world might ameliorate the just punishment of her loved ones in the next.' Her father was more sympathetic, but neither parent was enthusiastic about Catherine's retreat from the world. In turn, Catherine feared mightily for their souls. Indeed, she seems to have tortured herself to save her family. In her mind, she negotiated deals with Christ and his mother to save her own mother from hell, and her father from purgatory. Bell speculates:

> For the love she received from a belatedly understanding father and an all-too-worldly mother she felt obligated to be a good girl. So good and so special that her sacrifices in this world would save their souls in the next. To relieve herself of the burden of God's favour in allowing her to live when her sisters had died she became His humblest servant and dedicated herself totally to His work. She conquered the drives of appetite, sex, sleep and all material comfort; and if her punishments quickly took their physical toll, her will shaped the meaning of what she was doing.

Yet feminist historians warn against using a modern medical term to describe such a thoroughly mediaeval religious state of mind. Catherine was a product of a culture in which suffering, especially the self-inflicted sort, was admired and God was thought to be encountered through eating. Indeed, in a culture of scarcity, where harvests were easily disrupted and the rotation of the seasons was acutely felt, food carried more potent and charged religious symbolism than money or sex. To share food with strangers was seen as heroic generosity, while self-starving revealed, in Caroline Walker Bynum's phrase, 'the kind of courage and holy foolishness that marked the saints'. Food could be used to exert control, show renunciation, sustain life or produce suffering. It could symbolize both fertility and sacrifice. And this was even more true for women than for men, because in late-mediaeval culture it was women who prepared, managed and sometimes even *were* food. Mothers weaned. But saints 'exuded' sweet oils and other edible substances from their bodies, and were even said, like Catherine, to conjure food from thin air, as Jesus had done in the miracle of the loaves and fishes. Male saints tended to be dauntless men of action; female ones were mystics, levitated, developed stigmata, fell into trances, saw visions and supernatural signs. Caroline Walker Bynum tells us in her book *Holy Feast, Holy Fast* that mediaeval women often spoke of 'hunger' for God, but 'served Christ by feeding others, donating to the poor the food that husbands and fathers felt proud to save and consume'. Cases like Catherine of Siena, she argues, can only be understood in the context of their time. 'However absurd or vulgar some mediaeval practises and language may seem to casual modern observers,' she counsels, 'we do well [. . .] not to take offence.'

For Catherine was merely the latest in a line of food-phobic female saints of a sort that first emerged in the Low Countries in the late-twelfth century and set off a craze lasting nearly 400 years. Ida of Louvain 'ate only mouldy bread and, if food was served to her, she mixed it together in order to destroy any pleasant taste it might have'. Marie of Oignies mutilated herself out of guilt about eating, fasted for long periods and ate coarse black bread to tear her throat and make it bleed. Lutgard of Aywieres told a prospective husband: 'Go away from me, food of death, nutriment of villainy!' Dorothy of Montau suffered 'agonies of guilt over enjoying three small fishes, developed nausea at the sight or smell of food, ate so little she ceased excreting and would have gone without food entirely [. . .] had not her confessor intervened'. Such holy women, particularly numerous in Italy, were invariably 'devoted to the Eucharist' and this idea of God as food wreaked some of the strangest psychological and psychosomatic havoc. Saints' mouths were said to fill with the blood of Christ. A German nun saw the baby Jesus in a vision and told him: 'If I had you, I'd eat you up I love you so much.' Colette of Corbie went for long periods without food or sleep, developed stigmata and saw Christ as a child on a dish, carved up like a piece of meat.

The aptly named Christina the Astonishing survived terrifying food austerities and her habit of throwing herself into thorn bushes, threshing mills, freezing rivers and burning furnaces to live to the age of seventy-four. But she was an exception. Holy masochism did not usually coexist with longevity. Margaret of Cortona, penitent and patron saint of the mentally ill, 'struggled to conquer thirst', fasted obsessively and gave away whole loaves to the poor while keeping crumbs for herself. She spoke of her fasting as a 'war' to be fought 'until there is no life left' and duly starved herself to death at the age of fifty. The guilt-ridden Angela of Foligno, famed for her charity and theological brilliance, whipped and burned herself and starved to death as part of her search for 'God's love'. Near the end of her life, she had an urge to walk through town naked with dead fish and rotting meat hung around her neck confessing her gluttony and declaring: 'Come see this worthless woman, full of malice and pretence, receptacle of every vice and evil.' As a website devoted to Angela reminds us: 'Mysticism is characterized by an abnormal psychic state which may culminate in ecstasy. Such states are sanctified when the individual is perfectly united with God and the whole personality is fully free; otherwise, it may simply be a sign of psychosis.' Then there was Clare Gambacorta of Pisa, who mixed ashes with her food to spoil the taste, ate only scraps from others' plates and inflicted extreme pain on herself to divert attention from her aching stomach. A chorus of singing angels was said to have greeted the birth of Columba of Rieti, who grew up, like Catherine, to cut off her hair, self-flagellate and deprive herself of sleep. Columba also mixed ashes and dirt into what little food she ate, drank vinegar, licked dirty dishes, fell into trances while doing housework and once dropped into a fire a baby she was supposed to be looking after. When Columba finally starved herself to death, at the age of thirty-four, a fellow saint saw her soul as a 'radiance rising to heaven'.

Catherine was by far the most politically significant of these holy women. During adulthood her fame spread far beyond Siena and she was regarded as a living saint. She carved a reputation as a peacemaker and as advocate of a planned (but never-realized) new crusade against the Turks. Her most-celebrated achievement was helping to persuade Pope Gregory XI to bring the papacy back to Rome after the eighty-year exile in Avignon. It was, in the old phrase, a Pyrrhic victory with an unintended consequence: the Western Schism. Gregory died a year later and his successor, Urban VI, made himself so unpopular that the Church split. For the next three decades rival popes ruled in Rome and Avignon. The disappointment helped to kill Catherine. Her pleas for unity were ignored so, for a month in January 1380, she added refusal to drink water to her usual privations, slipped into a coma, partly recovered and died three months later at the age of thirty, her last reported words being, 'Blood! Blood!'

Catherine's remains are so close by it seems almost rude not to visit. A short walk from the bus stop at Largo Argentina brings me to her tomb under the main altar of the main Dominican church of Santa Maria Sopra Minerva. She is portrayed in a gleaming white marble effigy. The light is poor but the tomb is beautiful. As I wonder what it might be like to be a believer a proper pilgrim stops by, prays fervently, bows to the tomb and takes a photograph. I still can't imagine. In 1638, frescoes from the room where Catherine had died were brought to the church and are now in a space behind the sacristy. At the door, I ask a priest where I might find the original site. He directs me to the Piazza di Santa Chiara, down the little street opposite the church. The fourteenth-century building is long gone, but at number 14 the spot where Catherine and her disciples lived is marked by a little chapel, the Cappella del Transito, restored in 1999, which is in the same building as a tiny nineteenth-century theatre which is now run as the Teatro dei Comici. In 1999 Pope John Paul II declared Catherine a patron saint of all Europe. Catherine, he said, had been tireless in her commitment to resolving conflicts. She had admonished churchmen and political rulers alike and declared in an 'uninhibited, powerful and incisive tone' that 'in a society inspired by Christian values there could never be grounds for conflict so serious that the reasons of force need prevail over the force of reason'. A more ambiguous picture emerges from the story that lies behind the panel of the Catherine memorial in Rome.

Let the bas-relief set the scene for us: Catherine is crouching like an unusually calm wicketkeeper. In front of her is the bowed, kneeling figure of a muscular young man dressed in a loincloth. Above him stands an equally buff executioner, also semi-naked, poised to strike the death blow with a sword resembling a large kitchen knife. Catherine is about to catch the head. The image is based on the most celebrated of all Catherine's nearly 400 letters, her description to Raymond of her ecstatic participation in the beheading in the main square of Siena in 1375 of a political prisoner (or spy) called Niccolò di Toldo. The political background was complex: an increasingly bitter struggle between the Pope and the Tuscan city states, led by Florence, over the issue of mastery of Italy. The tension would soon explode into a three-year bloodbath known as the War of the Eight Saints, and this would end with defeat for Florence, the return of the papacy to Italy, and a massacre in Cesena by papal troops. For now, though, Toldo, a young nobleman who had infiltrated the anti-papal government of Siena, was waiting to die for his crime. The scene was set for Catherine to stride to centre stage via the medium of an exceedingly odd love story. Her letter is only a few pages long, yet its flamboyant shape-shifting erotic imagery generates remarkable heat. And its soaring masochistic spirituality takes us to the heart of her conviction that blood is the only nourishment anyone really needs.

Catherine's letters 'are like sparks of a mysterious fire, ignited in her ardent heart by Infinite Love', said Pope Paul VI. And of all her letters, this one arouses special admiration.

'In all the Lives of the Saints there are few episodes more striking, and none more profoundly moving,' said one of Catherine's modern hagiographers, the expert on vampires and witches, Montague Summers. The letter is generally considered metaphorical and allegorical, 'a parable in praise of Charity', according to Harvard scholar Joan del Pozzo, which should be read 'in the light of its ethical/spiritual complexities, and its duality as a melodrama and a sermon'. The drama is modelled on Christ's Passion, with Toldo in the role of Jesus and Catherine as Virgin Mary. Yet Toldo's severed head and spurting blood are real enough. And this fits the picture too. As Frances Stonor Saunders puts it: 'Nowhere in mediaeval literature is the proximity of the pious with the violent more immediate, more unsettling than in Catherine's letters. With their martial language and spectacular surplus of blood, they are like a battlefield, the site of a gruesome parody of the holy mysteries.'

The letter opens with a typical flourish: 'I, Catherine, servant and slave of the servants of Christ, write and recommend myself to you in the precious blood of the Son of God, desiring to see you plunged and drowned in that sweet blood, all aglow with his burning charity.' That's metaphorical burning, drowning, slavery, sweetness and God all in one sentence . . . and she's just getting started. Having further advised Raymond to 'acquire the little virtue of true humility born of self-hatred which, in turn, is born of love' she moves to her exciting news: 'I have taken a man's head in my very hands, and been so deeply moved that my heart can hardly conceive it or my tongue relate it and I am sure no eye has seen or ear heard the like. God's will was at work [. . .]!' Catherine explains that she visited 'the person you know about' (Toldo), and helped him make confession and prepare for his execution. Leaving aside a certain spiritual one-upmanship here (she succeeded in converting the sinner where others had failed), it's the eroticism that catches the eye. Catherine transforms Niccoló's fear into joyful embrace of death. When Toldo asks her to be with him at the end, she promises to do so. Next day, she returns and 'greatly consoles' him by taking him to hear Mass and receive Holy Communion, something he has not done before. But Niccoló is 'still fearful that he might not be strong when it came to the point'. So far so this has been relatively normal for the anguished stuff that took place between condemned men and religious comforters.

But now Catherine launches into uncharted territory: a delirious passion in both senses of the word. God, in his 'boundless and burning goodness', suddenly makes Niccoló fall *in love with* Catherine (as a stand-in for God). He rests his head on Catherine's breast and begs her to be with him at the end so he can 'be all right and die happy'. She responds hotly: 'I was aware of sudden joy, of the odour of his blood in some way mingled with that of my own, which I hope to shed for sweet Jesus my bridegroom. As my own yearning increased and I sensed his fear, I said to him: 'Courage, dearest brother. We shall soon be at the wedding. You will be going to it bathed in the sweet blood of God's Son and with the sweet name of Jesus [on your lips]. Don't let it slip from your mind for an instant. I shall be waiting for you at the place of execution.' At this, Niccoló tells Catherine 'lovely things' such as: he is happy that his 'soul's delight' will be 'at the blessed place of my execution' and is impatient to consummate their love.

Frustratingly, Niccoló has to wait in prison a little longer; but Catherine hurries to the place of wedding/beheading, the city's crowded central square. She climbs the wooden scaffold, mentally screens out the throng, talks to the Virgin Mary and gets a feel for the coming climax by putting her own head on the block. Finally, Niccoló arrives 'meek as a lamb', sees Catherine and begins to laugh. Catherine makes the sign of the cross and tells him to put his head on the block: 'Down with you to the wedding, brother! You will soon be in the life that never ends.' Niccoló obeys and Catherine stretches out his neck for him – and for the executioner. As Niccoló murmurs the words 'Jesus!' and 'Catherine!' the blow falls. Catherine exults: 'I received his head into my hands, while my eyes were fixed on the divine Goodness as I said: "I want it!"'

With Catherine now happily covered in Niccoló's blood, Christ appears on the scene like 'the light of the sun' and receives 'into his own the blood that had just been shed'. In 'a fire of holy desire', Niccoló's blood merges with the blood of Christ and Niccoló's soul enters the 'mercy-filled store-house' of Christ's side. 'How indescribably moving it was to see God's goodness; to see the gentleness and love with which he waited to welcome that soul – with the eyes of his mercy fixed on it – as it left the body and was plunged into his open side, bathed in its own blood that now possessed merit through the blood of God's Son.' Before the wound closes, Niccoló turns and does 'a lovely thing', 'one last gesture that would melt a thousand hearts'. He looks back, 'like a bride who pauses on the bridegroom's threshold to look back and bows her thanks to her escort'. In the space of a few lines Catherine has given us a blood wedding and bewilderingly rapid switches of sexual identity. Niccoló, the husband, turned into a bride. Catherine, the bride, became a male escort. Jesus revealed his female side. Catherine is now 'serenely at peace' and 'so impregnated with the scent of blood that I could not bear to remove the blood itself that had splashed onto me'.

The letter concludes with Catherine urging Raymond to imitate Niccoló's martyrdom, the better to dedicate himself to their work in the Church.

Viewed from a traditional Catholic perspective, it is a beautiful story. As heroine and leading lady of her own drama, Catherine is 'remarkable for her compassion, sensitivity, vulnerability, and dauntless courage in confronting overwhelming forces', says Del Pozzo. Catherine and Niccoló 'are joined in a crescendo of increasing intimacy, are separated by the executioner's axe, and are finally "wed" through munificent Divine Charity. Their bittersweet execution/"love story" reveals Catherine's extraordinary, seldom-displayed narrative powers; it celebrates Toldo's gallantry and Catherine's faith, and underscores the spiritual "first Truth" that God is Love.' And, from another perspective, Stonor Saunders again: 'for all the theological justifications, Catherine's joy at being splashed in the blood of a decapitated man – an experience she sought to prolong by not washing – suggests that she was now suffering from a full-blown neurosis'.

Historians have revealed a political aspect. Thomas Luongo, author of *The Saintly Politics of Catherine of Siena*, suggests that the letter represents something of a powerplay. It is the first thing Catherine writes to Raymond, future leader of the Dominicans in Italy (and the man mainly responsible for Catherine's later elevation to sainthood). The letter, written at a vital moment in Catherine's burgeoning public career, also demonstrates her authority and establishes a public role for herself. 'On one level

Catherine here was just telling Raymond what happened to her, using a letter to share experiences with an absent friend. But the meaning of the story was much more far-ranging: an audacious presentation of her identity and authority as well as the nature of her involvement in politics.' Moreover, this political role was murky in the extreme. According to Stonor Saunders, Niccoló was a spy working for Gérard du Puy, brutal de facto ruler of Perugia and cousin of Pope Gregory, and had been sent to destabilize Siena's government, to the advantage of the papacy. While du Puy pleaded for Toldo's life to be spared, this does not appear to have occurred to Catherine, despite her status as a local holy woman. Du Puy, meanwhile was intimately allied with the terrifying English mercenary Sir John Hawkwood, and with Catherine's friend, Raymond. Raymond, in turn, was a key player in all this and other intrigues, and used Catherine as cover. Catherine, who was busy urging Hawkwood to stop killing Christians and instead fight in the Pope's hoped-for crusade against the Turks, recognized that she was an instrument of papal policy, and seemed to enjoy the frisson of spying. She acknowledged in several of her letters that her movements were being dictated by the Pope, and she invited his prelates to use her and other 'servants of God [as] spies' in order to gauge popular sentiments in the conflict between the papacy and Tuscany. Luongo quotes a bitter view of Catherine recorded by the Florentine chronicler Marchionne di Coppo Stefani. 'She was esteemed like a prophet' by her supporters. 'But by the others she was held to be a hypocrite and a wicked woman.'

In our age Catherine has come to be revered and marketed as a symbol of democracy, peace, internationalism. In 1970, when Pope Paul VI declared her, alongside Teresa of Avila, one of only two female Doctors of the Church (a third, Thérèse of Lisieux, was appointed in 1997), he praised Catherine's 'inherent wisdom, the lucid, profound and inebriating assimilation of divine truths and of the mysteries of the faith'. A campaign to have Catherine declared co-patron saint of Europe bore fruit in 1999, when John Paul II appointed her to the post alongside Bridget of Sweden and Edith Stein (the philosopher and Carmelite nun murdered at Auschwitz because she was born Jewish). Catherine, said the Pope, had been 'tireless in her commitment to resolving the many conflicts which afflicted the society of her time'.

But just how did the food-loving nation of Italy come to choose a food-phobe like Catherine as its national saint? (She shares the role with the male saint Francis of Assisi – who was also not a big eater, though his abstemious lifestyle was comparatively moderate.) The answer lies in a deal between the Church and Fascism. Catherine's cult never stopped developing after her lifetime. Shortly after her death she was promoted in Siena by Church and civic authorities, and in Rome mainly by the Dominicans. Even her body is shared. Her torso, arms and legs are buried at Santa Maria Sopra Minerva but her head and a finger went to Siena, where they became holy relics. Catherine was declared a saint eighty years after her death by the Sienese Pope Pius II. For hundreds of years, the Sienese and the Dominicans promoted Catherine. In the fifteenth century inspiring accounts of Catherine's life helped deepen the religious obsession there with blood. By the sixteenth century the ascetic, mystical Catherine was seen as a model for nuns. In the nineteenth and twentieth centuries, the cult of the holy virgin took on new political significance. Historian Gerald

Parsons has tracked the twists and turns of her cult in detail. During the Risorgimento, the movement that led to the creation of the modern Italian state, she was promoted as a nationalist icon. By the early twentieth century she was being depicted as a backer for the Italian invasion of Libya and a supporter of the Italian army in the First World War. Even before Mussolini her name had become associated with aggressive Italian nationalism and 'the vocabulary of crusade'. But in the 1920s it got worse.

The Dominicans and politicians in Siena launched a campaign to have Catherine declared a national saint. Mussolini, whose father had hated the church, regarded religion with contempt. But the political advantages of having the Church on his side were too great to ignore. He and the Vatican negotiated the mutually beneficial Concordat and Lateran treaties of 1929, granting the Vatican numerous privileges and harnessing the influence of Catholicism for the Fascist cause. Pope Pius XI declared the deal had 'restored God to Italy and Italy to God', while Mussolini basked in international prestige and extra support at home. In this context it became useful for Catherine's champions to promote her in ever-more explicitly pro-Fascist terms. She became 'the most Italian of the Italian saints', the embodiment of the supposed ancient virtues of *italianità* and *romanità* ('Italian-ness' and 'Roman-ness') beloved by Mussolini. Her sense of discipline and devotion to hierarchy and unity made it possible to see her as a role model for Fascist women. In 1932 she became patron saint of the official Fascist girls' movement. When Italy invaded Ethiopia, using poison gas and committing other atrocities, young members of the organization raised money to send a painting of Catherine to Italian soldiers. Italy's bishops praised the war, and Catherine's vision of moral renewal and Italian unity under the papacy was likened to Mussolini's vision of moral renewal and Italian unity under himself. Unveiling the bust of Catherine that still stands on the Pincio, a Fascist politician praised the new 'spring-time of spiritual rebirth which shone with the actions of Italy's eminent *condottiero,* Benito Mussolini' and claimed that Catherine wanted the Pope in Rome because she believed Rome should rule the world. The Archbishop of Siena described Mussolini as the 'great man' of the twentieth century and declared that both Catherine and the Fascist dictator were heroes of the same mission of peace. The process culminated on 18 June 1939, three months before the start of the Second World War, when Pius XII – 'Hitler's Pope', in Rupert Cornwell's controversial phrase – declared Catherine *patrona* of the Fascist state. Six months later Mussolini, who as a young Socialist had denounced religion as man-made and a tool for controlling the weak-minded, pledged his personal support for the lavish renovation of the Sanctuary of St Catherine in Siena. With the outbreak of war, Catherine found herself hymned as protector of an Italy 'returned in our times to Imperial greatness'. Church leaders prayed to Catherine to protect Italian servicemen and help secure victory. An inspiring booklet for soldiers of Catherine's thoughts and quotations was published under three headings: *Believe, Obey, Fight* (Mussolini's slogan). At the newly inaugurated annual festival devoted to Catherine, a bishop delivered blessings to troops from the turret of an armoured car parked in front of her basilica, San Domenico.

After the war, Catherine was rebranded yet again and slowly stripped of her Fascist associations. She became, first, a protector of Italian soldiers, then protector of *Allied* soldiers as well, then inspiration for post-war reconstruction, and later a patron of Italian peacekeeping soldiers on United Nations missions. Catherinian festivals, conferences and journals now deal with themes of peace, justice and service, emphasizing the country's new commitment 'to the ideals of peace, justice, fraternity, and by participation in the community of European nations'. Still, it's hard to forget one particular photograph from the Second World War: it shows the main square in Siena awash with flags, military uniforms and 'Roman' salutes as the mummified head of St Catherine is paraded in a jewelled glass box to inspire Italy's soldiers to fight for Hitler on the Russian front.

X: The Ricotta

'Only those who are mythical are real'

The Centaur, Pasolini's *Medea*

I used to think I was the only person who knew this place even existed. The Caffarella Park is a wedge of rugged hills, farmland and buried ruins thrusting into the city from the south-east, near the catacombs and the Appian Way. At one time the area was papal hunting ground. By the late-twentieth century, it was a favourite haunt for heroin addicts and transvestite prostitutes. Around the time of the year 2000 Jubilee the park began to gentrify. Over the last few years, volunteer groups have sprung up to keep it tidy. Walkers and mountain bikers now share its rugged paths and weekends are a time for guided tours of nature trails and archaeological treasures. Still, though, hardly anyone seems to have clocked my favourite spot. It's a ten-minute walk from the old flat and this is how you get there. Enter the park opposite the school on Via Latina, head past the kids' playground and the sandy court where old men play boules and follow the path up a gentle slope to the area fenced off for dogshit. Then down the steep hill by the white horse to where the athletes and bodybuilders exercise, but turn off the main path and climb the big hill to the ridge, ending up on the ridge above the sheep farm. From here it's just another few minutes on the dirt path to the left. Stick to the path as it winds around the big holes, which are ancient villa ruins, and follow it all the way to the sweetest spot. Mind the nettles, now, get comfy among the tall grasses, savour the fragrance of wild mint and give yourself over to one of the great views of the city. To the south is a sweeping twelve-mile vista of the Alban Hills, Ciampino Airport and the Pope's summer residence at Castel Gandolfo. Below, a little river and its valley and, on the far side, a sacred wood, gentle-looking slopes and the little cave of the Egeria Nymphaeum. To the north you can see the gasometer at Ostiense and the tops of office buildings on the Cristoforo Colombo. Birds fly by at eye level, there's a warm breeze, and just listen to the sheep and the church bells! And almost no one's ever even known about this! Except Pier Paolo Pasolini, Orson Welles and the entire film crew, that is. Pasolini shot his crucifixion scenes for *La Ricotta* here.

The movie is a half-hour masterpiece of black comedy and deeply Christian satire – although, hidden inside a tedious portmanteau movie from 1963 called *RoGoPaG*, it's almost as obscure as its location. The title is derived from the names of the four contributing directors, Roberto Rossellini, Jean-Luc Godard, Pasolini and Ugo Gregoretti. But Pasolini's segment is by far the best. It got him prosecuted under an old Fascist law and also earned him a four-month prison sentence for blasphemy, though he never actually went to jail. The ricotta in question is a cheese made from sheep's milk which, rather wonderfully, can these days be bought freshly made from the little farmhouse I just mentioned, a few yards from the movie location. The ramshackle building is about 400 years old. Romanian shepherds tend the flock. The cheese is softer, less chalky in texture and much tastier than the ricotta in supermarkets and it comes in the little white-plastic colander that gives it its shape. Eat ricotta with vegetables, bread or as a pasta filling and it's quite a delicacy. Historically, however, it has a different meaning: it was one of the staple foods of the Roman poor. And, in Pasolini's *La Ricotta*, the cheese becomes a powerful metaphor.

On my little hilltop, Orson Welles plays a film director shooting the crucifixion scene of a kitschy religious epic of the sort often made in Cinecittà in the 1950s. The atmosphere on set is rude and irreverent. The crew booze, dance to pop music and persuade one of the girls to do a striptease. Attempts to shoot a scene of Jesus being taken down from the cross dissolve in nose-picking and laughter. Pasolini's vision is rooted, as it often was, in his profoundly Christian sensibilities, even though he loathed the Church for its sexophobia and hypocrisy. Here he unsuccessfully tried to head off trouble by declaring in a caption before the film starts: 'It is not difficult to predict that this story of mine will produce biased, ambiguous and scandalized judgements. In any case, I want to state here and now that, however *La Ricotta* is taken, the story of the Passion, which *La Ricotta* indirectly recalls, is, for me, the greatest event that has ever happened and the books that recount it the most sublime ever written.'

In the English-speaking world Pasolini is known as a maker of poetic, dazzling, pain-filled films like *Accattone*, *Il Decameron* and *Theorem*. In Italy the memory is different. He is seen as a novelist, poet and political activist who also happened to make films. He is certainly not considered the equal of the likes of Rossellini, Visconti, Fellini and Antonioni. Pasolini, by contrast, was a formidable, contrarian left-wing intellectual figure, daring and highly original, his too-brief life a continuous scandal. Defiantly gay and a defrocked Communist, he was often reviled and widely misunderstood. Pasolini was usually in conflict with almost everyone, not least himself. Maria Callas was madly, unrequitedly in love with him. And he had powerful enemies: the Vatican, Christian Democrat politicians, Fascists, the Mafia. His films depicted the poor not so much with respect as with adoration: he saw the untamed, uncorrupted underclass as the last bastion of integrity in society. Pasolini's last, posthumously released picture, *Salò*, a relentlessly dark allegory and depiction of Fascism and sadism, remains perhaps the most despised and controversial movie ever made. Yet Pasolini, who was murdered in 1975, has come to be regarded as a symbol of integrity, honesty and courage. In retrospect he has become something of the Conscience of the nation, even a quasi-religious figure in an increasingly secular land. The 'great blasphemer, grand criminal, supreme sage' got important things right. Long before the Red Brigades, Pasolini predicted Fascism from the left. Two decades before *tangentopoli*, he denounced Italy's rulers as hopelessly corrupt and demanded they be put on public trial. Long before the coming of Silvio Berlusconi, Pasolini warned of the dangers of TV and mass consumerism.

In *La Ricotta* his main character, Stracci, is the deeply poor actor playing the good thief crucified alongside Jesus. Stracci is desperately hungry, and no one will give him any food. The crew and other actors mock him. The director is barely aware he exists. When there's an on-set banquet for the director's friends, Stracci is excluded. Even when he finds food the star actress's yapping dog eats it all. Finally Stracci manages to con a small amount of money, runs down the road and buys ricotta, with which he stuffs himself. Finally comes his big scene. He's tied to the cross and hoisted up; and, just before the cameras roll, a bunch of glamorous VIPs appear. Stracci is forgotten again. As the party unfolds, he suffers with indigestion on his cross. By the time the director is ready to shoot again Stracci is dead. He is a modern Jesus. He has died for others' sins.

'It's a perfect little film, and very funny,' says one of Pasolini's modern champions, Fulvio Abbate, novelist, newspaper columnist and one-of-a-kind YouTube commentator. 'It's a masterpiece from an artistic and moral point of view, but I would call it an "involuntary masterpiece" because it's not a real film, just an episode.' The director's banquet from which Stracci is excluded is a metaphor for class inequity, but the key image is of a crown of thorns lying in the basket of food. The ricotta was chosen solely for its symbolism as the classic food of the *burini*, the poor of the countryside and the edge of the city. Pasolini himself ate little and never had much interest in food. 'He had more of a sexual hunger than a food hunger,' Fulvio explains. 'In [his unfinished last novel] *Petrolio* there's a description of sex with fifteen people and the description of pricks, one after the other, is very dramatic. It's very dark, obsessive. And that's why he's not hungry for food. He's hungry for sex, but in a bulimic way: he'd have a huge amount of sex, and feel guilty afterwards. He never had any sort of a Dionysian relationship with food.' The two main women in Pasolini's life cooked for him: his mother, Susanna (who appears memorably as the Virgin Mary in *The Gospel According to St Matthew*), and his friend the actress Laura Betti (who plays a selfish diva in *La Ricotta*) nursed him through a period of illness with a stomach ulcer and became the keeper of

Pasolini's artistic, poetic and political legacy.

There's plenty of food in *La Ricotta*, but it serves mainly to torment. The rich people mock Stracci's desperation. Even the diva's dog eats his food. This is because the alimentary meaning of the film is the exact opposite of eating. 'It's not about food,' says Abbate. 'It's about hunger. The theme of hunger recurs a lot in Italian popular cinema and theatre. Hunger is also the reason for the great emigrations. Here, Stracci is not just hungry. He has a *terrible* hunger. It is the atavistic deep hunger of the poor, a hunger from his ancestors. He represents the poor of Rome through the centuries. And he finds it impossible to accumulate food in a capitalistic way because his hunger is so extreme he hasn't got time. When he dreams, he has only one dream: an end to his hunger. And when he has food, he eats until he dies.'

XI: The Asparagus

'If a person is rubbed with asparagus mashed in oil, he
will never be stung by bees'

Pliny the Elder

With a slightly bashful '*Ciao*', Valeria's uncle Ezio
enters the living room in a green camouflage jacket
and dark forage cap. A rifle is slung over one shoulder and
he carries a plastic bag full of enough small dead birds to
feed us all. I sense a connection between the gun and the
birds. He eyes me suspiciously, and says, 'I've heard about
you.' It's quite an introduction to the most famous member
of the family. His woodland quails and thrushes, later
stuffed with bacon slices and pan-fried with laurel leaves,
turn out to be surprisingly delicious.

Valeria's family lives in Rome. Their apartment even has
a view to the back lot of the Cinecittà Studio. Their collective soul, however, resides in a village about an hour's
drive south, near Arpino, which is where Gaius Marius and
Cicero used to live. To a rootless cosmopolitan like me, the
family's sense of being rooted in such a place seems rather
magical. Valeria's big-hearted grandma, widowed when
young, is known for the warmth of her personality and

the expertise of her cooking. Last month she made pizza for forty guests. Because of her dark skin, her neighbour – a sheep farmer and one-time *carabiniere* – used to call her *La Bella Mora* (the beautiful Brunette). When drunk he would stand outside the house serenading her with love songs or shouting rude things about Romans. In her seventies now, she grows olives and raises chickens in the field above her house. The chocolate biscuits she bakes in industrial quantities at Christmas are famous far and wide. The Albanian refugees she took in nearly twenty years ago have flourished and become a second family. Her own family traces itself back at least 300 years, but there's stuff in this district so old it makes the Etruscans look like parvenus. By legend, Saturn, god of the harvest, founded the place and the original inhabitants were mythic Pelasgians. Historians insist that Volsci and Samnites lived here before the Romans, but a few hilltops away are the remains of a megalithic city. Its walls are made of smooth polygonal stone and there's a pointed arch, unique in all Europe. Archaeologists speculate that the structure may predate Stonehenge; locals prefer to think the walls were built by a race of one-eyed giants, hence the local name: 'The Walls of the Cyclops'.

Ezio, meanwhile, is a devoted Communist and works at a beekeeping cooperative that makes honey, royal jelly, wax and soaps. His greatest joy is to be in nature, hunting, walking, savouring the turning of the seasons, communing with the mountains and forest. This he usually prefers to do alone. So to be invited, as we just have been, to join him to search for wild asparagus is quite an honour. The asparagus here is prized and quite different from cultivated varieties. It has slight, feathery fronds, a woody stalk and a delicate, sharper, perfumed taste concentrated in the spear-shaped tip. Pliny the Elder praised its nutritional and medicinal qualities (a splendid remedy for jaundice and toothache) and maintained that wild asparagus was the only sort worth having. He scorned the 'gluttony' of cultivation and heavy-headed varieties. There are, however, drawbacks to wild-asparagus hunting. It is something of a plant-kingdom recluse and a master of disguise. It grows not in sociable colonies but in ones and twos, scattered deep in the woods, camouflaged and hard for a novice to spot.

I'd heard of asparagus expeditions around Mount Tuscolo and on the slopes and groves around the strange Albano Lake at Castel Gandolfo, where the Pope goes for the summer. A plant as enigmatic as asparagus seemed to fit with a volcanic lake known for its black sands, crystal-clear water and unexplained disappearances. But something lurks out here too. The best time of year for asparagus, early spring, is also the season when vipers come out to play. Not so long ago these snakes had all but died out. But vipers keep the rodent populations under control, so, as part of a programme to maintain ecological diversity, government helicopters spent a season dropping young snakes into the deepest parts of the forest. The reseeding worked and the viper population returned to pre-Second World War levels. I've never met one, and they're reputed to be shy, so I'm not worried. But the women in the family are phobic. *La Bella Mora* is so frightened by snakes that if she glimpses one on TV in a nature documentary she'll run out of the room. Valeria recalls walking near the house when she was eight with her when a large, black, non-poisonous serpent (not a viper) slithered from a wall and dropped in front of them. Grandma screamed, 'O God!' and fled, leaving Valeria behind. Valeria begins to think it might not be a good idea to go down to the woods today. To make the point, she shows me the Wikipedia entry on viper-bite symptoms: 'rapidly spreading acute pain, followed by oedema and discoloration. Severe haemorrhagic necrosis may occur within a few hours. Vision may be severely impaired, most likely due to degradation of blood and blood vessels in the eyes. The venom has both coagulant and anticoagulant effects.' Ezio assures us he hasn't seen one in many years. Vipers run (or slither) away when they feel vibrations from human footsteps. Anyway, they're far more interested in eating mice than they are in biting us. We'll wear thick boots, be careful and we'll be fine. And he'll bring a tourniquet.

We head straight across the field and climb towards the hill. Grey clouds, saturated colours, drizzle. Past a small vineyard, all string and growing posts, a tree lies rotting in the red-black mud. We enter the woods, which are steep and a thicker green. Leaving the narrow path, Ezio starts spotting and gathering. 'There's one . . . And there. See?' At first, all I see is a mass of tendrils, leaves and branches. I study his dainty, quick movements, try to notice what he notices, and begin to get the hang of it. Here is where the spears grow. Behind, Valeria, still nervous, pauses every now and then to stamp her feet to frighten anything in the undergrowth. Ezio reassures her. I begin to spot distinctive, lighter feathery plants, but for each one I see Ezio has five; and, where most of mine already had their spears plucked, Ezio is picking fresh ones. After a while, I have just six. He has a whole sheaf. Valeria has a dozen. We are strung out now, busily exploring our own patches of forest. Up ahead, Ezio has stopped and is studying an object near his feet. 'You should come and see this,' he says softly. 'What is it?' 'It's a viper.' I can just make it out, a pale coil part-hidden among dead leaves. His calm makes me calm, but by the time I reach him the snake has scuttled. But Valeria's face is white and she's shouting, 'Where is it? Where *is* it!?' She's properly frightened now. We have to leave. She half walks, half runs, pausing to stamp and shout. Ezio says: 'It was such a beautiful beast. It wouldn't have hurt you.' She calms down only when we reach the road.

Back at the house, Grandma is appalled by news of the close encounter: 'You saw a viper? A real *viper*? You actually *saw* it?' She shakes her head at the horror. 'And what did you *do*?'

'We came home quickly,' says Valeria. 'What do you do when you see one?'

'I've never seen one.'

'Never?'

'I've never seen one, and I never want to.'

Grandma is happy to have the asparagus, though, and prepares our little bundle for supper. She washes them individually, cuts away the woody stems, then fries them with pancetta and serves with spaghetti. It's really nice. Haemorrhagic necrosis might have made it less so.

XII: The Wafer

I'd been hoping to locate the very best Communion wafers in Rome and report on how they are manufactured, but I cannot. Most of Rome's Communion wafers are made by nuns in special workshops behind closed doors in cloistered convents. These, obviously, cannot be visited. However, Sister Maria Concetta of the Clarisse Convent of the Immaculate Conception in Albano Laziale has very kindly agreed to talk me through the process by telephone.

Me: 'Can you explain how Communion wafers are made?'

Sister Maria: 'We have a contemplative vocation and the idea is to offer a service to the Church and to the liturgy. Everybody knows the importance of the wafer. Once it is consecrated in the Eucharist celebration, it is transformed into the body of Christ. This is very important for us because through the wafer we produce, and through the words of the consecration, we obtain the body of Christ. It is of vital importance in the life of a Christian because it gives us the real "alive" and true presence of the body of Christ. And the only real presence we have of Christ is in the wafer of the Eucharist.'

Me: 'So it's important to make something pure?'

Sister Maria: 'Of course, of course! So for us as producers of the wafer this is not just a job, it is also to sustain the convent. But we really devote our whole attention, delicacy, hygiene and perfection where possible. Because everything is transformed into the body of Christ. The rules of the Church require us to use pure water and flour. And we are aware that these will become the body of Christ.'

Me: 'So you prepare spiritually? Do you pray before you begin? What ingredients do you use? Can you take us through the whole thing?'

Sister Maria: 'There is no preparatory ritual. But there is an attitude and a sensibility from us. As in our other workshops, before starting a job we make the sign of the Cross. There's a simple prayer, a simple invocation to the Lord. In this workshop in particular there is a heart that beats also because we are aware that the job will soon become the body of Christ. Before starting any action every good Christian makes the sign of the Cross. It's a normal good habit. It's the symbol of our salvation. As to the choice of the ingredients, these come from the rules of the Church. Water and flour is the secret, like the *pane azimo* [Jewish matzo]. The *pane azimo*, which was chosen by Jesus for the Last Supper. Other ingredients are absolutely not allowed, so we have to take maximum care that it's only water and flour.'

Me: 'Where do you get these?'

Sister Maria: 'We use drinking water that is passed through a filter in the workshop so we can have it as pure as possible. As regards the flour, we have a deal with a mill that does it for us in a certain way, in the way it is supposed to be. According to the rules, it is a delicate process and we need to have a flour that responds. In other words, the grinding of the flour has to be done in a certain way, to have the right level of humidity inside the flour. Otherwise the *cialda* [wafer] will all break once they are packaged. So we need the right level of humidity before cooking. It's all in the pure flour and there's no adding chemicals or other stuff. Absolutely not.'

Me: 'Do you do this analysis or the mill?'

Sister Maria: 'We do it in cooperation with the mill. But we can also control it from here.'

Me: 'You use a local, secular mill?'

Sister Maria: 'It's not really close. It's quite far away.'

Me: 'What's its name?'

Sister Maria: 'I prefer not to tell you.'

Me: 'Is it considered a privilege in the convent to do this work? Is it only the older nuns who do this?'

Sister Maria: 'Do you want to know about my community in particular? Well, there are the young sisters who work on the machines that produce the wafers, and the older sisters are occupied in the phase of wrapping. The wafers are counted. There are little and big wafers and they are weighed on electronic scales and put in special little bags.'

Me: 'So how exactly does the wafer-making work?'

Sister Maria: 'There are various phases: the phase of cooking, and the phase of humidification. First the water and flour are mixed into a paste called *pastella* and we know how to recognize when it's ready. It has to be worked in a certain way. The nuns say it has to be "smooth like silk". And from there it passes directly to the electric machines where the wafers are cooked.'

Me: 'What do the machines look like? Are they ovens?'

Sister Maria: 'They are *piastre* [presses/plates]. We have little cabins with plates inside and each machine produces two wafers simultaneously. From there they go into the humidification cell, which softens the wafer so it can be cut.

Otherwise it would break into too many fragments. You cannot cut the wafer once it has left the machines. It needs to be humidified, but this humidification must not ruin the wafer. Everything has to be calculated with precision, electronically. If the humidification is not right the wafer is too hard to cut. If you overdo the humidification the wafer loses its fragrance, which is almost the fragrance of fresh bread. And we pay a lot of attention to every detail because we know what the wafer will become.'

Me: 'So it's quite technological? You control everything electronically?'

Sister Maria: 'Yes, for the production we do. After the phase of humidification it passes to the phase of cutting and we have machines to cut the wafers. There are small wafers for the people, bigger wafers for celebrants and even bigger – fifteen centimetres in diameter – for the co-celebrations, when there are several priests together. The cutting is done with specific machines.'

Me: 'And then?'

Sister Maria: 'After the cutting there is the phase of packaging. The big wafers are counted one by one. The small ones are weighed. Everything is precise. We put them in pre-printed bags, which show the expiry date and the ingredients and the name of the workshop. And then the bags are sealed.'

Me: 'Do you have to wear particular clothing? Gloves? Masks?'

Sister Maria: 'Yes, we wear all white. Our overalls are like habits. Normally our habits are brown, but in the wafer workshop they are white. We don't use masks or gloves. And we don't have hats, but we do cover our hair with part of the uniform that is a cap by itself.'

Me: 'The picture I'm getting is that you're almost like doctors performing surgery. Is it like an operating theatre? It must be very clean. Is the room tiled? Do you have fluorescent lighting?'

Sister Maria: 'No! It is much simpler and warmer. We're not at the level of an operating theatre! But it is very clean and tidy certainly.'

Me: 'Antiseptic?'

Sister Maria: 'No, no. But certainly maximum cleanliness. The environment is covered with tiles so there is maximum cleanliness.'

Me: 'What is the ceiling made of? Stone? What lights do you have?'

Sister Maria: 'We use neon light and we have a false ceiling suitable for the hygiene and to insulate the sound of the machines.'

Me: 'How many people are involved?'

Sister Maria: 'Only some of the nuns are involved. It's a pretty large community. We are twenty-three in total and six nuns work in the wafer workshop. If we need more people, then more nuns get involved. We all help each other. The community is like a family. The number depends on the time of year. It's not like a factory. We are like a family.'

Me: 'When are you busiest?'

Sister Maria: 'Because of where we live, near Rome the demand for wafers is spread throughout the year. And we are near Castel Gandolfo and in the summer the Pope comes and there's a big influx of spiritual groups and congregations. But all this is harmonized according to the spiritual life of the community of the convent. We have time for prayer, time for training, time for the "fraternal life". If the nuns who make the wafers have to go on a course, others take their place. It's not like a factory. It's a family life.'

Me: 'How long do they work each day in the workshop?'

Sister Maria: 'We start at eighty thirty, after morning prayer, and go on till twelve thirty, more or less. Then, in the afternoon, it's from three fifteen until five forty-five or six o'clock. But again it depends on the time of year and the obligations of the community.'

Me: 'Where do the wafers go? Who are your clients?'

Sister Maria: 'We first privilege our local diocese, which means the parish churches, but also outside. Also we supply Catholic bookshops who sell them retail to individual churches.'

Me: 'Mainly in Rome and Lazio?'

Sister Maria: 'Also other regions. But sometimes we have to say no because our own community life has to come first. From work comes sustenance for our convent, but we can't let the work affect our liturgical life.'

Me: 'Do wafers from different convents taste different?'

Sister Maria: 'I hope that each wafer workshop keeps faith with the ingredients demanded by the Church.'

Me: 'But if each workshop is supplied by a different mill, isn't it possible that the wafers taste different?'

Sister Maria: 'Certainly. Maybe one difference comes from the type of wheat. It's all natural, but there are different types of cultivation of wheat nevertheless. The place and the quality of the soil might make a difference. That might slightly vary the final taste.'

Me: 'Is it something you've ever noticed?'

Sister Maria: 'When I've found myself in other convents I have noticed a difference. But it also depends on the cooking, on the way of cooking. Some workshops cook it a bit longer, so it has a taste of cooked bread. Some prefer it a bit underdone.'

Me: 'So there is a difference between wafers?'

Sister Maria: 'I think so, but it doesn't compromise much in the end. Another important factor is the conservation of the wafers. If the wafer is kept in a dry place and the expiry date is respected it remains tasty. But if it is kept in a damp place, as often happened in old convents, the wafer will be affected. There are workshops that prefer to produce thin wafers, and that changes the taste as well. We advise our priests not to buy too many at once, so they won't get too damp. Once you open the bag and leave it in a damp, closed sacristy the taste will change. The wafer is like bread. It immediately absorbs odours, moisture, and all these factors compromise the taste and the wafer itself.'

Me: 'Who picks the design on the wafer?'

Sister Maria: 'When we buy the *piastre* we can choose from among different symbols. The symbol is printed by steel *piastre* during the cooking phase. We prefer the Cross.'

Me: 'You can have other symbols?'

Sister Maria: 'We can have an ear of wheat or a chalice. But we definitely prefer the Cross.'

Me: 'And what about the bags?'

Sister Maria: 'The bags are sealed and have the logo of the monastery, which is SCA – which stands for Sorelle Clarisse Albano [Sisters of the Cloister of Albano] and inside the letter C is the bell tower of our church. We designed this ourselves.'

Me: 'How central a part does wafer production play in your lives? What else do you do?'

Sister Maria: 'We try to be independent and self-sufficient. Work in our convent has a double aim: sustenance of the community but also helping people who are poorer than us. This comes from our Franciscan spirit. Being Clarisse, we feel this very strongly. Work should not be a matter of prestige but of helping people who need us. We are twinned with the nuns of Santa Teresa of Calcutta and some missionary places in Africa. But we also work with families in the area who are in great distress. One of our other workshops makes objects from olive wood.'

Me: 'Tell me about your order.'

Sister Maria: 'We are Clarisse Daughters of Saint Clare and St Francis of Assisi. In other words, we are Franciscans, but Clarisse of the second Franciscan order, so we have a cloistered life of contemplation. There are also the so-called Franciscans nuns who live an apostolic, active life. But our priority is praying.'

Me: 'Are you mostly Italians? Or also nuns from abroad?'

Sister Maria: 'No, at the moment we are all Italians.'

Me: 'Well, thank you very much. You've been very kind. I'm sorry to keep you on the phone so long.'

Sister Maria: 'It's been a real interrogation! But the whole community wishes you good luck with the book.'

XIII: The Cat

'It was I who made Fellini famous, not the other way around'
Anita Ekberg

It's the best-known image of modern Rome. But does anyone remember exactly why Anita Ekberg and Marcello Mastroianni end up in the Trevi Fountain in *La Dolce Vita*? That's right. Cat food. He, the mediocre gossip journalist, has been driving her, the voluptuous, unattainably beautiful blonde film star, around Rome all night. Finally she gets out of the car, finds a cute white pussycat and is seized by the desire to take care of it. 'Marcello, we must find some milk,' she says. 'Where are we going to find milk at this time of night?' he says forlornly. While he trudges off, Ekberg and her pussy wander the deserted little streets and meow at each other. She balances the fluffy little creature on her head. Then she sees the fountain, and cannot help but wade in like a sea goddess. By the time Marcello returns with a glass of milk he's rather brilliantly acquired, she is cavorting in the water and has forgotten entirely about the cat. She tells Marcello to join her. Gamely, he gets in too. He worships her beauty. She anoints him with a few drops of water. He's too overwhelmed even to touch her face. Suddenly day breaks and someone switches off the fountain.

The scene was shot on a cold March night and took nine hours to complete. Ekberg, well-padded and used to Swedish winters, barely noticed the temperature. Mastroianni shivered continuously, drank an entire bottle of vodka to keep warm and ended up drunk. The scene has entered popular memory both as erotic climax and profound expression of modern Italian identity. But it was hardly a triumph for the image of the Latin lover. Around Ekberg, Mastroianni's character is like a lost puppy and never even gets a kiss. When he takes her back to her hotel, he gets punched out by her boyfriend. Yet the film saddled Mastroianni with the reputation of being the sexiest man in Italy, supposedly the world's sexiest country. The image stuck to him no matter how hard he tried to subvert it. In later films he played cuckolds, gay men, a pregnant man, an array of 'wretches', as he put it, 'where sex didn't even enter the picture'. Film critic Jacqueline Reich devoted a whole book to deconstructing Mastroianni's screen persona: 'Rather than the Latin Lover,' she said, 'he is the *inetto*, the Italian incarnation of the schlemiel or antihero.' The roles he played reflected masculinity in crisis in post-war Italy. She interprets the fountain scene as symbolic castration and points out that his character fails to accomplish anything in the course of the movie. He is a 'semi-prostitute' in his work, emotionally impotent with women and he actively chooses passivity. 'Mired in mediocrity, he succumbs to the temptations of bourgeois and aristocratic decadence.'

Well, all right, if you insist. But we love Mastroianni. How can anyone watch him and not be charmed by his combination of beauty, elegance, daring and self-deprecating humour? *La Dolce Vita* was his first work with Fellini and they went on to form one of the most interesting actor–director double acts in history. Everyone knows that Mastroianni came to be seen as Fellini's alter ego. Not everyone knows their relationship was rooted in food. Mastroianni was an old university friend and acting colleague of Fellini's wife, Giulietta Masina. But what really drew the director to the actor was the way Mastroianni ate. 'We would see each other sometimes in restaurants,' Fellini told his friend and biographer Charlotte Chandler. 'He was always eating a lot. I noticed that because I have a natural affinity with people who like to eat. You can always recognize a person who likes to eat, not because of the quantity he consumes but because of a sort of gusto – a person experiencing true pleasure. So first I noticed Marcello because I felt this restaurant rapport with him.'

Food defined much for Fellini. His parents had met when his father worked in a pasta factory, but by the time Federico was a boy the marriage had soured. His father spent as much time as possible away from the family home in Rimini, selling wines and cheeses around Italy and having affairs. Federico's lonely mother wanted him to grow up to become a priest. Federico's father hoped he'd be a food salesman. Federico wanted to be neither. Many years later, though, he found himself in a meeting with film financiers and it struck him that he'd ended up following his father after all. Only difference was that while his father's customers loved and understood the food he sold, the money men neither liked nor comprehended his movies. Fellini always sensed his father through the medium of food. As a boy he felt guilty about eating at all because his father was always away, supposedly working hard to put food on the family table. They always had enough but Federico came to think of his dad as a tall carafe of fine olive oil.

As a youngster Fellini thought 'hungry' meant having an appetite. In Rome as a struggling writer in the 1940s, he discovered a different meaning. 'For breakfast, if I sold some of my writing, it meant more and better rolls, and a second or third coffee. I discovered what hunger pangs were.'

He later recalled that his first impression of Rome was of people eating. 'Everywhere people were eating with total pleasure things that looked impossibly delicious. I looked in the window of the restaurants and watched spaghetti being wound round forks. There were more shapes of pasta than I had known existed. Resplendent cheese stores, the smell of warm bread emanating from the bakeries, the pastry shops . . . I couldn't afford those pastry shops as I wanted to, because I didn't have enough money for even one meal a day – in addition, of course, to breakfast. So I determined that I would become rich enough to eat as many pastries as I wanted.' He was always impressed by the 'monumental rudeness' and 'gigantic vulgarity' of the city. He was in love with both qualities from the start. 'It is a kind of liberation,' he said later, 'a victory over the fear of bad taste, over propriety. For anyone who observes the city with the aim of expressing it creatively, it is an enrichment, an aspect of the fascination that Rome inspires.'

At one point he thought it might be fun to run a restaurant. Later, he realized he didn't want the responsibility, only the pleasure, of such places. He also compared film-making to cooking: 'I am like a chef in a kitchen with a lot of ingredients, some strange and some familiar, who says, "What shall I cook today?" Then I get inspired and start mixing and stirring, and a new dish is created. This is only an analogy. I cannot cook at all. When I was very young, a long time ago, I thought I might have an interest in learning to cook, but it turned out my only interest in cooking was in the eating of what was cooked.'

Food and drink usually also had sexual connotations, as the TV commercials Fellini made towards the end of his career made explicit. In an ad for Campari a dissatisfied young woman stares out of the window on a train, flicking a TV remote control to change the view. Mountains, pyramids, icebergs, forests? They all bore her. Then a big man wearing a scarf takes the control, and a picture of the tower of Pisa appears beside a giant bottle of Campari. She brightens. In a spot for the Banca di Roma, an elderly man has a nightmare about financial insecurity. This is represented by an idyllic sexy meal in the countryside with a beautiful woman who suddenly ties the man up in the path of an oncoming train and straddles a tree branch to watch his demise. For the pasta manufacturer Barilla, Fellini showed us a beautiful woman in a restaurant being offered an array of complicated-sounding French dishes. She'd rather have rigatoni – and *al dente* at that, meaning 'firm'. 'Yes, the innuendo is intended,' said Fellini. 'The pleasure of eating and the pleasure of sex are closely linked.'

Fellini became Italy's most celebrated film-maker. He ate many pastries. In the process, he transformed himself from being a skinny boy embarrassed about his thinness to a big man perpetually worried about by his waistline. On one occasion he dropped a crumbly hors d'oeuvre at a party. He was mortified. Had he ruined the white wall-to-wall carpet? He thought of standing on the spot to hide his crime, then running out when everyone left. Then he looked down and realized his stomach had caught the hors d'oeuvre, which he ate quickly before anyone noticed.

More important than contributing to his girth, though, the eateries of Rome fed his creativity. From his favourite tables in various *osterie* and *trattorie* Fellini smelled, nibbled and drank in the city. One favourite was Il Fico in Grottaferrata, a place to whose onion omelettes Mussolini had once been partial. Fellini became close friends with Il Fico's owner, Claudio Coccia, and cast him in small parts in several films. Fellini even invited him to the ceremony in Los Angeles when he received his honorary Oscar. (Coccia didn't go because he was afraid of flying.) Other places Fellini loved included the Tuscan restaurant Girarrosto Toscano in Via Campania, the Cesarina in Via Brunetti, Le Tavernelle in Monti (where the panna cotta is now called *La Dolce Vita* in homage), Harry's Bar in Via Veneto and Colline Emiliane in Via degli Avignonesi. Wherever Fellini ate, he held court, charmed and entertained and was, in turn, courted, charmed and entertained. On napkins and tablecloths he drew dreams, scenes and stories. Many of these rude, joyful impromptu artworks were shown at an exhibition at the Complesso del Vittoriano in 2009 and revealed themes from his movies presented in a style even more whimsical, self-referential, playful and sexual. Fellini and writer Ennio Flaiano actually wrote and designed *La Dolce Vita* and *8½* during long sessions at the Fiaschetteria Beltramme restaurant in Via della Croce. Producer Dino De Laurentiis felt only one actor could play the role of the journalist in *Dolce Vita*: Paul Newman. Fellini had another idea and one evening in 1959 invited Mastroianni to Beltramme to discuss the part. They ate, drank, laughed, chatted. Finally, Mastroianni asked to see the script. 'Give it to him, Ennio,' said Fellini. Ennio handed over one of Fellini's drawings, which showed a man with a huge penis floating on his back surrounded by half-naked women. Mastroianni took the part.

The fountain scene in *La Dolce Vita* is remarkable. But the coda Fellini added twenty-seven years later is more moving. In *Intervista*, Mastroianni and Ekberg, in colour now and no longer glamorous, sit together and see the scene projected onto a sheet. Marcello kisses Anita's hand. They sip *grappa*. To the sound of Nino Rota's most plangent piano score, they watch their beautiful young black-and-white selves. As the film ends, she wipes away a tear.

XIV: The Strawberry or the Chocolate

'Elisir di sì perfetta/di sì rara qualità/
  Ne sapessi la ricetta/conoscessi chi ti fa'
('Elixir of such perfection/such rare quality/
  I wish I knew your recipe/and who made you')
                              Donizetti's *L'Elisir d'Amore*

Scattered across the dark tarmac of Via Albalonga are dozens of cars, all stationary and driverless. Normally the word would be 'parked', but these vehicles are stranded at crazy angles. Doors and windows gape. Music blares eerily as if drivers were taken by surprise and had no time to turn off their radios. In a Hollywood movie, mayhem such as this would signify, at the very least, a sneak attack by aliens. Here in the grey inner suburbs of Rome after midnight, a more intriguing force is at work.

An hour ago my flatmate Boris called to ask if I wanted to go somewhere 'special'. 'Special?' I queried. '*Really* special!' promised Boris, declining to divulge details. Boris likes his surprises. How could I say no? So he swung by in his battered Audi, brought me here and parked with his customary panache. Boyish, skinny and floppy-haired, he stands beside me now on the crowded pavement. As does half the beautiful youth of Rome, it seems, all pouting, shouting, posing, flirting. Immaculately coiffed and manicured boys from Piazza Bologna dance attendance on tight-jeaned temptresses from Testaccio. These nervy, happy Romans are all queuing to get into a spangly-fluorescent café with a vaguely suggestive name: 'Pompi'. '*This* is the surprise?' I ask. 'You'll thank me,' says Boris.

Presently three of his friends join us. One is his ex-girlfriend Laura. Small, dark, pretty and melancholy, she works at the Ministry of Culture. More to the point, she still yearns for Boris but the feeling is no longer reciprocated. A few months back, when she and he were still living together, Boris realized he was gay. He's just back – glowing – from a weekend with his new love, a skinny, boyish stand-up comedian from San Francisco. I'm not sure it's wise for Laura to be here. My sense of anxiety is heightened by the arrival of Silvia and Riccardo in their trademark punk-goth black-leather outfits. Silvia is a biologist and kick-boxer; Riccardo works at a checkout at the Ikea store in Anagnina. Normally they're a delight, but tonight they've had a blazing row and are glowering in silence.

As I begin to have very bad feelings about all this, I reflect on the sheer oddness of the scene. If Pompi were some hyper-cool American or British big-city nightspot, it would probably be a club or bar or music venue. The hepcats around me would be dressed differently, and they would probably be looking forward to a night of dancing, drinking, drugs or sex, or quite possibly all four in sequence. One thing they would definitely not be doing would be queuing for half an hour for a few dollops of sickly looking pudding on a little white plastic tray. Yet that, as Boris explains, is precisely what we intend to do. But this is no mere pudding parlour. Its full name is: Pompi: Il Regno del Tiramisù – Pompi: the Kingdom of Tiramisu. We're on the threshold of the most-celebrated *dolce* in the city.

Tiramisu derives its name from the Italian words *tirami su*, meaning 'lift me up' or 'pick me up'. Recipes around the country vary slightly, but generally involve mascarpone cheese, sponge or 'lady fingers', coffee, raw egg, sugar and chocolate. Often liqueur and cream are mixed in too. The result can be almost impossibly rich. The dessert's true origins are hidden by myth. One tradition has it that it was invented in the seventeenth century in Siena for a visit by Cosimo III de'Medici, the Duke of Tuscany. Hence tiramisu's supposedly ancestral name: Zuppa di Duca (Duke Soup). Another claim is that the dessert was born 200 years later, in Turin, supposedly created at the request of Italy's first prime minister, Camillo Benso, Conte di Cavour, who needed it to sustain him during the exhausting work of unifying the Italian state after the *Risorgimento*.

All nonsense. Tiramisu is a thoroughly modern invention, created in 1971 in the northern Italian town of Treviso. But authorship is disputed. A pastry chef called Carminantonio Iannaccone, who now lives in Baltimore, insists he devised it to show off his skills. Meanwhile, one Mrs Alba Campeol, co-owner of the Becchiere restaurant in the same town, claims she invented it, with some help from *her* pastry chef, Loly Linguanotto. This version is supported by food historian Pietro Mascioni, who tracked down Mrs Campeol in 2006. The version of the genesis she told him was this: 'When my son was born, I was very weak, and my mother-in-law, to help me recuperate some energy, gave me a zabaglione. A simple one like the kind we make in Treviso, egg-yolk and sugar beaten together, with a bit of mascarpone cheese. That time, my mother-in-law also added a bit of coffee to it. 'Eat,' she told me, 'It will lift you up.' It was so good that when I went back to the restaurant I said to [Linguanotto], "Why don't we try to make a dessert out of this?" He had an idea to make layers of *Savoiardi* [lady fingers] cookies dipped in coffee. Then we added the cocoa topping. It was then that I remembered my mother-in-law's words, and we called it *tiramisù*.' Mrs Campeol suggested that her creation should be seen as essentially medicinal rather than frivolous: 'Please don't put any liquor in the *tiramisù* because we give it to children and elderly people for energy.'

Like Frankenstein's perfect new human, however, this cheerful coffee-based dessert has developed a life somewhat different to that intended for it by its creator. Far beyond Treviso, word of Mrs Campeol's pick-me-up spread. First the entire Veneto, then all of Italy succumbed to its sweet and caffeinated charms. By the late 1980s tiramisu had crossed the ocean and made a big impression in America, a moment captured by Nora Ephron in her 1993 romantic comedy *Sleepless in Seattle*. The Tom Hanks character is uncomfortably back in the world of dating and a little nervous about an exotic new word he's been hearing. 'What *is* tiramisu?' he asks his friend. The friend teases him: 'You'll find out ... You'll see.' Hanks admits his anxiety: 'Some woman is going to want me to *do it* to her and I'm not gonna know what it is.' The joke plugs into legends associating tiramisu with sex. One is that prostitutes in Venice used it as a pick-me-up between clients. Clients, too, are said to have deployed the stuff as a kind of seventeenth-century Viagra.

There would have been a biochemical basis: huge shots of caffeine, energy-giving sugar and performance-enhancing carbohydrates might have been just the thing for a long Venetian night. One of the rudest of Italian slang words is *pompino*, meaning 'blowjob'. Is this where Café Pompi gets its name?

On the pavement, we are edging ever closer to the door and thereby to the payment counter where we will hand over three euros to obtain a paper slip entitling us to a single portion of either chocolate- or strawberry-flavoured tiramisu. (The strawberry is a Pompi invention.) While Riccardo and Silvia's sulk seems to have softened, and Laura and Boris engage in impressive eggshell-walking, I've been noticing the behaviour of the crowd, which is, unmistakeably, in party mode. This is a date place. I get chatting to a couple, Enzo and Chiara, from Monteverde Nuovo. 'It's our special place,' they say when I ask why they bothered to make the journey. 'We've been here four times already.' Is there some aphrodisiac quality to the tiramisu? 'No it's just nice. And it's our place.' At last, we all pay and reach a counter where two men in waiter uniforms are handing out portions, like soup from the back of a Salvation Army truck. 'Strawberry or chocolate?' asks one. 'Chocolate,' I say, and receive a flimsy tray piled with unappetizingly snowy goo garlanded with brown powder. I have to be careful not to drop the whole thing on the pavement. I move away and pick up a scoop. Meanwhile, Boris, Laura, Riccardo and Silvia have all made the same choice. All the tables in the warm brown interior of the restaurant are taken and there's a line of people waiting for seats. We step outside again and find all the tables near the entrance busy too. Eventually, we find a spot next to some rather smelly wheelie bins.

To be honest, I've never much liked tiramisu. Encountered in restaurants and at dinner parties, I always found it soggy or stodgy. How could this be different? With trepidation, I take a first mouthful. The gel turns out to be cool, soft, light and startlingly smooth. As it hits my teeth and tongue and mouth-roof the tiramisu somehow melts and explodes and soothes all at once. Yikes! The second mouthful is like the first, only now attended by a soaring bliss. Boris is watching my reaction. 'Pretty good, eh?' I'm nodding frantically and smiling like an idiot. Distantly, rationally, my brain calcu-lates that any combination of sugar and caffeine would be pushing my chemical buttons. But that wouldn't explain the sheer erotic pleasure of the thing as it dissolves. It wouldn't explain the creamy ecstasy. Greedily now, I'm gulping mouthful after mouthful. It's all over far too quickly ... Immediately I want a second helping, but sense that perfec-tion cannot be doubled. Riccardo and Silvia have apparently forgotten their row; the tension between Laura and Boris seems to have evaporated. I brim with goodwill towards all humankind. I catch Boris's eye again and say: 'Thank you!'

In ancient myths and legends, love potions are noxious and the cause of terrible tragedies. True, in 'Love Potion Number Ni-i-ine' the only really bad thing that happens after drinking Madame Rue's concoction is kissing a cop on thirty-fourth and Vine. Likewise, in Shakespeare's *A Midsummer Night's Dream* all the love-potion-inspired chaos is sweet-natured. But the mediaeval tale of *Tristan and Isolda* hinted at the darker truth, and when such potions appear in Roman and Greek myths they are invariably the stuff of nightmares: Lucretius is murdered by a jealous woman with a love potion. Greek women who used erotic magic to get a man usually ended up poisoning the object of their lust by mistake. And was it not it a toxic love potion that triggered the terrible madness of Caligula? Dodgy ingredients were partly to blame – horse semen, moon juice, frog blood, body parts of murdered children, and so on. And it was not until the nineteenth century, and an extraordinary collaboration between a frequent musical visitor to Rome and a writer whose name actually means 'Happy Romans', that the problem was solved.

Gaetano Donizetti and Felice Romani's delicious comic opera L'Elisir d'Amore (The Elixir of Love) showed that, to be truly effective, aphrodisiacs ought to contain no active ingredients of any kind and consist solely of heart, craft and artistic magic. Legend has it that they created their classic in 1832 in barely the time needed now to make a proper tiramisu. Romani, borrowing from French and Italian sources, took just a week to mix the ingredients for his elegant, gentle, funny libretto. Donizetti, who married a Roman and had his first great hit in Rome, whipped up his sweet and satisfying score in less than a fortnight. (Indeed, some of his best work was done at incredible speed and under pressure. When told his rival Rossini had taken more than two weeks to finish The Barber of Seville, he commented: 'I'm not surprised; he always has been lazy.') Opera and pudding share something else, too: seemingly fluffy and inconsequential confections, they are made with such precision and balance they taste of the sublime.

The opera was Enrico Caruso's favourite and still packs a punch. In his movie Match Point, for example, Woody Allen used a recording of Caruso singing the famous aria 'Una Furtiva Lagrima' ('A Furtive Tear') to extraordinary effect. The opera's deeper magic, though, lies in its effortless-seeming lightness of story. Nemorino, a penniless rustic, is hopelessly besotted with a beautiful richer woman called Adina, who treats him with contempt. In desperation, Nemorino buys an 'elixir of love' from a flashy quack called Dulcamara (the name means 'bittersweet') who claims to be the benefactor of all mankind. But the 'elixir' is just a normal bottle of wine, and it doesn't work quite as advertised. Frantic now, Nemorino imagines he just needs a more powerful hit, so he signs away his future and agrees to join the army just to get enough money to buy a second dose. Because this is an *opera buffa*, all turns out well: Adina discovers Nemorino's sacrifice and realizes she loves him passionately after all. Meanwhile, unknown to him, his rich uncle has died and left him all his money. As every woman in the village throws herself at him, Nemorino chooses Adina, and thanks Dulcamara's miraculous drink for changing his life. To wild acclaim, Dulcamara takes all the credit and rides off into the sunset claiming that his potion not only cures all ills but also makes you rich!

All this, I suppose, makes the modest Roberto Pompi, owner of Café Pompi, a sort of heroic Dulcamara in reverse, an anti-Dulcamara. Self-effacing and reticent at times to the point of monosyllabism, Mr Pompi insists against all evidence that his magic mixture is utterly prosaic and has no hidden powers: 'Oh, no. I think people come here because they appreciate the high quality of our product. That's all there is to it.'

Hang on a minute! I've been to Pompi a few times now. I've been entranced by both strawberry and chocolate flavours (just as good as each other). And I've seen those giant takeout trays of tiramisu people buy to take home. There has to be more to it than that!

I ask what distinguishes his tiramisu from others, but Roberto refuses to divulge significant details. Nor is he willing to say much about how his tiramisus are made, though he does insist the recipe is 'very simple' and no baking is involved. The ingredients are simply melded together and left in a fridge to bring out all the flavours. He's not even very forthcoming about the family history. The Café was founded in 1962 by his father, Giuliano Pompi. At first, Pompi was in the Via Flavia and sold ice cream, cake and coffee. Sometime during the early 1980s, Giuliano took a fateful holiday in the ritzy skiing resort of Cortina d'Ampezzo, encountered a version of Mrs Campeol's creation and brought home the recipe. Since then, everything about it has changed. 'In our recipe today there is perhaps nothing left of the original,' says Roberto, but he is evasive and mysterious about the details, saying only: 'It was our skill to make the original recipe better and bring it to a high level.'

He point-blank refuses to discuss competitors. 'It's not that I'm boasting. I just don't want to even talk about other people's tiramisu. But I will say this: we use only very high-quality products. Other people have different systems because they want to make tiramisu quickly. They use sponge cake, *pan di spagna*. Absurd! Some use *savoiardi*. Obviously, we do not use such ingredients! Our cookies are made exclusively for us. I cannot say what they are exactly, but they are very like *Pavesini* [a sort of light, sweet cookie brand], thinner than lady fingers and very crunchy. Almost like a baking biscuit.' How do you make the tiramisu soft and smooth? 'There is a "system of cold". The product is put into the freezer and "beaten with temperature", as we say. We have a machine for this, which first brings the product to the right level and then preserves it at the right temperature, just the way we want it. After that, the product is put in the freezer. This is the last stage.' I'm confused. How do the changes in temperature make the tiramisu soft? Gnomically, he says: 'There are no tricks. We use no tricks.'

In *L'Elisir d'Amore*, the shameless, flamboyant Dulcamara tells outrageous lies about his potions. Roberto, by contrast, is dark-suited and reluctant to claim any credit. His head is shaved, his beard goatee, and he walks with a slight limp. He looks like an injured Lazio soccer player. His tiramisu is self-evidently a boon to all humankind, yet he plays this down and disavows all knowledge of magical properties. What do your customers say about your 'product'? 'Well, I think they like it.' What kind of words do they use? 'Oh I don't know . . . They say it's "sublime", "fantastic", "tempting", "embarrassing". I do remember one funny thing. One night, after we closed, we had a message from a man whose wife had a craving for tiramisu in the middle of the night. So she sent him here and he put a note through the door begging us to open up and make tiramisu for her immediately.' And did you? 'Well no, we only got the message the next morning. We never heard from him again.'

I simply don't understand how you can say there's nothing aphrodisiac about all this! Eating your tiramisu is obviously an extraordinarily pleasurable, sensual thing to do! Everywhere I look here I see couples playfully feeding each other little forkfuls! Smiling at each other! This stuff *is* the elixir of love! How can you say there's nothing sensual about any of it? 'Oh, now you are pushing it. OK. People come here, and they buy our tiramisu. And they like it. But anything else is none of our business. I really don't know what they do when they get it home.'

XV: The Body

'For my flesh is meat indeed, and my blood is drink indeed'

Jesus, Gospel of John (6:55)

It's lunchtime, and talk turns, as it often does, to great issues of the day. For instance, coffee is running low, but is it really worth travelling twenty-two stops on the metro to get new supplies from Castroni's near the Vatican? 'Absolutely!' says Liberato. Can *biologico* beef from a herd near Fiumicino Airport be considered truly organic if the cows spend most of their lives breathing aviation fuel? And why, on a recent visit to London, were fresh anchovies so damnably hard to find? Something about this arcana inspires me to raise the subject of Eucharistic-wafer manufacture, whereupon Nadia chips in with an observation of huge significance.

'The Eucharist is very important,' she says. 'It's a very important symbol of Jesus.'

'I don't think so,' I reluctantly correct her. 'I don't think it's a symbol. It's actually Jesus.'

'Eh?'

I explain as best I can. As I understand it, the Church has for many centuries been most firm on this point. In the

1960s, when liberals put about the idea that the Eucharist was merely 'symbolic', Paul VI slapped them down with an encyclical. The Church continues to insist, as a matter of absolute importance, that in a correctly conducted Mass the Eucharistic wafer becomes Christ because the 'real presence' enters. This happens through a mysterious process called transubstantiation whereby wafer and wine, the other Eucharistic ingredient, continue to look, smell, feel and taste like wafer and wine but are miraculously transformed. To eat a consecrated wafer is therefore to eat Christ, and this is very good. Nadia was educated by what must have been very liberal nuns. Although she thinks of herself as a non-believer she has a picture of Padre Pio in her car and last month visited the shrine of Divino Amore to pray for Valeria to finish her PhD. She regards me quizzically for a few seconds, weighs my words, then bursts out laughing. 'But that's *ridiculous*!'

Spoken like a true, vaguely post-Catholic, secular-ish, thoroughly modern Italian woman. Nadia's reaction is also a good example of a profound rupture with the not-so-distant Roman past. Assailed by scandal and doubt, the Church is a shadow of its previous all-powerful self, and plenty of modern Italians find its teachings, including those on the Eucharist, hard to swallow. It's not easy to get an exact fix on this phenomenon. A Gallup poll from almost twenty years ago found that only 30 per cent of Catholics in America believed in the 'real presence'. But the figure has been disputed, and, anyway, Italy doesn't go in for surveys in quite the same way as America, so no one knows for sure.

Instead, to sample attitudes to the Eucharist, I conduct a quick survey of people I know. Valeria makes the sign of the cross when she enters a church, but she believes no dogma, hasn't been to confession since she was twelve and considers the Eucharistic rituals 'creepy'. When I ask my devout brother-in-law, Sean, if he believes in real presence, he answers enigmatically: 'It's a mystery.' The great Bible scholar Geza Vermes recalls his experience as a young priest in Hungary and Belgium: 'The Eucharist was just one of the things you did and you didn't think about it very much. Mass was just part of the daily routine and the wafers tasted of nothing.' Valeria's devout colleague Chiara says: 'Being a Catholic means, among the other things, believing that Christ himself, with his body and blood, is in that wafer you are eating and in that wine you are drinking, after they have been consecrated by the priest at Mass. This is one of the dogmas of the Catholic Church we cannot explain through reason; it's simply an act of faith.' Cristiano, a research biologist who grew up in a traditional, observant Catholic family in Umbria says: 'It's not the same Italy as twenty or thirty or one hundred years ago. I don't know anyone who believes the Eucharist is literally the *actual* body of Christ. Who can believe such a thing? I take it as a symbol, and it's a very good symbol. My wife's family is even more Catholic, and I think they all feel the same way.'

Yet if there was a prize for most-important foodstuff in the history of Rome, the Eucharistic wafer would probably be the only candidate. It has been a source of inspiration, devotion and power. Wars have been conducted in its name. It has defined a culture as well as a religion. It united the faithful. It split the Church. It is, by any reckoning, a highly remarkable little biscuit. And it used to carry a very much more potent and unsettling charge than it does now. As Piero Camporesi makes clear in *The Consecrated Host: A Wondrous Excess* – one of his studies of a subject to which he often returned – the somewhat vegetarian modern view sits oddly with the ancient 'abominable grandeur' of the rite:

> The sensibility of believers and ecclesiastic doctrine [. . .] have over time nearly obliterated this bloody offering, anaesthetizing and reducing it to little more than a symbolic act. They have edulcorated and disincarnated it, reinterpreted it merely as a trope. In other words, they have unconsciously rejected the awesome notion of Transubstantiation, and have refused its intolerable weight. The image and feeling of bloody totemic rite during which unworthy sons swallow the raw flesh of their Father (of a Father who, most perfect and pure victim – the only one worthy of his glory – has already immolated himself before his Creator) weighed on the conscience, at least until the 18th century, of all those who received Communion.

Christians believe that Jesus instituted the Eucharist at his Last Supper, which was also a Passover supper. According to Luke, Jesus breaks bread, gives it to his disciples and tells them: 'This is my body which is given for you. Do this in remembrance of me.' He then adds that the wine after the supper, 'poured out for you is the new covenant in my blood'. A growing number of modern scholars, however, have cast doubt on the historical basis for this version of events. One of the most influential has been Vermes, emeritus professor of Jewish History at Oxford University and foremost authority on the Dead Sea Scrolls. In a series of books starting with the groundbreaking *Jesus the Jew*, written in 1973, Vermes showed that what can be discerned of the man and teachings of the Jewish Jesus of history are at odds with the redeeming saviour Christ of Christianity. 'The religion of Jesus and Christianity are so basically different in form, purpose and orientation that it would be historically unsafe to derive the latter directly from the former,' he has written. He believes that Jesus would have been baffled by such concepts as his own divinity and resurrection, the virgin birth and the Trinity. Nevertheless, he regards Jesus as a formidable and inspiring teacher whose teachings, rooted in the traditional Judaism of the first century, should be taken very seriously indeed. Catholics often tell him his books have 'deepened their faith'.

Regarding the origin of the Eucharist, in his book *The Passion*, Vermes points out contradictions in New Testament accounts of the Last Supper. The Synoptic Gospels (Mark, Matthew and Luke) differ from each other in small details but are contradicted on key matters by John's Gospel, which was written later. Following the synoptics means believing that Jesus was executed during Passover, which, for Jewish religious reasons, could not have happened. If John's version is correct, Jesus was executed on the *eve* of Passover. Vermes concludes: 'Jesus held a common meal with his apostles which turned out to be his last. It was not a Passover supper, nor did it contain the institution of the Eucharist.' Moreover, given that Judaism, then as now, absolutely forbade even the consumption of bloody animal meat, the chances are slim that Jesus could have said to a Jewish audience the 'shocking' things John has him saying in John, 6:35–59 ('He that eats my flesh and drinks my blood has everlasting life [. . .] For my flesh is meat indeed, and my blood is drink indeed. He that eats my flesh and drinks my blood abides in me, and I in him'). As Vermes notes in another book, 'In Jesus's own society, profoundly rooted in blood taboo, the suggestion of drinking a man's blood would have filled his listeners with nausea.'

Vermes has lived on the fault line between the two religions. He was born Jewish in rural Hungary in 1924 and later converted to Catholicism, as his parents had done. They were murdered in the Holocaust but he was hidden in a monastery. He left the church in 1957, not over theological matters but for the love of a woman whom he married. He takes a gently amused view of the manner in which Jewish rituals involving bread and wine ended up as cornerstones of a crucial redemptive rite of Catholicism: 'It's what the producers of Yiddish versions of Shakespeare used to say: "We have translated – and improved."'

The most important figure in the development of the Eucharist, as in so much Christian thought, was Paul, whose first letter to the members of the gentile church he had founded in Corinth described the Last Supper and paved the way for the Gospel accounts, which were written later. (Corinthians 11:23–26: 'The Lord Jesus, on the night he was betrayed, took bread, and when he had given thanks, he broke it and said, "This is my body, which is for you; do this in remembrance of me." In the same way, after supper he took the cup, saying, "This cup is the new covenant in my blood; do this, whenever you drink it, in remembrance of me." For whenever you eat this bread and drink this cup, you proclaim the Lord's death until he comes.') Paul talks about the Eucharist as a communal meal and in the early Church that's what it was. Only much later did it evolve into the highly stylized ritual we know today. And only in the high Middle Ages did the Eucharist move to centre stage in Catholicism. The doctrine of transubstantiation, later to receive intellectual support from Thomas Aquinas, became

Church dogma only in 1215, with the Fourth Lateran Council. The Pope presiding over this development was the austere and terrifying Innocent III.

The Eucharist became ever more important in the decades that followed. Into this tiny wafer, virtue, holiness and authority were loaded. Popular enthusiasm for the sacrament also increased. The host was unlike other sacred objects that depicted the source of power, for it was the source itself. As Miri Rubin puts it in her book *Corpus Christi*, claims made for the Eucharist contained the potential for all kinds of trouble: 'the ways of access to Christ's body and its uses and abuses were constant sources of tension and conflict as the body was packaged, used, experienced, touched, carried, smelt and contemplated'. Naturally, only one institution had monopoly rights in the rituals, use and deployment – the Church. Equally naturally, it asserted these privileges with vigour to extend its hegemony. Because the emphasis at this time was more on display than eating, increasingly exotic and inspiring methods were devised. Priests held the consecrated host aloft. Ever more splendid monstrances were created. Following a miracle in Bolsano where a doubting priest found blood seeping from a newly consecrated wafer, a new festival was created: the feast of Corpus Christi (Body of Christ). Now Christ, hidden inside his wafer, could be adored more fully, taken from the church and carried in procession through the streets. Not for nothing does Raphael, in one of the key religious images of the Renaissance, make the host the centrepiece of his Vatican fresco *The Triumph of Religion*.

But there was a dark side too. In the fifth century, as warfare raged about the nature (or natures) of Christ, communion became a weapon against members of rival factions in the main centres of Christendom. In Constantinople a man became famous as Cyrus the Spitter because he spat out a host and was then tortured to death for the offence. In the Middle Ages, first in Paris, and later and more often in Germany, Jews were accused of 'host desecration' and tortured and massacred. Among Christians, philosophical objections developed. In late-mediaeval Europe, Lollards, Hussites and other heretics began to see the Eucharist and its rituals as symbols of political and social privilege. Voices began demanding alternative ways of gaining access to God. The Eucharist could not be reformed. It could be either accepted or rejected. As new ideas about the Eucharist developed they inevitably turned into attacks on the faith itself.

During the violent convulsions of the Reformation and Counter-Reformation the Eucharist was the 'hinge on which the symbolic world turned', says Rubin. Luther believed in real presence, though not in the Catholic dogma of transubstantiation. Zwingli, Calvin and Cranmer rejected real presence outright. Protestants developed a variety of alternative symbolic masses. In the new atmosphere, street processions of the host, epitome of the Catholic sacramental system, were violently contested as opposing world views clashed. In Geneva, Protestants stormed the cathedral in 1535, desecrated the tabernacle and fed consecrated white hosts to animals. Positions hardened. Protestants viewed the Catholic Eucharist as a source of pollution and disgust. Catholics saw it as Christ's sublime flesh and blood, a cause well worth fighting for. In the 150 years of religious war between north and south Europe that followed, the Eucharist became 'a militant emblem of a struggle unto death'.

Not surprisingly the Council of Trent, great ideological centrepiece of the Catholic fight-back in the age of the Counter-Reformation, reaffirmed the doctrine of 'that wonderful and singular conversion of the whole substance of the bread into the Body, and of the whole substance of the wine into the Blood – the species only of the bread and wine remaining – which conversion indeed the Catholic Church most aptly calls Transubstantiation'. In other words, Christ was still in the wafer, and the Church would do whatever it took to safeguard this treasure.

One of the reasons Galileo was charged with heresy may have concerned the Eucharist. The theory of atomism in his book *The Assayer* threatened to undermine the Church's claim (based on the physics of Aristotle) that while the *'substance'* of the bread and wine changes when the magic words are said, its *'accidents'* of taste and appearance do not change. Galileo's atoms theory would have made the accidents the result of tiny, unchanging particles of substance. A much less well-known case, but one more revealing of a lost Roman world of thought, feeling, fear and aspiration, is that of an eighteenth-century conman called Domenico Spallacini. For theft and procuring, he had been sentenced to prison and to five years in the galleys of the Pope's fleet but managed to escape. He then went on the run posing as a properly ordained priest. In this new role he began to enjoy celebrating the Mass in prestigious basilicas and churches in Rome. Says Camporesi: 'He was an excellent imitator and a first-class actor and he slowly succeeded in identifying with the role which he had discovered, performing it with passion and dedication. He may perhaps have been fatally attracted by martyrdom, by a ruinous and secret vocation. He was not what you might commonly call a good shepherd, but undoubtedly he had a profound knowledge of his profession.' His mistake was to revisit Loreto, a town where he had committed several robberies. He managed to say Mass twice in one chapel and again in the church of Saint Anna, and to pass off consecrated and non-consecrated particles of host. And then his luck ran out. Spallacini was recognized, arrested and sent to Rome. After being found guilty by the Inquisition, this 'false priest' was taken to the Campo dei Fiori, hanged and then strapped to an iron stake and burned to a crisp. In an even stranger case, a man was hanged for stealing a ciborium (an ornate container for consecrated hosts) and its contents. Oddly, the thief, who stole on behalf of a wealthy client, had no interest in the ciborium but in the consecrated wafers inside, some of which he kept. Camporesi, who relates the story in *Fear of Hell*, believes consecrated host must have been a commodity so precious that 'it was worth risking one's life for it'. There must also have been a clandestine black market for sacred unleavened bread, with a network of dealers, buyers and sellers.

Both my friend Arpad, who writes and researches on Catholic political history and converted to the faith from Lutheranism, and Valeria's colleague Chiara speak appealingly about the emotional and spiritual experience of receiving the sacrament. 'It's not like eating, and it's not symbolic. It feels like an encounter,' says Arpad. 'It's certainly very charged. Even as a convert you quickly realize it's the essence of Catholicism. You have the feeling you're encountering a god, not a person you eat. It's a meeting rather than an eating.' For Chiara, eating the host means opening herself to Christ, 'who comes into my body, which is the temple of his Holy Spirit, and this "meeting" can make me stronger, new, regenerated. The path of a Catholic never ends. You are always walking on to the path of faith through better and worse, through ups and downs, through silence and dialogue. It's difficult to put into words some deep emotion related to your own spiritual self. What I can say is that most times, after receiving the Eucharist, I feel a sense of quiet, other times it feels like crying as if I were suddenly aware of my weaknesses, my smallness, and my intense need of His presence in my life. Then, see, I am human, so some other times it happens that I go and receive the Eucharist with thoughts (I mean distractions) in my mind which prevent me from treasuring that moment as something really extraordinary as I am receiving Christ himself.'

But eating was once precisely the point. Pre-modern Catholics, says Camporesi, understood and experienced the Eucharist as something transforming and disturbing: 'the mysterious force of the sacred host and the holy wine-cum-blood was perceived as a sweet and awesome drug, a fragment of sacred flesh which, estranged from reality, led elsewhere, opened dimensions which were unknown to the senses and broadened and transformed the conscience (albeit temporarily)'. It was 'the particle into which a hidden and invisible god had prodigiously fallen', the 'miracle of miracles' which exorcised the possessed and healed the lame. Saint Cyprian said martyrs faced death happily when fortified by the host – the 'bread of angels' which 'surpassed the flowers of the tastiest things, and exceeded all the sweets that can flatter our senses'. Those who ate it might be infused with 'happiness, sweetness and spiritual pleasure'.

It could also be terrifying. Transubstantiation was understood to be an alimentary phenomenon that highlighted the chasm between the sublime Christ and the foul physicality of humans: 'Disgust for the slippery human guts, a labyrinth of worms and a sinkhole of filthy liquids, and horror of the slimy womb, the dark cavern which Christ did not abhor, were added to the repugnance for the mouth and stomach; they became part of the new *via crucis*, part of the path leading down into the unpleasantly wet crevices of the "infamous body" into which, having been swallowed by the foul mouths of wretched persons infected by every vice, the Most Holy Body, the "undefiled sun", fell.'

So much did the rite imply the descent of the pure into the impure, the absorption of the holy by the unclean, that the officiating priest often felt 'like the executor of a supernatural act of occult violence'. He was a 'necromantic mediator', summoning Jesus 'in the guise of the body and blood of a slaughtered lamb; whereby, at this point in every Mass, the Redeemer dies again mystically without really dying, at once alive and as if murdered'. It was the 'great mystery', the 'dramatic apex of divine participation and supernatural presence'. The delicate moment of transubstantiation could take place only through precise observance of every rule. But the process was also fraught with danger, for it might open the door to mutations, apparitions, miracles: 'In the prodigious alchemic balance of divine permutations, the heavenly and the demonic could explode into a war of conflicting powers.' By bringing life out of dead matter, the Mass seemed to dislocate and violate natural laws. It overturned laws of nutrition and digestion too. Normal food was altered by digestion. With the Eucharist it was the other way around: food transformed the swallower but remained unchanged.

For those receiving the host it could be even more troubling. When a communicant swallowed the host, 'all the terrifying images associated with this act – the body of the purest lamb entering the filth of the digestive apparatus, the divine flesh polluted by contact with mucous membranes, the juices of the corruptible flesh and the rot of the bowels – must have returned to his mind and seized him with vertiginous horror'. Moreover, receiving the host in the mouth or oesophagus didn't really count. Divine grace could manifest itself only after the host, 'having reached the warm bag of the stomach, had been melted into mush by the warmth of this natural oven'. The seventeenth-century Jesuit theologian Jean-Baptiste Jure wondered: 'O sovereign and incomprehensible Majesty, is it really possible that, though You are in Heaven, I can see you in my stomach, where you have come after making so many miracles and turning nature upside down? I tremble all over and am seized with awe whenever I think of this infinite favour [. . .] I believe, without the slightest doubt, You are, soul and body, inside my stomach.'

Thus, the stomach and digestive tract became the focus of minutely detailed contemplation as theologians 'followed the descent of Christ's body into the antrum, the damp and smelly bowels'. Rigorous fasting from midnight preceded morning communion because to allow other kinds of food into the stomach, even inadvertently, would be sacrilege. But, in an age without toothbrushes, what happened if small bits of food stuck between teeth came loose in the night and were swallowed accidentally? St Thomas Aquinas concluded that such particles would not imperil the process 'because they are swallowed not by way of food but by way of saliva. The same holds good of the unavoidable remains of the water or wine wherewith the mouth is rinsed, provided they be not swallowed in great quantity.'

Problems arose at every stage of the host's passage through the body. To achieve ideal fullness of grace, the natural warmth of the stomach had to function as perfectly as possible. This was one reason why the sick could not receive the host. Conversely, it was thought that the more (and more often) a healthy person could eat it, the greater the benefit. Worshippers might therefore ask for several hosts at a time. And what happened if the host was accidentally vomited out? Well, as long as it retained some of its bread-and-wine qualities, this vomit too deserved to be adored; and if it was reintroduced to the stomach it would still produce full beneficial effects. Then there was the question of how long Christ's presence in the host lasted, and how long He took to be fully digested and assimilated. Generally, this was thought to take about an hour, but the length of time varied according to 'the character and temperature' of each individual stomach. According to Roman doctors consulted by Cardinal Juan de Lugo in the early-seventeenth century, the digestive process took about a quarter of an hour for priests and about one minute less for laymen. Some experts took the view that the effects of grace started the moment *all* host fragments reached the pit of the stomach. Others believed only a *single* piece was required. And then? 'When, after having thus kept our Lord, the species are digested and He ceases be with us corporeally, we must pray for him not leave us,' wrote Saint-Jure. 'But since you have decided to go away corporeally, and that I be thus mortified, I submit to Your holy and divine will and accept this, however bitter, separation.' At what point along the digestive tract did the host turn to something else? Saint-Jure regarded the final destiny of the 'accidents' (the bread and wine), and the mysterious events that accompanied their putrefaction as the last stage in a series of 'miracles and prodigies that nature can only contemplate with dread'.

A story written by the fourteenth-century theologian Domenico Cavalca reveals that doubts about the doctrine did exist and had to be countered. The tale concerns an ancient hermit who does not believe Christ is really in the host. Two other hermits pray to God to show him his error and take him to Mass. The bread is placed on the altar for consecration, and a miraculous vision occurs:

All three saw a young child on the altar, and when the priest started breaking the Host, it seemed to them that an angel came down from Heaven and divided the child in two with a knife, and collected his blood in the chalice. When the priest divided the Host into several parts to give Communion to the people, they saw that the angel was also dividing the child into several small parts. And when, at the end of the Mass, the hermit went to receive Communion, it seemed to him that he alone was given a part of the bloodied flesh of that child. Seeing this, he was filled such dread that he screamed and said: 'My Lord, now I really believe that the bread consecrated on the altar is Your Holy body and the chalice, that is to say the wine, is Your blood.' And immediately it seemed to him that the flesh had turned again into bread and he received Communion. Then, the other two hermits told him: 'God, knowing that to eat raw flesh horrifies human nature, ordered that this sacrament assume the guise of bread and wine [. . .]'

'Believers, particularly in earlier centuries,' explains Camporesi,

> were quite conscious of the bloody fragments of divine flesh that descended into their stomachs in the guise of the Host. To their horror of the anthropophagous act, in itself nefarious, was added their sacred dismay at the thought of introducing illicit portions of an incommensurable food – global fragments of heavenly flesh – into their infamous bowels. The child slaughtered by the angel, his flesh cut up into small bloody bits [. . .] reflects this profound attraction-repulsion towards the sacrificial mystery [. . .] emphasized further by the mention of the irrepressible disgust which the idea of digesting provokes in the deepest recesses of the self.

The cannibalistic aspect of God-eating was unmistakeable and well-understood. In case anyone missed it, Saint Alphonsus de Liguori, Doctor of the Church, Bishop of Rome's Sant' Agata dei Goti church and one of the giants of eighteenth-century Catholic theology, spelled it out: 'What a refined expression of love, Saint Francis of Sales says, would we see in the act of a prince who, seated at his table, sent a portion of his meal to a pauper? And what if he sent him his entire meal? And what if he sent him his own arm to eat? In the Holy Communion, Jesus not only gives us part of his meal to eat, or part of his body, but his entire body.'

XVI: The Ice Cream

'In Korea, we're more famous than McDonald's'

Leonida Fassi

On 4 May 1938 the most-celebrated *gelato* master in Rome, Giovanni Fassi, drove in his own limousine to the Quirinale Palace. With him were his six-year-old son, Leonida, and one of the oddest food consignments in history. For the defiantly moustachioed Signor Fassi the journey was a matter of pride. He was delivering in person a set of ice-cream cakes he'd been asked to make for one of King Victor Emanuele III's most special banquets. The king's guests that night were Benito Mussolini and Adolf Hitler. They were celebrating their new alliance and paving the way for the future wartime 'Pact of Steel'. To mark the occasion, therefore, Fassi fashioned desserts in the shape and colour of special Italian flags. For the red, white and green of the *tricolore* he used strawberry, cream and pistachio. And on top of each flag he set a little frosted black swastika.

Politics, of course, was the very last thing on his mind. Receiving the prestigious cake commission had felt more like a moment of triumph, even revenge. Many years earlier Fassi had worked at the very palace to which he now returned. But his job as a young assistant pastry chef in the royal kitchen had ended the day the king ordered his staff to shave off their moustaches. The king believed that nothing should be allowed to detract from the magnificence of his own facial hair. But this was a principle young Fassi, who was greatly attached to his own 'tache, was not willing to accept. He therefore walked away from the royal household and struck out on his own. Whereas his father Giacomo ran a small kiosk near Barberini selling ice and beer, Giovanni's first venture was a little *pasticceria* next to the Piazza Navona. There he sold pastries and simple ice cream and did well enough to move, eight years later, to much bigger premises on the Via Piave, where he created a grand café. That business also thrived. But in 1927 he sold it to his sister and embarked on what all his friends and family warned him was an absurdly risky enterprise.

For the colossal sum of a billion lira he bought and lavishly decorated a high-ceilinged palazzo on the Via Principe Eugenio. It was 700 square metres of retail and workshop space just off Piazza Vittorio Emanuele, one of the city's main commercial centres. Taking advantage of new refrigeration technology, Fassi now set about creating an eating establishment of a kind Rome had never before seen. He called the new building the *Palazzo del Freddo:* the Palace of Cold. It would close from the end of October to March, because obviously no one in their right mind would want to eat frozen delicacies in winter. The rest of the year, however, he would make available to ordinary Romans a commodity in many flavours that was once reserved for the grandest popes, aristocrats and members of royal families: handmade ice cream.

The Roman *gelateria* was born.

'Everyone told my father, "You're crazy", and, "It will never last",' recalls Leonida, now a dapper, radiant and energetic man in his late seventies, emphasizing points by quietly jabbing with his unlit cigar. 'But my father was right. It was an incredible success. Even now no one else has such a big place.' Giovanni Fassi turned out to be more than thirty years ahead of his time. *Gelaterie* would become common in Rome only in the 1960s. He also buttressed the appeal of his excellent ice cream with a range of appealing gimmicks. One of his best ideas – still going strong – was to devise a way to keep *gelato* cold and fresh without surrounding it with ice, which would inevitably melt: he used dry ice and inaugurated a Roman custom. Especially on Sundays, instead of buying traditional cakes or flowers to take as gifts to friends and relations, bringing a package of dry-ice-packed Fassi ice cream became fashionable. Fassi also proved himself something of a marketing genius by pioneering a sophisticated takeaway service called *telegelato*, whereby boxes of ice cream could be whisked by train throughout Italy and by air as far away as Paris and London. Fassi's products proved popular with everyone, including the city's new rulers. Former air ace and leading Fascist Italo Balbo, Mussolini's designated successor, was one regular. And when Balbo became governor of newly conquered Libya his chauffeur continued to come to Fassi's for ice cream, which was promptly flown to Tripoli.

I think I know how Balbo felt because one hot summer, when I lived around the corner, I too became addicted to Fassi's *gelati.* I visited as often as possible, and slowly worked my way through all twenty-two flavours, three scoops at a time, in different combinations in little cups and cones. Compared to my stuffy apartment Fassi's seemed heaven: physically cool, emotionally warm. Its marbles, old ice-cream machines and posters from the 1920s made me nostalgic for a world I'd never known. The clientele was an appealing blend of tourists and locals and on one memorable occasion I recall a great party of Franciscan monks sweeping in, all wearing brown habits and sandals. On busy nights the throng in front of the great marble counter was three or four deep. I was always faintly astonished, though, by the presence on the wall, among the other bits of memorabilia, of a newspaper clipping reporting the story of the *gelato* for Hitler. I was never sure if this was innocent or creepy. The clipping is long gone, and when I ask Leonida about it, he looks sad. 'Well, it's not a beautiful thing to tell,' he says. 'But Italy was different then and, for my father, it wasn't a political thing. He remembered only that he had had to leave his job at the royal household and now he was coming back in his big car. He was so proud. I remember him saying to me: "I left here as a servant, and now I've come back as a *padrone*!"' The pride endured. Leonida remembers a day in the early 1950s when an elegant old man in a threadbare dress coat came to the shop and asked to see Giovanni. The two chatted for a while, and when the man left he asked, 'Who was that?' His father told him: 'That was the Master of the Pasticceria of the Royal Family. He is retired and poor now, but that was the man I used to work for.'

A barely heard but more significant conversation from a few years earlier is etched powerfully into Leonida's memory and still makes him proud. 'It was 1943 and I was at home playing with the cat when two people came to see my father. The woman had a bag, and they were talking very secretively. I didn't know why, but I was suspicious. Many years later I found out what happened. These people were Jewish. They had a shirt shop in Piazza Vittorio, and when the Nazis started rounding up Jews they came to ask my father for help. Of course he said yes. He had a little house in the country near Monte Mario and that's where he hid them. Every week he took food there. He told us he was taking food to his brother, but actually he was helping the Jews. My father always said, "I don't care or think about politics," and, "It's better to mind your own business." But he saved this Jewish family.'

During the early stages of Italy's involvement in the Second World War the Piazza became a tented city for Italian troops en route to North Africa or Russia. As the soldiers waited for their trains from nearby Termini station, they sought entertainment at the Ambra Jovinelli Theatre and refreshment from Fassi's. As the 'Pact of Steel' crumbled to dust, however, ingredients became scarcer. Without milk and eggs for the 1942 season, Fassi sold only *gelati* made of fruit. By July 1943 the sugar had run out too, so he shut his great shop. When the US Army arrived the following year they inaugurated a new era, requisitioning Fassi's and turning over his workshops to making industrial-style ice cream in large quantities for the American soldiers. As the now-teenaged Leonida wondered how the sweet-toothed, luxury-loving Americans had ever won the war, his father had a more pressing business question to decide. The head of the American Red Cross in Rome made Giovanni an offer he could refuse. He proposed a partnership to create a company to make industrial ice cream for the mass market. Giovanni responded: 'I've only had one partner my whole life, my wife, and I'm not looking for another.' He preferred to remain faithful to his vision of *artigianale* (handmade) ice cream, a higher-quality product not suitable for industrialization because it could be kept fresh only for a few days. When the Americans left in 1946, Giovanni bought back the equipment and restarted the *Palazzo del Freddo*. And Isner founded Algida, now owned by Unilever and part of one of the world's biggest ice-cream manufacturers.

By the 1950s Fassi's had been restored to its former glory. In 1961 Leonida took over the running of the business from his father. He has gone on to win numerous awards for the quality of his products and for his ethical approach to business. But in the 1990s changes in the Esquilino district brought Fassi close to disaster. The piazza had seen many changes since being built at the end of the nineteenth century as one of the largest squares in Europe. In the early years, its great colonnades housed an upmarket shopping centre. Rome's biggest, most important wholesale food markets were nearby in the area west of the main railway lines, and most of the shops had been Jewish-owned. In the sixties the surviving Jews moved away to Viale Libia, the shopping area on the Via Appia Nuova, and to the city centre. The Piazza became famous instead for its wedding-dress shops. By the late nineties, however, another change had occurred. The area had become a dilapidated Chinatown. While the wholesale market moved to Ostiense, Chinese businesses began to take over. The Chinese had little interest in ice cream, and the wedding shops started to disappear, replaced by non-retail outlets for Chinese clothing warehouses.

'The Esquilino changed completely,' says Leonida. 'At one time it was one of the most important commercial areas. After the war it looked exactly as it does in *Bicycle Thieves*. You know the scene where they go to the flea market looking for his stolen bike? That was filmed near here. Later, Rome expanded and this area became less important. But at least we were famous for the wedding shops. There were thirty-two of them and when people came to buy or look at wedding dresses they also liked to come in here and eat *gelati*. And then everything changed. No one came to the Esquilino any more to buy wedding dresses and we lost all our occasional customers.' Another problem was caused by traffic engineers who, in 1995, set the street's tram tracks on raised concrete, making it impossible for cars to park outside Fassi's. 'We lost a lot of customers. We had to end table service and the business was nearly completely killed.'

In the noughties, however, things began to recover. The city eventually relented and took away the concrete barrier. Even better, a new generation of young Chinese-Italians grew up to develop a taste for *gelato*. Fassi's now has plenty of local customers again and Leonida sees an advantage. 'China is becoming the richest power in the world, so it's good to be with them! I think you'll see a change in the Chinese businesses here. At the moment, they're mostly warehouse outlets, but soon they'll go back to being retailers and it will go back to being a business area.' He is also proud to have kept his standards high and his prices low. Fassi's *gelati* are still reckoned the best in the city, and cost about 30 per cent less than those of his rivals. Meanwhile, the company is growing in the Far East. 'In Korea we're more famous than McDonald's!' It's a franchise operation, he explains. 'We give them assistance, though we're not so involved.' There are now seventy-two Fassi branches in South Korea and every Korean who comes to Rome feels a trip to see the original is as essential as visiting the Colosseum. The same company is now trying to develop the Fassi brand in Thailand, China and other parts of Asia.

These days the business is run day to day by his children and grandchildren. Leonida has spent his life working to develop his father's vision. But in one respect he is trying to do the opposite. 'My father never thought of ice cream as a thing to eat in the winter. For him, winter was a dead period. But I want to change habits. It's true that traditionally people, especially older people, prefer pastries when it's cold. But I believe you should also eat ice cream in the winter. It's common in other parts of Europe. And now we are seeing a generational change. Older people still prefer pastries. But young people now come in here and have a *gelato* for lunch. Ice cream is a foodstuff like any other. Our product is high quality and very nutritious – and it only costs three euro. Have a coffee as well and that's a proper lunch. So this is my dream now. I want to make ice cream a popular product both for summer and winter. It may take five or ten years but I think it's going to happen. Everything is going to change!'

XVII: The Mushroom

'I'm not hungry'
Monica Vitti

The water tower at the edge of the city looks like a giant mushroom. It is known as the Mushroom, and there's even a restaurant at the top called the Mushroom. But you can't eat this mushroom, and the restaurant specializes in 'Italian Sushi'* instead of mushrooms. So the thing just squats there, a fifty-metre metaphor for anxiety, alienation and the impossibility of human relationships in the modern world . . . in mushroom form.

Holy ground in Rome is made and found in many different ways. For the frail old lady in black I used to see there, the church of Santa Croce in Gerusalemme was evidently sacred beyond words because she knelt on its cold marble and prayed to the gold box said to contain a piece of the genuine True Cross. For others, a visit to Santa Maria Maggiore must be moving because it's where snow miraculously fell one

* The Italian Sushi at Ristorante Il Fungo consists of cooked (rather than raw) fish wrapped in lettuce (instead of seaweed) and dressed with balsamic vinegar (instead of soy, ginger and wasabi). Search for this dish in Osaka and your quest will be a long one.

August night in the fourth century to prove the Virgin Mary really had visited Pope Liberius in a dream. Then there's the spot where martyred virgin St Agnes miraculously sprouted hair to preserve her modesty. It happened, and it happened right here. There's plenty of stuff for the secular too. Who can look up in the Sistine Chapel and fail to derive at least a small buzz from the thought that Michelangelo di Lodovico Buonarroti Simoni himself was once up there, lying on his back for four years atop a forest of wooden scaffolding to paint the ceiling? It really did happen right here. No place on earth is more chock-full of sacred places. There are cloisters, relics, shrines, statues and monuments all over the city.

My personal favourite has no religious connotation and concerns the other Michelangelo. The location is a nondescript corner at the crossing in EUR where Viale del Ciclismo (Cycling Street) meets Viale della Tecnica (Technology Street). The corner is reached down a winding road from the Mushroom and is the site of one of the miracles of the twentieth century. It's a miracle that doesn't need to be proved or sanctified because you can just rent or buy it in DVD form, or watch bits on YouTube. Dario Argento will support me in this claim. When I mentioned the final seven minutes of Michelangelo Antonioni's *L'Eclisse* (*The Eclipse*), he went into raptures: 'God, it is maaaaarvelllous!! Especially during the eclipse when you see the buildings in the last seven minutes! Wooowwww!! My God! MY GOD!!' When I suggested that the scene may even be the greatest seven minutes in the history of cinema, Dario paused, thought carefully, then nodded: 'Yes, it may be.' He paid his homage to Antonioni's film by quoting it in *Tenebrae*. I shall honour the seven minutes in a different way, by following the film's hitherto neglected trail of food and drink.

In the early sixties Antonioni came to be acknowledged as one of the masters of cinema on the basis of three bleak and brilliant black and white films: *L'Avventura* (*The Adventure*), *La Notte* (*The Night*) and *L'Eclisse* (*The Eclipse*). These movies were said to have changed cinema. They explored the idea that human relationships had become all but impossible in the dehumanized modern world of big money and big industry. The films have sometimes been mocked for their supposed pessimism, but looking at them now they generate more of a sense of exhilaration. How could anyone be so bold? Antonioni's lost, suffering characters are memorable. The beauty of his images is unrivalled, and he tells his strange stories in a completely original way, with steely panache.

The trilogy starts in Rome with *L'Avventura*. Listless, luminous Monica Vitti (Antonioni's muse and lover) collects her best friend Anna from a house in the *periferia* and they head off together with a group of bored rich people for a holiday cruise. When they take a day trip to a tiny rocky island Anna mysteriously disappears. So they all look for her, frantically. Then they keep looking, only a bit less frantically. Then they look desultorily. After a few days they forget about her completely and carry on with their lives as if she'd never existed. Watching it now you're thinking: are you even *allowed* to do this in a movie?! Well, if you're Antonioni, if you're a once-in-an-artform genius and you've just carried out a bloodless coup against everything cinema has ever been before, you can do what you like. Vitti is beautiful in a way no other actress has been, and Antonioni's storytelling and imagery are transcendently arresting. The whole thing is done with such aplomb it makes you want to jump up and smother the screen with kisses. (Alfred Hitchcock thought along similar but less daring lines the same year, killing off his main character after twenty minutes in *Psycho*.)

When *L'Avventura* appeared in 1960 it was considered a revolutionary challenge to conventional cinema. It looks even more radical now. Meanwhile, the great man was working on his next masterpiece, *La Notte*. This features a successful couple, Marcello Mastroianni and Jeanne Moreau, wandering around Milan, going to parties and falling more and more out of love with each other with every passing frame while their best friend lies dying in hospital. The closing credits of *Life of Brian* mocked: 'If you enjoyed this film, why not go and see *La Notte* [. . .] one of the most vapid and depressing movies of all time.' Or, as one critic quipped: 'Cold, harsh, dark – and that's just the drinks.' Laugh if you like, but *La Notte* was one of Stanley Kubrick's ten favourite films and I'm sticking with Stanley. And then came *L'Eclisse*, the boldest of all, a movie which, among other things, inspired a young Italian–American film student called Martin Scorsese. Some critics have compared it to great music. Others call it a poem. But it's made of celluloid like regular movies, it has pictures, and it tells a story. It's just that the story breaks every rule of storytelling and comes up with something better.

Aristotle said stories should have beginnings, middles and ends. *L'Eclisse* begins slap-bang in the middle of an ending. That's quite a flourish in itself. Two Roman lovers (she stunning in a black dress; he stunned in a white shirt) have been up all night talking and are now at break-up point. The couple, Vittoria (Monica Vitti) and Riccardo (Francisco Rabal), stare at and past each other. She has the air of an anguished saint, her blonde hair catching the light like a halo. She arranges objects in an empty picture frame and curls into a ball on the cream-coloured sofa. She opens the curtains and stares at her own reflection and up at the famous Mushroom. (The film was shot at the height of the Cold War, so this is usually interpreted as symbolic of an atomic mushroom cloud.) Riccardo just wants to make her happy but Vittoria no longer loves him, though she doesn't know why. She leaves, and walks past the Mushroom. He follows in a car then insists on walking her home. Four years later, for *Blow-Up*, Antonioni painted all the grass in a London park because he didn't like its natural shade of green. With Rome, though, he took no liberties. Unlike, say, Fellini, Antonioni always made a point of filming the city just as it was. So, as Vittoria walks to her apartment, the director is giving us a topographically precise depiction of EUR.

The concept of food makes its first appearance as soon as the broken couple reach Vittoria's building. Riccardo, in denial, points to Giolitti's, the grand café on the banks of the EUR artificial lake, which is evidently one of their places. 'It's open,' he says brightly. 'Don't you want breakfast?' Softly she replies: 'I'm not hungry, Riccardo, I'm not hungry.' Alone in her apartment she stares at the wind in the trees. A theme has been established. Vittoria's difficulties with men will be paralleled by her lack of interest in food. She is too cloudy and contemplative to need sustenance. While others munch or nibble, she floats through the entire movie without a sip or a bite.

We next see her getting out of a taxi in Via de Burrò to visit her neurotic mother at the Borsa (stock market), a bear-pit of capitalism, where she will meet Piero, her mum's stockbroker, played by the irresistible young Alain Delon. Piero is restless, energetic, boyish and so thoughtless he never seems to contemplate anything. He eats hungrily. The odds on he and Vittoria making it as a couple can be calculated by studying the famous shot that occurs almost as soon as they meet: they are seen as tiny figures separated by a huge granite column. Antonioni shows the stock market as an arid and emotionally brutal place. On this day everyone makes money, including Vittoria's mother. Outside in the Piazza di Pietra, she haggles and buys pears at a stall that also sells watermelon, zucchini, apples, potatoes, *insalata riccia*, lettuce and white organic grapes. (Food, it seems, is a commodity too.) Vittoria averts her eyes from the fruit and turns away airily. 'Are you eating with Riccardo?' asks her mum. 'Yes,' says Vittoria.

Later, literally up in the clouds on a jaunt in a private plane, Vittoria seems briefly happy. She notices a cloud that 'looks lit from the inside' and wants to fly into it. At the airfield, she gazes contentedly at vapour trails but avoids a café where a waitress suggestively pours beer for a male customer. Next day Vittoria goes back to the stock market. Her mother scatters salt to bring luck, whereupon the market crashes. The pandemonium in the market is extraordinary and violent. Voyeuristically, she follows a fat man who has lost fifty million lire to the nearby Bar della Borsa, where he takes a pill with mineral water and draws pictures of flowers. From inside the bar, Piero offers to buy her a drink. As she accepts, he turns away, grabs a croissant and orders an iced coffee for himself. While he rushes about the café munching a croissant, Vittoria picks up an abandoned drink, contemplates the glass and puts it down again. They go to her mum's apartment, discuss poverty and the father she never knew. Piero tries to kiss her, but she turns away. Her mother arrives and he says she'll make food. Vittoria leaves.

The next day, she joins Piero once more to watch as his sports car is pulled from the lake, with the body of the drunk who stole it still inside. Piero is more worried about the damage to the car than he is about the corpse. Our lovers go for a walk. He steals a glance down her blouse. They end up at Giolitti's but don't go inside. They continue to flirt and circle each other, attracted but never consummating. Finally, they walk towards their most charged location: the street corner where Tecnica meets Ciclismo. Modern apartment buildings line one side. The other has a little garden, behind which we see the floodlights of the Olympic Velodrome. Facing that is an unfinished building, a wooden fence and a water barrel. Approaching the building, Piero says: 'When we get there I'm going to kiss you.' Suddenly it's an electric moment. Halfway across Vittoria says: 'We're halfway.' They reach the other side. She smiles alluringly. Wind rustles the trees. He leans forward to kiss her, and she pulls away. She looks cloudy again. She walks away.

Next day they meet again at the same place then head to the apartment of Piero's childhood, where he offers her a drink, which she declines, and a box of chocolates, which turns out to be empty. But at least they kiss, first like prisoner and prison visitor, through a pane of glass. Then they're in his office, cuddling and laughing on a dark sofa. They seem happy, and promise to see each other every day. They arrange a date for that evening, at the usual place. As she walks downstairs Vittoria's cloudy look returns, and she slumps. Upstairs, phones start ringing and Piero looks cloudy too. On the street outside, she looks up at the trees, then down at the camera and walks out of frame.

The next seven minutes cannot adequately be described, but are both beautiful and terrifying. The camera returns to

the street corner and waits for Vittoria and Piero to show
up. At first, all is calm. In long-shot we see the half-finished
building, and behind, on the hill, the Mushroom. A nurse
pushes a pram; sprinklers water the lawn. The images of
these ordinary things are exquisite and unsettling. We
observe bricks, scaffolding, the fence, the water barrel,
which is leaking now. The camera lingers on the shadow of
a tree and the surfaces of the street, then slides along a row
of shuttered kiosks outside the stadium. A sense of unease
begins, aided by plinking piano chords and softly discord-
ant trumpets. A man who is not Piero crosses the street. A
bus arrives, disgorging passengers we don't recognize. A
gardener turns off the sprinklers. More water flows from
the barrel into a drain. We see ants, droplets, the strangely
beautiful effect of water flowing over pavement dirt. A few
strangers pass. A couple on a balcony point at vapour trails
in the sky. With relief, we see a blonde woman who must be
Vittoria. She turns. It is someone else. Darkness begins to
fall. Another bus stops and disgorges more strangers, who
walk away into the night. As darkness envelops the scene,
street lamps flicker on, and we cut to a close-up of one of
them, blindingly bright. The trumpets rise to a crescendo
and the chords of the piano become thunderous, apocalyptic. A graphic hurtles into close-up: 'The End'.

The scene has been interpreted in many ways, including
the idea that it is simply abstract. Antonioni himself firmly
rejected this, and deployed a metaphor of eating: 'The seven
minutes have been called abstract, but this is really not so.
All of the objects that I show have significance. These are
seven minutes where only the objects remain of the adventure; the town, material life, has devoured the living beings.'
Like much of Antonioni's work, the scene is metaphysical:

he seems to open the way to fundamental truths by showing things which are also other things. Martin Scorsese's take on it is satisfying. In his *Voyage to Italy*, a documentary about Italian cinema, he recalled being excited by the film and fascinated by Antonioni's vision of an impersonal world where finding real love was like trying to grow flowers through concrete. The Vitti and Delon characters try to keep their relationship going but have simply lost the will. That the film carries on when they fail to show up produces something extraordinary: 'Antonioni leaves us with nothing but time staring back at us. The world becomes a kind of shell around the absence of these two people. In other words, it's not what's there, it's what isn't there. It's a frightening way to end a film, but at the time it also felt liberating. The final seven minutes of *Eclipse* suggested to us that the possibilities in cinema were absolutely limitless.'

Antonioni went on to make a few more great movies – *Red Desert, Blow-Up, The Passenger* – and a few less great ones. But nothing quite matched the heights of those last seven minutes. When in 2007 he died, at the age of ninety-four, his body lay in state on the Campidoglio. At his funeral his friend the German director Wim Wenders said Antonioni had created a new image of twentieth-century man and Daniela Silvero, star of his late film *Identification of a Woman*, declared: 'For Italian cinema, he represented everything.'

Things have changed a little for some of *L'Eclisse*'s locations. In the centre of town, the Borsa closed in 1997 and became an art gallery (the stockbrokers moved to Milan). The fruit stall and the pharmacy are long gone. The Bar della Borsa, where Piero failed to buy Vittoria a drink, is now a fancy restaurant. Down in EUR, from the outside, the house where Riccardo and Vittoria break up (on Via dell'Antartide) looks much as it did in 1961, except a mass of ivy now grows around the front gate, and the view from the house of the Mushroom has been blocked by new building. The park through which Vittoria walked with Riccardo has disappeared under luxury apartments and mansions. The largely empty, monochrome streets have filled with cars of many colours. For the last couple of years the Mushroom has been shrouded in scaffolding while its great concrete legs are restored. Disgracefully, the city has permitted the dome to be disfigured by mobile-phone masts and advertising hoardings. (Why not stick ads over St Peter's and the Pantheon?) Giolitti's is still going, but it is no longer visible from the entrance to Vittoria's building. The windows on her old apartment are now covered with security grilles and the block has an electronic entry-phone system. In the middle of a nearby grass patch that saw Vittorio and Piero in a brief moment of joy there's a small memorial to the victims of the 9/11 terror attacks on America. At the corner of Ciclismo and Tecnica, the half-finished building of the film has become a fifty-year-old building that houses an agency for civilian victims of war. The Velodrome's floodlights have disappeared along with the Velodrome itself. One fine day in 2008, the long-abandoned showpiece, built for the 1960 Olympics but reclaimed by nature when the foundations started to sink, was demolished with high explosives. A big crowd came out to watch and there were *oohs* and *ahhs*. Now it's a hole in the ground waiting to become a water-sports centre. The spot where Piero promised to kiss Vittoria has turned to rough grass. The trees are taller. There are still vapour trails in the sky.

XVIII: The Lamb

From *Science in the Kitchen and the Art of Eating Well*, Pellegrino Artusi, 1891:

> To stew a lamb's head, do not cut it in half crosswise like the maidservant whose master told her to divide it in two. It was this same gifted girl who on another occasion skewered some thrushes on a spit from back to front.
>
> Cut the head lengthwise along its natural division and put both pieces in a large pan. But first sauté some chopped garlic and parsley in olive oil, and when this has browned, stop it from cooking with a ladleful of broth. Toss in the lamb's head and season with salt and pepper. When it is halfway done, add a bit of butter and a little tomato sauce or tomato paste, and finish cooking with more broth if necessary.
>
> This is not a dish to serve to guests, but for the family it is inexpensive and tasty.
>
> The part around the eyes is the most delicate.

XIX: The Fish Marbles

'Romans, especially in the imperial age, became total masters of the fish world'

Livio Jannattoni, *La Cucina Romana e del Lazio*

I've started eating raw fish at half-time. This is because Finnegan's, the Irish pub in Monti where I watch Arsenal games, serves no real food. After the first forty-five minutes, therefore (or sometimes after ninety), I find myself drawn to the new sushi place on Via dei Serpenti (Road of the Snakes). Japanese food in Rome is still considered newfangled and this sushi bar is part of a chain that has been doing well in fancier parts of the city. Better still, the place overlooks the Piazza della Madonna dei Monti. Up the street to the left is a good *gelateria*, an *alimentari* specializing in fiery Calabrian food, a fine-looking expensive fish restaurant I've never actually been in, and a trio of Indian eateries, including the Maharajah. A couple of hundred metres the other way, at the end of a traffic-fume-filled canyon of brick and looming like the great marble-clad, statue-heavy beast it once was, stands the Colosseum.

As with almost anything one can ever say about Rome, each element of the above paragraph has a back story, and everything is connected, though sometimes obscurely. Finnegan's, for example, is more institution than pub: an unofficial social centre for English-speaking ex-pats that generates large amounts of jollity and serves cheese-and-onion crisps. Monti, meanwhile, a network of ancient cobbled streets, remains one of the most authentically Roman of neighbourhoods. Albeit gentrifying fast, it is still full of working-class families who've lived there for generations. On hot summer nights, and even cold winter ones, the gorgeous little Piazza of the Madonna (named for the big church next door) attracts the young to its lovely eight-sided fountain to flirt, drink beer, strum guitars and eat ice cream. By day, dogs drink from a bucket below the *nasone*. Kids play football against the door of the Ukrainian Church. The square is popular with makers of TV commercials, students, business and theatre folk. Other regulars include a quartet of white-hatted Colombian buskers, always singing the same ghastly version of *Arriverderci Roma*, and a tramp called Angelino who is treated kindly by all. And off in the distance the lost marbles of the Colosseum . . . Which make me think of fish.

In classical Rome, marble was ubiquitous to a degree that probably can't even be calculated. Great temples, palaces and bathing establishments were swaddled and dripping with marble statues and marble slabs on the floors and walls. Vestigial ruins of some of these places remain. But the marble is long gone. What happened to it all? You may think that barbarian invaders – Vandals, Goths, Langobards and the like – were the guilty parties. But you would be wrong. Marble was much too heavy for conquering armies to carry off in any quantity. The marble of Ancient Rome was ravaged, ransacked and wrecked by the Romans themselves.

During and after the epoch of imperial decline Rome became tiny and disintegrated. Literacy rates collapsed along with Rome's political, military and economic power. From its second-century peak of 1.5 million the city's population almost halved by 400 AD. It was down to a quarter of that a century later. The horrors of the sixth-century Gothic Wars, when the eastern empire tried to recapture Rome and the city endured siege after siege, reduced the population to just 30,000 (and left Rome in the hands of the popes). At various low points in the Middle Ages, barely a few thousand were clinging on.

Naturally, the city's fabric was torn up too. As early as 500 AD, even before the sieges, Rome had fallen into a state of 'shabbiness'. Economic collapse meant that little food got through and the great estates outside the walls had long been abandoned. Without drainage, the countryside turned to malarial swamp (and remained so until Mussolini). Inside the Aurelian Walls, sewers and aqueducts gradually disintegrated, colonnades and granaries collapsed, precious stone and metal was looted from public buildings. The pilfering of such materials, said Richard Krautheimer, the great German historian and expert on post-imperial and papal Rome, became a Roman custom. And the most important organization in town, the Church, became both the 'main culprit' and 'principal beneficiary'. Christianity had little use for the old buildings. For more than a thousand years, like a buzzard slowly devouring a horse, the little new Christian city nibbled its way through the carcass of the fallen giant. The original St Peter's, for example, was a jumble of classical columns, bases, capitals and entablature. The green-speckled marble columns of the Lateran Basilica were nicked from an old temple. Sometimes the church was making a political and religious point, as in the sixth and seventh centuries, when churches were deliberately erected in and around the Forum, Palatine and Capitoline to Christianize the pagan heart of the old city. At other times, ordinary and usually desperate Romans were simply using whatever materials lay at hand. The unimaginable vastness of the legacy of empire still lay all around. The process of melting, burning and hammering away the statues, marbles and most of the stonework of the Colosseum was the work of dozens of generations. In the nineteenth century, Stendhal lamented:

> Why, what a thing of splendour were this site of Ancient Rome, had not her fatal star decreed, as crowning outrage, that the *Priests* should build their new metropolis upon the very ruins of the old! What glory might our eyes not still behold, were all those ancient stones – the Colosseum, the Pantheon, the Antonine Basilica, together with that fabulous wealth of monuments, now razed to the ground that *churches* might be built instead – still proudly standing within their ring of deserted hills.

Some of the worst destruction was wreaked at the very moment when appreciation of the culture of antiquity was at its highest. The various church and palace building booms of the Renaissance, Counter-Reformation and Baroque eras involved unprecedented vandalism as the Church oversaw the sack of ancient places for building materials. Many old monuments became quarries, complete with their own wrecking crews and kilns (for turning ancient marble into cheap lime, an ingredient in plaster). The artist Raphael was appalled by this destruction, and wrote to Pope Leo X:

How many popes, Holy Father, having had the same office as Your Holiness, but not the same wisdom nor the same value and greatness of spirit; how many popes – I say – have permitted the ruin and destruction of antique temples, of statues, of arches and of other structures, that were the glory of their founders? How many have consented that, just to obtain pozzolanic soil [for making cement], foundations should be excavated as a result of which buildings have fallen to the ground in a short time? How much lime has been made of statues and other ornaments? So that I dare to say that this new Rome we now see, however great she may be, however beautiful, however ornamented with palaces, churches, and other buildings is nevertheless built of lime produced from antique marbles [. . .] It should therefore, Holy Father, not be one of the last thoughts of Your Holiness to take care of what little remains of the ancient mother of Italy's glory and reputation.

Raphael, father of the modern conservation movement, persuaded the Pope to set up a new body to supervise the old marbles. Yet destruction continued. Most of the stone and marble in the present St Peter's Basilica came from classical sites. Sixtus V, the Counter-Reformation pope, is revered for opening up the city and laying out Baroque Rome's street plan, but he also destroyed as much as he could of the remnants of the 'filthy' pagan city of antiquity. As architectural historian Jukka Jokilehto put it: 'Some ancient monuments were destroyed while others were repaired and dedicated to Christian purposes. The ancient associations were obliterated as far as possible, and new inscriptions were cut into the stone. Symbolically, these monuments then demonstrated how Christianity had conquered heathenism.'

But in one place at least some ancient marble survived. Why? Because marble had qualities never fully appreciated by the architects of ancient Rome: it was a good surface from which to sell fish.

The place in question was the Portico of Octavia the still-standing columned relic at the entrance to the Ghetto. The combination of history, archaeologists and city planners has now rendered the place all but incomprehensible. There are paths on two levels (mediaeval street level and, two metres down, classical street level), a tangle of walkways and a little bridge. In classical times, however, the area must have made perfect sense because it was part of one of Rome's great public spaces (and almost entirely covered in marble). The 2,000 years of sometimes violent, often squalid and occasionally uplifting history reflected by the ramshackle Portico started in Republican times. The Portico started as part of a colonnade built around twin temples to Juno and Jupiter. Later, the emperor Augustus rebuilt it and named it after his sister, Octavia. Now it was on a grand scale: a covered walkway with nearly 300 marble and granite columns – that's more than the present St Peter's Square – enclosing a space bigger than a modern football pitch. The Portico, lined with statues, was on the route for state occasions such as military triumphs. Titus passed through on his return after crushing the Jewish Revolt. More often the Portico provided elegant shelter from the rain or sun for audiences of the vulgar entertainments at the nearby 11,000-capacity Theatre of Marcellus. At other times people must have simply promenaded on the lavish marble paving, amid statues and artworks. Earthquake and fire damage was repaired towards the end of the imperial era, under emperors Septimius Severus and Caracalla.

As Rome entered what Petrarch later called the dark ages, the city split into two. Most of the population retreated to the tiny, crowded *abitato* (as it came to be called) on the west and east banks of the river by Tiber Island. This area included the Portico. Outside, in 90 per cent of what had been the walled city, lay the uninhabited *disabitato*: 'a dangerous waste of forest, vineyard, and garden, interrupted only by the irregular masses of Rome's fortified monasteries and the fortress-towers of its barons, by hamlets scattered around the major churches and the militarized hulks of Rome's vast ruins.' (This according to Ronald G. Musto in *Apocalypse in Rome: Cola di Rienzo and the Politics of the New Age*.) Old tenement houses, mansions and public buildings and spaces crumbled to ruin and became fields interspersed with small settlements and farms. As late as 1870, when modernity arrived, the space between the Colosseum and the Palatine was still farmland.

Meanwhile, back at the Portico, the old Augustan columns, temples, statues and marble paving stones had long since been demolished, burned or plundered. By mediaeval times the great old space had been filled instead with houses, fortified towers, churches, monasteries and convents. On the Portico itself, two damaged pillars were damaged by earthquake and replaced with a brick arch. In the eighth century, a small church was built between two pillars at the back. The Portico soon became part of a graveyard. Bodies were dug into the earth at first and, when space ran out, the floor was raised and new masonry tombs or ossuaries (for bones only) inserted. Each tomb contained several corpses. But by the twelfth century space was exhausted; burials stopped. The cemetery now became a fish market. Soon the little church changed its name to Sant'Angelo in Pescheria – St Angelo in the Fish Market. Even allowing for the skeletons under foot, the new spot was cosier and handier. It also provided a chance to put to use a dozen or more huge white-marble slabs from Augustus's original Portico. Supported by bricks or, in some cases, fallen ancient capitals, they became permanent fish stalls.

Legal documents from the church discovered by historian Robert Brentano reveal touching details of life around the market in the fourteenth century. Church officials controlled the slabs and rented out space on them to fishmongers on annual leases. Those who could not afford a whole slab would lease a half. These leases were highly prized, being traded or passed down from father to son. Having a fish-slab lease was reckoned to be as good as owning a shop or farm or vineyard. In one case, for example, rent on a slab was two florins a year, while the price for a fishpond across the river was three florins – plus an additional fee payable in herring. In one transaction, a fish-seller called Pietro Corre strikes a deal with fishermen from Terracina who, for a fee of seven florins, promise to supply fish. In another deal, a fishmonger returns money he has borrowed from a money-lender in Trastevere. We learn that a member of a prominent fish-selling family called Paolucio di Lorenzo Ponziano was known as *Capograsso*, meaning 'Fathead'. A fishmonger called Ponziano leaves money in his will for oil for the lamp to light an image of the Virgin Mary.

By the Middle Ages the city was caught between feuding warlord families. One of these, the Savellis, moved into the old Marcellus Theatre and turned it into their personal fortress. In 1347, the locally born politician and mystic Cola di Rienzo, who dreamed of ending corruption and restoring Rome to greatness, launched his short-lived revolution from the Sant'Angelo. In the sixteenth century, the Confraternity of Fishmongers adopted the church as their own. Jews from the Ghetto next door were whipped into the church to hear conversion sermons. In the seventeenth century a smaller oratory opened next door, called Sant'Andrea dei Pescivendoli (St Andrew of the Fish-Sellers). Above its door there's still a bas-relief of the saint posing with a dead fish and a set of scales (for weighing fish). An inscription above the door is dedicated to 'those who sell fish'. Nearby is a marble plaque on a wall reminding fish merchants to give the heads of their fish, up to and including first fins, to city officials. (Fish heads, particularly those of the sturgeon that lived in the Tiber, were prized for making soup.)

Paolo Giovio, the noted sixteenth-century physician, historian and aide to Pope Clement VII, published a book about Roman fishes in 1524 called *De Romanis Piscibus*. This hardbitten chronicler and eyewitness to the horrors of the Italian Wars and the Sack of Rome was utterly devoted to fish, and believed the Ancient Romans had been too. For example, he attributed classical affection for the moray eel to sentiment rather than gourmet sensibilities. 'I don't believe the Ancient Romans praised the moray because they were very tasty but because they lived a long time,' he declared. 'They can become so tame that they take food from your own hands.' He recalled that Crassus had cried when his moray died (he even gave it a proper burial) and Antonia, daughter of Drusus, made earrings out of moray fins and owned an eel so tame she could put little gemstones on its eyes. Less charmingly, Giovio noted that morays could also develop a taste for human flesh and criminals condemned to death were sometimes chopped into little pieces and fed to them.

Regarding the fish of his own day, he recommended the sea bass (*spigola*) found in the Tiber and suggested fishing for it 'between the two bridges' because the waters there, rich in nutrients from the city's sewer outflows, helped the fish grow nice and fat. He also offered cooking advice. Fish whose meat was 'dry', like white bream, should be eaten roasted and dressed with cheese and vinegar. Fishes with 'fat and tender meat', like *orata* (gilt-head sea bream) were best cooked over a slow fire and brushed with oil, vinegar and salt. The *triglia* (red mullet), meanwhile, being neither fat nor liquid nor fibrous but firm and flaky, had a 'very pleasant taste' and were easy to digest. The best way to cook and eat them, he said, was over a grate and with a 'flavoursome' topping of fried parsley leaves, oil and sweet orange juice. One of the great chroniclers of ordinary life in Rome, poet Gioacchino Belli who wrote in Romanesco dialect, penned a sonnet called 'The Condiments' about one of the great issues of his day. Which is better for frying fish – animal fat or olive oil? Belli's answer: '*L'òjjo è la morte sua p'er pessce fritto*', meaning 'oil is the death of fried fish' (i.e., it's the only thing that suits the purpose).

Giuseppe Vasi's 1761 guidebook describes the market at the Portico as a place where 'every part of every kind of fish' is sold, but a guidebook printed in 1843 by John Murray, the late Lord Byron's publisher, described the market as 'one of the dirtiest quarters of Rome'. This judgement was endorsed by the American artist and writer William

Wetmore Story, who described the Portico as an 'uncouth structure' where a few beautiful original Corinthian fluted columns, 'cracked and crumbled by fire and defaced by time and abuse' stood amid general squalor. He wrote: 'Within the enclosure stands the church, and on the arch are the peeling frescoes of a Christian age, dropping daily with the decaying mortar. Nothing can be more melancholy than this spectacle. Everything has gone to ruin. Low miserable houses surround this splendid relic of antiquity. The noble columns are broken, stained, and walled up.'

He was even less impressed by the market itself.

Stone slabs, broken and grappled by iron hooks, stretch out on either side of the street, and usurp it so as to leave no carriageable way between them. If it be market-day you will see them covered with every kind of fishes. Green crusty lobsters, squirming crawfish all alive, heaps of red mullet, baskets of little shining sardines, large *spigole* [bass], sprawling, deformed cuttlefish – in a word, all the inhabitants of the Mediterranean are there exposed for sale; while the fisherman, standing behind them, slashes now and then a bucket of water over the benches and cries out his store. Is the market over – the street is deserted, the marble slabs are encrusted with scales of fish, the purchasers and the purchased are gone but the 'ancient and fish-like smell' remains, a permanent bequest, to haunt the place.

Fishmongers themselves came under attack from a Jesuit priest called Father Antonio Bresciani who called them 'the most idle and uncouth mob of the lowest scum'. They were, he said, people with no trade, they throw themselves down in the market places to pick up waste and scraps of food and resell them to the dregs in the remotest corners [of the city] for a few pennies. These people, always hanging around with thieves in gambling houses, do not speak the common language, but an ugly, sly jargon, which cannot be understood by anyone but themselves. They are always planning to swindle the gullible; ready for a coin to aid and abet in night smuggling, in revenges, in illicit love affairs and in any evil action, as long as they can snatch some money. They mainly have truculent ugly faces and shrill and hoarse bad voices: always barefooted, ruffled, filthy and in rags.

The old fish market closed in 1877. The marbles, broken, battered museum pieces, remain.

XX: The Black Rice

'Between 1958 and 1962, China descended into hell [. . .]
The experiment ended in the greatest catastrophe the
country had ever known, destroying tens of millions of lives.'
Frank Dikötter, *Mao's Great Famine*

There was nothing quite like Sonia's tiny, cave-like Hang
Zhou restaurant. Go at peak time to the grotto on the
corner of Via Merulana and you'd probably wait more than
an hour for a table. But you wouldn't mind because when
you were finally seated and the food arrived, the perfumed
black rice seemed a wonder of the world and the dishes
came steaming, fragrant and decorated with little sculptures of pussycats, pagodas and walruses made of carrot
and radish. Elfin waitresses seemed to hurry and glide
simultaneously between the crowded tables. And Sonia
herself, owner, impresario and resident diva, appeared like
a glamorous little lighthouse, sweeping the room with her
10,000-megawatt film-star smile (an empress among queen
bees). The walls were no less striking. Over the years they
had acquired a coating of photographs: snapshots of film
stars posing with Sonia – '*Hey! It's Nanni Moretti!*' – pictures
from Sonia's TV appearances, mugshots of carroty cats. And

at the back, in a little alcove, as Yuri would say, a shrine to Chairman Mao Zedong. I could never work out if this was some kind of weird ironic joke. But to eat prawn ravioli under a dozen cheery propaganda posters of the author of the Great Leap Forward and the Cultural Revolution as he waved to happy peasants was an experience offered nowhere else in Rome.

In May 2010, Sonia moved from the grotto to a new place four times bigger, in the heart of Chinatown, right across the street from Fassi's on the Via Principe Eugenio. It's still the best Chinese in Rome, her waitresses glide even more elegantly now, and there's so much space you don't even have to queue. A little of the old magic has been temporarily mislaid, but the process of coating the new walls with the old pictures is coming along nicely.

The genesis of the restaurant lay in the slow process of China's opening up to the outside world, which began in the seventies. The rapprochement with Nixon's America was aided by 'ping-pong diplomacy'. In Italy, 'ravioli diplomacy' played its small part when China's State Alimentary Service decided to improve China's image through food. Via the Chinese embassy in Rome, a high-quality Chinese restaurant for Rome was proposed. Traditional Chinese restaurants employ a roster of specialist cooks, but there was money for only one chef. A man with the requisite talents was duly identified and recruited and arrived in 1981 on a single-year contract at the city's first Chinese restaurant, in Trastevere. There the cook attracted the attention of Sonia's uncle. 'He went to see how he cooked, and was very impressed!' she recalls. When the cook returned to China, the uncle followed, desperate to persuade him to return. 'At first he refused because in China he had lots of people to help him and here he had to do everything himself. He used to spend all his free time doing the little sculptures. So my uncle went to his home in Beijing and said he could bring whoever he wanted. Eventually he said yes and came back to Rome, this time with his whole family. And he stayed almost fifteen years. We were so lucky to have him for so long! As we say in China, he turned out to be a tree of money.' The current Hang Zhou chef is Sonia's brother-in-law and learned everything, even the animal sculpting, from the great man before he left. 'He taught him to do every single thing with great patience, personally!'

Sonia herself arrived in Rome in 1991 and worked at the restaurant. When the uncle left in 1997 for Germany, where his son lived, Sonia took over. She started by asking the cook to develop new dishes, and then started getting customers involved by asking what they wanted. 'You always have to be very careful to make sure you give the customers something they like,' she advises. Even so, Chinese food still requires translating for Italians. Pasta parcels like wan-ton are always 'ravioli'. Chinese noodles are 'vermicelli'. All over the city, to this day, Chinese food tends to be served one dish at a time in the Italian fashion, rather than *insieme* (all at once). Even now, Sonia daily faces the Chinese equivalent of the *Big Night* scene where WASPs at an Italian restaurant in 1950s New Jersey enrage the chef by demanding spaghetti and meat sauce with absolutely everything. Likewise, Romans assume that Chinese food means *fried* Chinese food. 'And it's not true!' says Sonia sweetly. 'In my menu you can find many different types of dishes, and the non-fried is better. It's more perfumed and has a better flavour.' Fried food takes four times longer to cook, too. 'But when I advise people on this they often say, "Yes, but I still want *fried* food," so I say, "OK." What can I do? I try to make sure there's a balance because some people will eat on time and others will not.' By contrast, some of her customers have spent time in China and know exactly what to order. She tries to keep everyone happy. 'I'm preparing a new menu now, with proper Chinese specialities, but before I do that I want to test them. The dishes have to be good. But to me it doesn't really matter if the dishes are Italianized or authentically Chinese. The main thing is they have to be cooked well.'

I ask about her signature dish – the perfumed black rice, which comes with prawns or vegetables, plain or spicy. 'Black rice is very special,' Sonia explains. 'It's called *riso nero dell'imperatore*, the black rice of the emperor, because in China it was never allowed for normal people. It was very rare and difficult to grow and anyone who had any had to give it to the emperor. Now, thanks to technology, it is possible to cultivate black rice, and production is changing all the time. Red rice is already common, and they're producing green rice, too, though I haven't seen any yet.' Here, black rice was a popular novelty, but Sonia says it's healthy too. 'In nature there aren't many black foods: black beans, black rice, sesame, black mushrooms. But our bodies need some of this element. It's good for the blood. It's healing.'

The old Hang Zhou was down the road from Santa Maria Maggiore, on the furthest edge of the Esquilino. The new restaurant is in the heart of Chinatown, which gets bigger all the time and occasionally arouses hostility. 'Chinese Out' graffiti can sometimes be seen on the pillars around the piazza, even posters for neo-Fascist parties. My friend Beppe broaches the subject. He says he's been living in Esquilino since 2001 and has lots of Chinese neighbours but doesn't find them easy to talk to. 'It's not easy to have a relationship with them,' he says. 'It's probably my fault. I should make an effort, try to talk to them a bit more. We brush by, but never talk. With you, it's different; it's easier to speak with you than with them.' Sonia says warm relationships depend on the individual, and on language. 'Many Chinese people live here, but it's as if they live in China. They are a bit closed. For me it's different because I have lots of Italian customers. But [many Chinese in Rome] work only with Chinese people, speak only Chinese, eat only Chinese food. I see the same thing in my kitchen. The people in there do not speak Italian at all! My cook, my *maestro,* has been twenty years in Italy but he doesn't speak any Italian. He says to me: "I speak with the pan every day; I don't need to speak with Italians!" So he doesn't. When he has to renew his visa and other documents, I have to help him.' But aren't they curious about the city? 'It depends on the person. Things are changing slowly with the children. The Chinese kids born here all go to Italian schools and they grow up in an Italian culture. My son speaks *romanaccio* [dialect]. If you turn away and only listen to him, you'd never know he's Chinese. So he already has a different culture, mixed. Not really Italian, not really Chinese. Half and half.'

She tells us about the famous wall pictures, which chart the restaurant's rise to celebrity status. The first actor to have her Hang Zhou picture taken was Catherine Spaak, a beauty who starred with everyone who was anyone in Italian and French film in the sixties and seventies: Mastroianni, Gassman, Belmondo, Sordi, Trintignant, Manfredi, Tognazzi, Vitti, Cardinale, Audran, Maria Schneider – even Tom Baker before he was Dr Who. The second was the TV starlet Valeria Marini. Sonia recalls: 'In 1997, Valeria came in and I was so upset I didn't have a camera to catch the moment. So I had the idea of leaving a camera in the kitchen. Since then, every time a famous person came we could take a picture. Slowly we covered the wall. I think it's cool!'

I have to ask about the Chairman Mao posters. What's he doing here? Sonia's answer is unexpected: 'Mao is a great man.' How so? 'Before the Revolution women were under subjection. A woman couldn't do anything. This changed in the new China, after Mao. Now women could go out of the house and do anything. Before Mao she had to hide all the time behind her husband. All she was allowed to do was cook and look after the children. And because of Mao's Revolution that changed. Women had more freedom, more possibilities. Go to Shanghai now and you see how things have changed. Now men are the ones who do everything at home. Before the Revolution men could not cook, only eat. Just sit at the table and eat. Now men cook, go to the market, buy food. They have become like women. Equal! More than here! I've been told that Italian men do not help at home. A Chinese friend of mine who lives with an Italian man says he doesn't help at home at all!' Chinatown has more female entrepreneurs than male ones. But there are still differences. 'Women are still the ones who serve the food. They're the waitresses, and men are the cooks.' Why? 'Because kitchen pans are heavy so you need a strong arm to handle them. The strong men can lift and flip the pans with one hand, so that's what they do. And the women with soft beautiful hands serve the tables.'

In 2002, Sonia's brother brought a Mao calendar from China and she proudly stuck it on the wall. 'You can't imagine how many people ask me about it! They were asking me to have a copy.' 'It's certainly different,' says Beppe gently.

'You don't see Mao in other Chinese restaurants.' 'Well, I put it up to remember Mao,' says Sonia. 'He was a great personality and after he died in 1976 many stories of miracles came out. He has become a saint.' She tells us two such stories. One concerns a farmer on whose wall a picture of Mao hung for thirty years. One day the man's son, who had become rich in the city, returned home and offered to repaint the house. The father accepted so he took down the picture of Mao and his son painted over the spot. Both were then astonished to see Mao's face miraculously reappear in the paintwork. 'The picture came back by itself where the picture had hung all those years! So the house became a shrine, tourists came, and now everybody knows the house where the picture appeared on the wall by itself.' The other story concerns a fearful multiple car smash in Canton in 1986. Almost everyone died, but at the centre of the pile-up one car was unscathed, its driver unhurt. 'People were amazed! Why did nothing happen to this man? Well, inside his car, they found an image of Mao! So everyone said, "Mao is like a lucky charm!" I believe in the power of Mao. I believe it is true. It doesn't happen with everybody. Only Mao. He brought luck to me as well. And one businessman was very clever and became very rich because he made little pictures of Mao for people to hang in their cars for luck, and he became a millionaire. See?' She is pointing to the ceiling and I notice for the first time that the little charms hanging down are these Lucky Mao charms. 'Just put one of those in your car and everything will be fine!'

XXI: The Horse

Flames lick and rumble in the great oven in the corner. On the far wall, Che Guevara stares heroically from a calendar ten years out of date. A pennant celebrates Italy's 2006 World Cup win. The wall is covered in pictures of cows, with little ceramic toy cows. Signs declare: 'WE SERVE ONLY MAD COW'. In another corner, abandoned or confiscated neckties dangle mournfully from a rack and a sign warns: 'TIES NOT ALLOWED'. From crowded wooden tables all around the sound of laughter, seduction and political argument comes bubbling and shouting. We're in one of Rome's most singular *trattorie* and the flamboyant waiter with high hair, goatee beard and red-star hoody is telling us about tonight's specials.

'We have an excellent horse steak, and shredded horse – which is really tasty . . .'

Just for a moment there I thought he said 'horse'.

'Did you say horse?'

'Yeah. Like I said, the horse steak is good, and the shredded horse is . . .'

'Horse like My Little Pony?'

'What?' He looks slightly offended.

'Horse like the only thing left to eat during the siege of Leningrad?'

Now he's cross. 'Hey! It's good meat. Now you tell me, Mr English Guy, what's the difference between eating a horse and eating cow or pig?'

He's got me. I can't think of a difference, except that the Lone Ranger's horse was called Silver, and he used to say, 'Heigh ho, Silver, away!' and off they'd go and I loved that. 'He's right,' chips in Valeria. 'It's normal. Anyway, you should try it for the book.' This reminds me of Elizabeth Bowen's line about typical Roman food she characterized as being 'For the hungry, the healthy, and those in humour.' I follow Valeria's advice.

The shredded is like a *bresaola* with rocket and parmesan. Mari has chunks of horse, which taste like beef, only drier, light and spicy. Anna tries the horsemeat kebab. Above our heads doggerel is written in blue crayon on yellow card:

> *Del cavallo sono ghiotto*
> *Sia di crudo che di . . . cotto*
> *Me ne mangio a profusione pranzo,*
> *cena e colazione*
> *All'anemico che 'esangue'*
> *al vecchietto che e' un po' 'brillo'*
> *fa saltare come un grillo*
> *lo stressato zio Cirillo*
> *da vigore da 'Mandarillo'*
> *alla donne poi se sa*
> *lui le aiuta*
> *a 'Procrear'!*

For horse I'm greedy
Whether it's raw or cooked
I eat lots for lunch, dinner and breakfast

The pale anaemic,
The tipsy old man
it helps to jump like a grasshopper
To the stressed uncle Cirillo
It give the energy of an old goat
Then to women as you know
it helps them
to 'procreate'!

I keep thinking about Silver. Then again, I have so much else to think about. Horse is one of the most accessible parts of a meal as surprising and tasty as any I've encountered since a sheep-brain-and-green-soda lunch in Tbilisi, Georgia. Horse isn't even the main event. The really spicy, interesting stuff is from Rome's distinctive working-class and Jewish-Roman cuisine. Thus, all served on beautiful wooden plates: peppers and cartilage. Oxtail stew, breaded bull testicles, offal with artichokes, sausage stuffed with radicchio. There's quail, too, and chard, chicory, lettuce, potatoes and broccoli and mushrooms. Not every dish is traditional or challenging. The vegetarian *carbonara* with zucchini, served on wood, is proprietor Tommy Spoletini's invention. Horsemeat is not common in the city, but Tommy loves it. 'It's quite original to have it in Rome. Our horse dishes are from Puglia and the Veneto. But it's really one of the cleanest and healthiest meats. Full of iron, doesn't have any cholesterol, doesn't cause any sort of illness. Pregnant women are encouraged to eat it, even raw, though it's not good for people with high blood pressure. That's the only problem with it. People used to sell horse blood in capsules for people with blood problems like anaemia. So it stays in the menu as a support. I developed it as a support because

it's very nutritious rather than something special and tasty
to eat. Horse steaks are the main thing with it. I used to
do horsemeat ravioli but I don't any more because it's too
complicated.'

All over the city *trattorias* are dying. Each year it gets
harder to find those simple, charming old-fashioned places
with paper tablecloths, no menus and an old retainer who
comes to the table to tell you what's cooking. Fading too
is the traditional working-class Roman cuisine of defiantly
tasty foods made from the most despised ingredients. Here
in the Via Sorgnana, in a hidden district of tiny, ramshackle
houses, Tommy, abrasive and charismatic, owner and sole
cook of Betto e Mary, has chosen to make his stand on
both issues. He has carved out a unique role in the city for
providing food that is defiantly Roman, and for updating
the *trattoria* tradition and making it hip.

'Roman food is like all the regional working-class
cuisines,' he explains. 'It's a cuisine based on leftovers. Rich
people took the prime cuts. The poor used what's left. So
we have things like oxtail and internal organs, intestines,
spines, lungs, liver, tripe. You find ways to make them tasty
and nice and with a certain energy.' Not only is it a tradition born of poverty, it is also in large part Jewish. 'Roman
working-class food is Jewish. So we don't use pork. Our
specialities are things like tail of cow, tripe, the heart, liver
and lung of lamb, lamb intestines, sweetbreads, which is the
thymus gland. And – oh yeah – balls. Bull testicles. They're
very tasty.'

The *trattoria* is named after Tommy's parents, Betto and
Mary, who used to run the place. In the early seventies they
returned to Rome after five years in San Francisco and opening a restaurant seemed an obvious career move because

Tommy's grandparents had a restaurant in San Giovanni. Over time, Betto and Mary made the Via Sorgnana popular. Their combination of traditional Roman food and vibrant atmosphere turned the place into a cult venue, and created something of an identity crisis. 'By the late seventies, basically, we had well-to-do people from Parioli, and work- ing-class people from this area and from San Lorenzo. So we had to decide which clientele to keep, whether to go up market or "popular". And obviously we chose for the work- ing class.' Now society has changed. Sandwiched between the Via Casilina and the main train line south out of Rome, this was a desperately poor and isolated part of the city in the fifties and sixties. It was also one of Pier Paolo Pasolini's favourite districts. The writer and film-maker probably visited the *osteria* in the days when it served only wine and beer. In those days if you wanted to eat here, you had to bring your own food. It's still a leftist, mostly working-class district, says Tommy, 'but you can't really tell any more'. When Betto and Mary retired, a decade ago, Tommy kept the menu going and adapted it to a younger clientele.

The key to his food, he says, is simplicity and natural- ness. Little in the restaurant is programmed or planned. This is because Tommy despises homogeneity. 'Being the same as everyone else, doing what everyone else does, is just rubbish, in every field. Beauty lies in the differences between people.' The banning of ties began as a joke after Tommy got married without one. It also happened to signal, rather neatly, that Betto e Mary would be the opposite of fancy places with a formal dress code. The mad-cow poster and the kitschy cow figurines had a different genesis. 'When the mad-cow meat crisis came in 2001 we very nearly closed. People were suddenly freaked out about eating meat and the restaurant was completely empty. I said: "OK, I'll give it a month and if no one comes I'll close forever." I was ready to do that. We put up this poster – "We only serve mad cow" – and for some reason it changed the situation completely. It was like an exorcism. After that we started putting cows everywhere.'

The contrast with the dozens of overpriced tourist restaurants in the city centre with their low standards and multilingual menus could hardly be more extreme. 'Obviously I don't think much of those places,' says Tommy, his gravelly voice loaded with sarcasm. 'If I thought they were good I'd do that stuff myself. I guess the difference is money. Usually when you open a restaurant you only think of making money, but to keep a place like this going you have to be thinking about something else too. I don't want this to be mechanical, a food factory. I'm more interested in the relationships with the people who come to eat, with the people who work here, with the neighbourhood. I'd rather transmit my tradition. Another problem with tourists is you have to let them taste all the dishes all the time because they don't know anything about this food. With Romans I earn more money because they know what they want, so it's much easier.'

The atmosphere in the place developed naturally and 'comes from inside'. Tommy says he's similar to his father and just kept his spirit going. 'I really believe in the soul of the place. This soul is transmitted to the people who come here, and to the people who work here. People who eat here, they naturally come back when they share this common soul. I don't have a selection process for staff. People just come and ask for a job. If we have room we take them. The ones who fit the atmosphere and style tend to stay, others leave. I'm not the one to decide.' He has no interest in expanding, and is unwilling to compromise. He doesn't cater for groups of tourists. And, despite the Pasolini connection and the fact that his brother Marco is a well-known film editor (*Gomorrah* was his work), Tommy even keeps a distance from movie people. 'Directors sometimes want to shoot here; and I've allowed a few scenes for little films, but I really don't like the atmosphere around cinema people. As soon as they become arrogant sons of bitches I say no.'

Will the tradition survive? Maybe not. At one time, Tommy hoped to open a school to teach Roman working-class cuisine, but raising money for the project proved difficult and conventional food colleges in the city were hostile. As the last generation of cooks of the traditional old Roman food retires and dies, Tommy is becoming the keeper of the flame and a guru. But he's getting tired. 'I don't have time to go around teaching, but people who are interested sometimes come here and I teach them what I know.' It's a hard business. 'Being here all day is exhausting. I'm responsible for everything because I'm the owner and the cook, so I go to sleep at three and get up at seven and I'm tired all the time and fall asleep everywhere.' Won't your children carry on the business? 'Actually, I'm hoping they'll do something else, because it's a big sacrifice. If you love it and you do it with your full heart, fine. But if you don't, it would feel like a prison sentence.'

XXII: The Blood

The Middle Ages are closer than you think. A few minutes' walk from the graves of Keats and Shelley, on a busy road leading to the river and the old industrial zone, stands a dingy-looking pub with frosted yellowish windows. I push through the doors of the Mastro Titta on Via del Porto Fluviale to be greeted by very loud thrash-metal music. It's eight o'clock and only just dark outside. In here, though, it seems to have been murky forever. At one table, someone is reading a menu by flashlight. And what an arresting menu it turns out to be. Not because of its rich selection of beers from around the world, or its unusually large selection of pizzas. Rather, it's the image on the front cover that's striking. The old engraving shows a group of figures on a small wooden stage in front of the Sant'Angelo castle. A stocky, middle-aged man with white hair, wearing a cravat, a workman's apron and sturdy shoes is holding something aloft. It has a long dark tail, a wider, dripping body and looks like a fish. At the man's feet there's a flaming brazier and a pair of tongs. Behind him is a heavy wooden shape like an empty door frame. Further back stand a priest and three stooped figures, their faces hidden by pointy hoods like members of the Ku Klux Klan. We see the dome

of St Peter's and statues of angels. By the door lies a voluptuous young woman in a billowing dress. But her hands
are tied. It dawns: the door frame is not a door frame. It's a
guillotine. And that's no fish. It's the woman's severed head.
Buon Appetito! Welcome to the restaurant named after one
of Rome's strangest showmen: the Pope's executioner.

The Pope's *what*!? That's right. These days the Church gives
the impression it has always opposed capital punishment.
The world's best-known living nun is probably Sister Helen
Prejean, the American anti-death-penalty campaigner. Pope
John Paul II, a man personally, profoundly opposed to state
killing, declared the justification for executions to be 'prac-
tically non-existent'. Yet from St Augustine onwards the
Church built elaborate structures of theological justification
for putting people to death, and in the Papal States, where
popes ruled for more than a thousand years as divinely
ordained kings, executions were elaborate ceremonies serving religious as well as judicial functions. Other countries in
pre-modern Europe (England, for example) put many more
people to death, and often for more trivial offences. But
nowhere else were miscreants dispatched with such sacred
theatricality. Even more peculiar, Rome's mediaeval-style
executions, carried out by various methods, some exceedingly bloody, continued right up to 1870. Which is to say
that, in Roman terms, this didn't stop until barely the day
before yesterday.

Down the centuries many men acted as papal executioners, but only one ever became a star. Take a bow
Giovanni Battista Bugatti, better known by the corrupted
version of his formal title *maestro di giustizia* ('master of
justice'): Mastro Titta. For generations, Roman mothers sang nursery rhymes to their children about the man

who sawed the wicked to pieces: '[. . .]*sega, sega Mastro Titta!*' More recently, Mastro Titta Productions was the name of a Roman punk-music label (logo: a dripping axe). Probably the best thing to ever happen to Titta's image was *Rugantino*, a popular romantic-comedy musical from the sixties featuring a song rhyming *gioia* ('joy') with *boia* ('executioner') and depicting the old brute as a cuddly, gold-hearted guy who runs a restaurant and whose real love is cooking. It did no harm that the actor playing Titta was chubby Aldo Fabrizi, one of Italy's best-loved performers, who had played the saintly priest executed by the Nazis in *Rome, Open City*. Fabrizi was also a gourmet, as was his equally adored sister, Sora Lella, who ran one of the most popular restaurants in the city, on Tiber Island. Meanwhile, Titta's work clothes – his big red mask and flappy red tunic still spattered with blood from his last job – remain on display at Rome's strange little Museum of Criminology near the Via Giulia, close to the Tiber. (When I went, I was the only visitor and was followed around the gloomy marble-floored rooms by a policeman. Did he think I was going to steal a guillotine?) Even odder was Titta's supposed memoirs, *Mastro Titta, Boia of Rome: Memoirs of an Executioner Written by Himself*, which is still available at all good Roman bookshops, a few dodgy ones and even here in the restaurant. Once my eyes adjust to the gloom, I noticed that the place is decked out with Guinness signs and shamrocks. Why? While I ponder that, I order a *wurstel* pizza, topped with little roundels of chopped sausage. It seems the right thing to do. The dish, surprisingly large, arrives burned around the edges, which seems apt, but proves surprisingly tasty when washed down with German white beer.

The guy who owns the place, Giorgio Chioffi, is large and taciturn and proudly identifies himself as ninth-generation Roman. He wears shorts, large, yellow-tinted shades, has a vivid tattoo of an American-football helmet on his right arm and wears a goatee beard. With his bulging T-shirt, chunky thighs and nineties-style demeanour he looks in fact like John Goodman in *The Big Lebowski*. Back in 1997 he was searching for a theme for a pub-cum-restaurant-cum-rock-venue, and lighted on Titta's name and image. 'I was looking for something that was very Roman but not so well known,' recalls Chioffi. 'Titta was a cute name, so I thought he would fit well with the idea of a pub. I thought: he only killed people who did something wrong and it's like that with heavy drinking. You want to get drunk every night and kill yourself with alcohol? Well, don't blame Mastro Titta. It'll be your fault!' Giorgio's first Titta restaurant was down the street and was much more spectacular. Visitors paid a small membership fee and descended to a huge basement, part dungeon, part hobbit-house, equipped with low wooden benches and decorated with instruments of 'correction'. Most of the macabre stuff is now stored at Giorgio's home and in the basement of the new building, which is, rather disappointingly, clogged with the bric-a-brac of its previous incarnation as an Irish pub. What do Guinness and Irish pixies have to do with Mr Titta? 'Well, it's not finished yet,' explains Giorgio. 'I ran out of money but it'll be just like the old place eventually.' He apologizes for the thrash metal, too. 'Normally it's rock from the sixties and seventies.'

Later, I sit down with the book that has defined Titta's image as a ghoul. It starts with quite a bang, describing his precocious debut: 'I began my career as an executioner for His Holiness, hanging and quartering in Foligno Nicola Gentilucci, a man who, taken by jealousy, had killed a priest and his driver [. . .]' The date is 22 March 1796. Seven years since the French Revolution kicked off, four years from the end of a century history remembers as the age of the Enlightenment, though this rather passed Rome by at the time. On that fateful day the monks would have comforted Gentilucci, assuring him that his confessed soul would go to paradise, but the man himself was about to become the first canvas of the executioner as a young artist. At the gallows, Titta wasted no time. As he tells it, as the condemned man finished the last Amen of his prayers Titta slammed into him and pushed him off the ladder with 'a magisterial blow'. He then displayed 'truly extraordinary dexterity' by jumping on his shoulders to 'perfectly' strangle him before stylishly spinning the body into 'several elegant pirouettes' to 'amaze' the crowd. Titta finished off with a splatter-movie flourish that might have made a Lucio Fulci or Mario Bava blanche: chopping off Gentilucci's head 'with honesty and accuracy', carving the corpse into four equal pieces 'like a most experienced butcher', then neatly impaling the bleed-ing hunks on spikes around the stage. Pretty impressive for a seventeen-year-old.

The youngster went on, as this weird book relates, to enjoy a phenomenal sixty-eight-year career as a 'teacher of righteousness', variously chopping, bludgeoning and hang-ing 516 people on behalf of six separate Holy Fathers. Most of Titta's victims were criminals, though some were political prisoners. Generally speaking, the more heinous a crime, the nastier a death Titta was required to inflict. Nastiest of all, though rarely used, was a mediaeval horror known as *mazzolata*, involving a mallet and a knife. At the moment of death, it was customary for fathers in the crowd to slap their son's faces as if to say: 'Don't let this happen to you.' Many executions were followed by carnival-like revels, yet Titta came to be detested by many Romans. Accordingly, he lived close to the Vatican in the Borgo Pio district and crossed into the main part of the city only when required. Killing people wasn't even his main job; he was paid just three cents a corpse and earned his living making trinkets for tourists. Instead, he seems to have felt an almost religious calling, to have been a pious man doing his duty. Looking back after being finally pensioned off at the remarkable age of eighty-five, Titta declared that his conscience was clear because people had to atone for their sins and he had simply carried out 'God's will' according to the 'instructions of His representatives on Earth'.

By turns salacious, solemn and cheery, this volume which has entered Rome's folk memory consists mainly of descriptions of the crimes Titta punished. This being Rome, some cases turn entirely on food. One such was that of a priest called Don Giovanni Lupini who 'loved generous wine and good food'. One night in 1800 he went to sleep happy after one of his peasants served him a big meal and some light, sparkling wine from his own vineyards on Monte Mario. During the night, thieves broke in and strangled Lupini in his bed. They then ransacked the house and pantry and cooked a feast in his kitchen. When they realized they couldn't carry away Lupini's wine, they opened all the taps and poured it on to the ground ('thus dispersing the grace of God', says Titta, an odd phrase to whose meaning we shall return). Food, inevitably, was also the men's downfall: they were caught when they sold the priest's hams and *caciocavallo* cheeses to a local grocer. After torture (routine in the Papal States at the time), the men were sentenced to an especially gruesome death: to be hanged, dismembered *and* burned. Titta duly turned his stage into 'a butcher's shop' and some of the resulting body parts were later displayed on the Sant'Angelo Bridge, a sight so ghastly that people entering the city turned pale and fled in terror. But, later that same day, a different reaction had set in: 'All the taverns of the surroundings abound in the curious, who drew hilarious, joyous and happy, as if they were attending a party.' The Roman public, he added, were 'convinced that the sentence was fair and did not believe that criminals deserve pity'.

Then there was Carlo Castri, a Sweeney Todd-ish wine seller who ran a nice little tavern in a beauty spot just north of Rome in Parioli, now Rome's richest suburb. In fine weather, customers travelled there from the city, as they now do to places like Arriccia, and Castri did well. In winter, though, when weeks went by without a single customer, he was known to force women 'to pay in kind' for food and he took to lurking as a highwayman, robbing and killing unwary travellers. Titta's memoirs go into some detail about the fine food with which he lured victims (roast venison, woodcock, noodles, pan-cooked chicken, egg *capellini*, salami, pecorino cheese, roast partridge, creamy milk, salami, fresh bread, bottles of 'topaz-coloured' wine from the vineyards of Montemarano) before explaining how Castri's reign of gastronomic mayhem ended. He killed two hunters but failed to bury them properly, leaving the heads sticking out. The subsequent execution was insanely gory even by Titta standards. Sentenced to hanging and quartering, Castri struggled and screamed 'like a madman' and wasn't even properly dead when Titta started chopping.

'The day was freezing, the north wind blew and his bowels were smoking, as if they were drawn from a boiling pot. In contact with the icy air the smoke condensed into fat on my hands, making them slippery. Before returning home it took me a pound of soap to clean up.' But the body parts continued to 'smoke' and rendered the gallows so disgusting it had to be destroyed. When Titta took it home and burned it, again producing a stench, his neighbours asked: 'Are you making sausages from the people you've hanged?'

According to the book, Titta rarely exults in his horrors. Many chapters end perfunctorily: 'condemned to *mazzolatura* and quartering, he refused religious comforts and died stoically'; 'arrested, tried and sentenced, he had his head cut off by me'. Before each job, he solemnly visited the Church of St John the Beheaded to make confession and take holy communion. This church, in Via dei Cerchi, was named after John the Baptist (whose own severed head, since you ask, can still be seen in a little glass box in the San Silvestro Church by the bus station), and was headquarters to the order of St John the Beheaded, whose monks played a central role in Roman executions. Before each ceremony, these Capuchins did their best to soothe and prepare the condemned for 'a Christian death'. When it was over, they gathered together the pieces of the body and buried them with ceremony in the church courtyard. In earlier centuries this had been considered a holy honour and an act of charity that gave dignity to the condemned. By Titta's time, the monks were seen more as acting on behalf of the state. Either way, everything about the execution ritual was religiose, marked by constant praying and sermonizing. The condemned man's last, slow journey by cart through the city to the scaffold deliberately evoked Christ's journey on the Via Dolorosa. The chanting, singing, pointy-hooded monks did their best to keep the prisoner as calm as possible with talk of the afterlife and by holding on sticks little paintings called *tavolette* before his eyes until the last moment. These pictures depicted the executions of Christ or St John the Baptist, and were meant to be encouraging. Circulating among the crowd, other monks passed alms boxes to raise money for prayers for the soul of the soon-to-be-departed. All these were old customs, but by Titta's time revolution was in the air and many prisoners declined religious 'comforts'. In 1828, for example, in Ravenna, in the north of the Papal States, four members of a revolutionary *carbonari* group who had tried to kidnap a cardinal and spark an uprising rejected the attentions of the monks and went to their deaths shouting, 'Long live Italy! Down with the Pope!' The men had 'greatly agitated His Holiness', says Titta, but the city was on their side. On execution day, Ravenna draped itself in mourning black and the streets were deserted. Later, Titta was obliged to leave town secretly, under escort. As a youth, at his first performance in Rome – before 'the most exalted ecclesiastical judges, illustrious personages of the papal court, ambassadors, ministers, noblemen and ladies' at Piazza del Popolo – Titta adopts a derisory tone about a burglar who struggled and protested that his death sentence was an 'abomination'. Without hesitation, Titta 'sent him to another world, where he could take his complaints about the justice of Rome'.

Generally, though, the great executioner was courteous to his 'patients', often offering them a pinch of snuff before killing them. He didn't like executing women because 'I have always considered woman to be intellectually and physically inferior to man and it disgusted me to have to exercise my action over this inferiority'. He admired those who 'died well, without cowardice, without fuss', who went out 'as Christians' or 'suffered resignedly, requesting forgiveness from God and men'. The death of a twenty-five-year-old robber 'was most edifying. He made a sincere confession of his misdeeds and showed repentance. He wanted to attend Holy Mass and receive the Eucharistic food before moving to execution. On the way from prison to the square he continued to pray aloud, with the comforters. He mounted the scaffold singing the Litany of the Blessed Virgin Mary and died as a saint.' Those dragged 'ignominiously' into Titta's presence earned his scorn. Then there were prisoners for whom the anguish of imminent death triggered various kinds of personality collapse. One man arrives at the gallows an 'automaton', another is 'catatonic', others are struck dumb or their hair turns prematurely white. A murderer, sentenced to bludgeoning and dismemberment, starts to rave, develops convulsive fever and slides rapidly towards insanity. To forestall the possibility of him either dying of his illness or going so mad he wouldn't understand his execution, the church authorities do the right thing: they order Titta to chop the man to pieces immediately to stop him 'cheating justice'.

Executions drew large crowds (Charles Dickens had to wait hours to get a good view), but audiences were volatile. Depending on the nature of the crime being punished and the drama on stage, Titta could find himself applauded or vilified. Not infrequently, the sheer splatter of the spectacle produced mass hysteria, cursing, screaming, fainting. At one beheading, Titta admits, a female spectator died of shock. At another, 'the emotion aroused in the audience who watched the torture was immense, indescribable'. The guillotining of 'incomparable beauty' Geltrude Pellegrini in

1838 – the execution seemingly depicted on the pizza menu – brought out voyeuristic instincts. The eyes of Pellegrini, who murdered her ugly old husband for love of a younger man, were 'full of mysterious languor and dazzling iridescence'. She had long, black, soft, shiny hair and fine, velvety skin 'of that pale golden brown which is the despair of painters'. A great throng saw her procession through Rome, with many witnesses observing through telescopes. When Titta finally displayed her head, the crowd was 'more stunned and excited than any I ever happened to see'.

Titta's descriptions tally with those of contemporary observers. Dickens, for example, was horrified by the 'show' when he saw Titta behead a man in the Via dei Cerchi: 'It was an ugly, filthy, careless, sickening spectacle; meaning nothing but butchery beyond the momentary interest, to the one wretched actor.' Lord Byron, who saw Titta guillotine three men in Piazza del Popolo in 1817, was more sympathetic:

The ceremony – including the masqued priests; the half-naked executioners; the bandaged criminals; the black Christ and his banner; the scaffold; the soldiery; the slow procession, and the quick rattle and heavy fall of the axe; the splash of the blood, and the ghastliness of the exposed heads – is altogether more impressive than the vulgar and un-gentlemanly dirty 'new drop', and dog-like agony of infliction upon the sufferers of the English sentence. Two of these men behaved calmly enough, but the first of the three died with great terror and reluctance, which was very horrible. He would not lie down; then his neck was too large for the aperture, and the priest was obliged to drown his exclamations by still louder exhortations. The head was off before the eye could trace the blow; but from an attempt to draw back the head, notwithstanding it was held forward by the hair, the first head was cut off close to the ears: the other two were taken off more cleanly. It is better than the oriental way, and (I should think) than the axe of our ancestors. The pain seems little; and yet the effect to the spectator, and the preparation to the criminal, are very striking and chilling. The first turned me quite hot and thirsty, and made me shake so that I could hardly hold the opera-glass (I was close, but determined to see, as one should, see every thing, once, with attention); the second and third (which shows how dreadfully soon things grow indifferent), I am ashamed to say, had no effect on me as a horror, though I would have saved them if I could.

In *Discipline and Punish: the Birth of the Prison*, Michel Foucault argued that public execution fulfilled an essentially political ceremonial function, utilizing 'an invincible force'. The idea was to show in the most extreme way possible the dissymmetry between a subject who violated the law and the all-powerful sovereign who enforced it. Moreover, the 'liturgy of punishment' affirmed the superiority of power. 'This superiority is not simply that of right, but that of the physical superiority of the sovereign beating down upon the body of his adversary and mastering it [. . .] the ceremony of punishment, then, is an exercise in "terror".'

But stranger meanings were surely at work on Titta's stage. It was the setting for swirling, primal dramas and dark echoes of old ideas about blood, sin and redemption. Especially blood. Titta seems disturbing to us because, like the repressive theocratic system he served, by the nineteenth century he was an anachronism. His career coincided almost exactly with the decades when popes tried desperately, and with no little cruelty, to fend off the evils of modernity: rationalism, secularism and liberalism. In 1870, six months after Titta retired (and a week after the Pope was officially declared infallible) Rome fell to the army of the new, secular republic of Italy and, amid scenes of wild popular rejoicing, ended the millennium of papal power of life and death over the city.

Titta embodied an older Catholic world, one steeped in bloody symbolism. 'From birth to death, the sight and smell of blood were part of the human and social pilgrimage of each and all,' Piero Camporesi tells us in *Juice of Life*:

> It was common to see gallows and scaffolds, executioners' carts smoking along the streets [...] heads impaled on stakes or nailed to doors, corpses left to rot and putrefy in the tower cages, cadavers hung on windows with hooks, 'quarters' abandoned at crossroads [...] the butcher shop that hacked up persons merged imperceptibly with the one that slit the throats of bulky beasts slaughtered in the open. Small animals were killed in kitchens and yards. Barbers, phlebotomists, pork butchers, midwives, brothers, hospitalers, opened, closed, cauterized veins with appalling indifference.

Camporesi, a writer surprisingly little known even in Italy let alone the English-speaking world, was one of the most interesting cultural historians of the twentieth century, part literary detective, part anthropologist of the past. His remarkable achievement was to penetrate the thought-world of pre-modern Europe, especially that of the poor, through an encyclopaedic knowledge of obscure, non-literary texts such as sermons and popular song. In books with titles like horror movies (*Land of Hunger, Fear of Hell, The Incorruptible Flesh, Anatomy of the Senses, The House of Eternity*) he summoned visions of past daily lives which were dark, fantastical. 'Camporesi', wrote Umberto Eco, his friend and Bologna University colleague, 'is a gentleman who walks into a room where there is a very beautiful rug on the floor – a work of art, and everyone has always regarded it as a work of art, with its patterns, and all those lovely colours – lifts it by the edge, turns it over, and shows us how, under the rug, worms, roaches and larvae have been swarming, a whole, unknown, *underground* life. A life no one has discovered. And there it was, under the rug.' Camporesi, he explained, was a *gourmet* anthropologist who saw the body 'as the locus and occasion of pain, torture, everlasting sufferings [. . .] He has looked and seen how human beings ate, cooked, how they smacked their tongues when they swallowed, how they aroused, with their ointments and elixirs, their very sexual capacities [. . .]' Eco also warned that his friend's work was indigestible, that it was best to sample it 'a sip at a time'. To do otherwise, would be 'like eating cream puffs for a week and nothing else, or swimming for a week in one's own excrement (and it would be the same thing).'

In *Bread of Dreams*, for example, Camporesi explains why pre-modern Europe seems so odd. Some of the things people believed and did in those superstitious, pre-industrial times seem to us outlandish, as if the entire population must have been off its head on mind-altering drugs. Camporesi's explanation is simple: the entire population *was* off its head on mind-altering drugs. All Europe, he says, had 'the appearance of an enormous house of dreams' where everyone, from crippled mountain-dwellers, to the people of the forests, towns and cities, lived in 'a suspended and bewitched condition, where portent, miracle and the unusual belonged to the realm of the possible and the every-day'. It was a 'febrile and sleepless society' on a 'collective journey into illusion'. With deep poverty endemic, starvation constantly threatened. In such circumstances, people ate pretty much anything they could lay their hands on. Bread was adulterated with poppy seed, hemp, darnel and other hallucinogens. Opiates were widely used, mass witchcraft believed in, exorcism common. Children were routinely drugged to put them to sleep. He tells of a seventeenth-century Roman doctor called Scipione Mercuri who recommends dabbing an ointment made of lettuce seeds, poppy seeds, rancid oil, saffron and vinegar, then adding a dose of white poppy syrup by mouth. 'Thus prepared and "seasoned", the infant was entrusted to the dark arms of the night. The initiation into controlled dreaming and the artificial ease of opium-induced sleep began with swaddling clothes. From infancy to old-age narcosis reigned supreme'. Almost every page imparts disturbing information about a lost world of the senses. It was a society made up of 'oiled, smeared, anointed and spiced, violently odorous and unbearably smelly' people. Men, women and children of every rank and station lived in 'a verminous universe unimaginable today' and were permanently infected with parasitic worms. 'Clinging to the narrow cavities of the intestines, masters of the entire territory bounded by throat and sphincter, [these worms] could neither be molested nor irritated, under pain of causing the decline of health into the abyss of illness.'

Unlike most academics, Camporesi tends not to develop straightforward theories or linear arguments. His work is more like an erudite, poetic nightmare, an unearthly lighting of a bizarre and ravaged landscape. Since just one of his elegant, cascading sentences tends to contain more ideas than some books, he's difficult to summarize, or even quote intelligibly. But I'll give it a go because *Juice of Life* (subtitled *The Symbolic and Magical Significance of Blood*) reveals much about the pre-modern Catholic culture of which Mastro Titta is so late and interesting a symptom.

'The red saccharinity of blood flows over the pre-scientific and religious imagination as an unsettling, real presence,' says Camporesi. In a culture obsessed with the sufferings and blood of Christ, the red stuff was 'knotted to life [. . .] to its passions, to its commotions [. . .] Life and salvation were closely tied up with [blood's] quality and its purity. In parallel fashion with human blood, but with unlimited miraculous content, the divine blood loomed over human beings' salvation and welfare.' This was a world in the grip of an 'ideology of blood' as intense as that of the human-sacrificing Aztecs. Suffering was virtuous and the ideas of divine sacrifice, regeneration through wounds, torture and bloodletting fundamental. At the core of all this lay the 'insane faith in the absurd'. Legions of Christian martyrs were celebrated as saints who had founded the faith 'with their blood'. Christianity's sacred places 'gleamed with the shreds of the bodies of those who had died in bitter, piercing pain'. Such men and women were revered as 'innocent victims, slaughtered lambs, champions of sacrifice'. The Church was 'this polyvalent mausoleum, this dissecting table, museum of sacred osteology, immense reliquary', a 'temple made of blood, a gigantic clot of blood, blood dripping like a ceremonial slaughter in pre-Columbian America, like a sacrificial pyramid'.

You begin, perhaps, to see what Umberto Eco meant. But there's so much more. Blood was 'thick with magical signification, mystical claims, pharmacological prodigies, alchemistical dreams'. It stood at the very heart of medicine. It was central to notions of purity and beauty. Inevitably, it was also food. In the kitchen, blood was the best 'sauce', the most prestigious stock, the 'finest juice'. Blood was 'family remedy, household drug, aliment of life'. Hence a near-universal taste for blood cakes, blood puddings, pastas of bloody flesh, boiled blood, blood fritters and 'doubtful pies of a gloomy blend whose "dark soup", distilled from bloody meat, constituted their dense, viscous, savoury stock'. From Spain came a whispered legend about cooks and confectioners who 'not infrequently used the blood of persons drawn and quartered, or the shreddings of torture victims, to concoct a sort of *vol-au-vent* or puff pie.'

In a culture where the torments of Christ were depicted in increasingly gruesome and anatomically precise detail, so, in the late Middle Ages, executions and tortures became increasingly sophisticated: 'bodies impaled, severed heads, members stripped and shredded of their skin, flesh torn with forceps, roasted, toasted, innards scattered about, body parts dismembered and impaled, crushed testicles, genitals cut off and stuffed in the mouth, witches, heresiarchs and sodomites burned'. This sort of thing 'evoked the image of the hell's kitchen, a city in shambles, where everyone, men, women and children (boys in particular) shared in the cruel fun of the mass sadism, enjoying the slaughter and torment with visceral rapture, in a collective projection now upon the person of the executioner, now upon that of the victim of the tortures – but always in the province of blood, of the squandering of life'.

Camporesi guides us through a cannibalistic world in which it was normal for apothecaries to sell oils, fat and other healing products derived from humans. Every imaginable body product was used, and every unimaginable one too: human faeces, urine, fat, ear wax, sweat, semen. Fragments of the crushed skulls of persons who had died violent deaths were especially good for you. '*Cranium hominis suspensi in pulvere reduce,*' recommends one pharmacological textbook: 'Grind to powder the skull of one hanged.' People had themselves bled to cure illness or ritually purify themselves when the seasons changed. Blood was used to stop haemorrhage and staunch wounds. Health-giving oils and salts could be derived from human blood, as could 'a ruby stone of wondrous efficacy and virtue'. Blood was the most important of the 'humours' which governed health. A sixteenth-century Bolognese doctor boasted that he used a 'quintessence' of human blood to cure the almost-dead: 'Suddenly I have seen them return, and in the briefest time become well. This [quintessence] is of much succour, and does great wonders in the case of diseases caused by blood, for it rectifies it, and preserves it, precisely as the fifth essence of wine, when a small quantity thereof is put in a cask full of wine, purifies and preserves it indefinitely, which other materials do not do.' A Franciscan apothecary left us a recipe for preparation and storage:

Draw blood from persons of warm, moist temperament, such as those of a blotchy, red complexion and rather plump of build. Their blood will be perfect, even if they have not red hair [. . .] Let [the blood] dry to a sticky mass, then place it upon a flat, smooth table of soft wood, and cut it into thin little slices, allowing its watery part to drip away. When it is no longer dripping, place it on a stove on the same table, and stir it to a batter with a knife [. . .] When it is absolutely dry, place it immediately in a very warm bronze mortar, and pound it, forcing it through a sieve of the finest silk. When it has all been sieved, seal it in a glass jar. Renew it in the spring of every year.

The blood of the blotchy was splendid enough, but the authentically divine stuff, available exclusively through the miracle of the Mass, was very much better. 'Divine blood' was 'a great and terrible reality'. It was the 'unique and precious balm, the exquisite of distillates', a 'revenge on the stagnant, foul, rotting waters of death'. According to St John Chrysostom, 'if the precious blood of Christ be taken with faith, any disease is snuffed out by this remedy'. Camporesi describes the Mass as a

darksome, complex rite in which the inexplicable tran-substantiation of wine into blood effected by the ritual invocation, by the celebrant's 'powerful' words, expresses one of the 'mysteries' of greatest tension, and is one of the moments of most uplifting desolation and unfathomable depth. It was a rite secret in part and incomprehensible to the faithful who shared in it, with words whispered by the priest lest they be caught by the profane, or worse, used for spells and evil deeds. Indeed it was the 'bloody' component of the sacrifice, the magical metamorphosis of wine into blood, that excited queer, paradoxical, morbid, vaguely vampiric attitudes. The cultic devotion to the

divine sacrifice and a convulsive, obsessive, almost mani-
acal taste for blood, are profoundly interrelated.

The dominating story of the age was the Passion, and
devotion to the tale became inseparable from ever-more
hideous depictions of Christ's suffering. An obsession with
his whipping and scourging 'took root in popular piety
and sensibility', as did a profound and morbid interest in
all the other horrors of the process of 'the murder of God's
son': 'the open wounds, the cloven chest, the palpitating,
fiery heart, [the] drippings of the butchered, outraged
flesh'. These gave body to fantasies of self-punishment and
remorse and 'indicated a horrible fall on the part of the
human being, and of God'. Depictions of the Passion reso-
nated with 'an emotional cache buried in the lower strata of
the collective consciousness, with its vague sense of guilt,
and the irrepressible need of that guilt for mass purification and expiation'. During Holy Week, 'the streets flowed
with blood' from mass-flagellations ('rhythmic floggings,
sing-song self-slaughters'). These were inspired by preach-
ers who would evoke the 'horrible, disgraceful spectacle'
of the flagellation and crucifixion of Christ with 'parox-
ysmal sermons', then 'tear off their clothing and scourge
themselves before dismal, horrified crowds, inciting to
penance and suffering, setting in motion the mechanism of
self-punishment [. . .] priming, in a process of criminal identification, the need for a purificatory bath of spilt blood'. A
preacher called Francesco da Montepulciano raved: 'There
will be blood everywhere. There will be blood in the streets,
and blood in the rivers, filled to overflowing, lakes of blood,
rivers of blood with great heads floating there, I tell you,
floating in the blood.'

In the hagiographies of saints, Christ's blood becomes an 'inebriating drug', 'stupefying, and narcotising, alienating and paralysing', a sort of combined wine cellar, bakery and butcher shop. Saint Frances of Rome longed 'ardently' for this blood because of her 'burning love' for Jesus. Saint Philip Neri, the 'Apostle of Rome', famed for his work with the sick, the poor and the prostitutes of the city, developed so intense a passion for divine blood that, when receiving communion wine, he left teeth marks on the silver chalice and licked and sucked 'with such affection that he seemed unable to detach himself from it'. If he had a nose bleed, Philip prayed to be allowed to bleed more. Eventually, 'The Lord being pleased to grant his prayer, one day [blood] issued in such a great amount that he lost his sight, and could no longer see; at other times it was as if he had fallen dead [. . .] Thus it happened with Philip, to whom the Lord granted to shed, time and again, entire basins of [blood]. And his last illness was nothing but blood.' Philip's blood, in turn, was mopped up, collected in a decanter and preserved by the faithful so it could be dripped into the mouths of patients during their final illnesses. At the last, the soul of the late-sixteenth-century saint Mary Magdalen dei Pazzi (who famously declared 'my soul takes pleasure from and exults in pain') 'was transformed into blood, so much so that she thereupon understood nothing but blood, saw nothing but blood, tasted nothing but blood, felt nothing but blood, thought nothing but blood, spoke nothing and could think nothing but blood. And all that she performed immersed and steeped her in the blood of Jesus.'

Maybe a restaurant named after the sanguinary master isn't such a bizarre idea after all.

XXIII: The Tomato Sauce

From *Science in the Kitchen and the Art of Eating Well*, Pellegrino Artusi, 1891

There once was a priest from Romagna who stuck his nose into everything, and busy-bodied his way into families, trying to interfere in every domestic matter. Still he was an honest fellow, and since more good than ill came of his zeal, people let him carry on in his usual style. But popular wit dubbed him Don Pomodoro (Father Tomato) because tomatoes are also ubiquitous. And therefore it is very helpful to know how to make a good tomato sauce.

Prepare a *battuto* [crushed mixture] with a quarter of an onion, a clove of garlic, a finger-length stalk of celery, a few basil leaves and a sufficient amount of parsley. Season with a little olive oil, salt and pepper. Mash seven or eight tomatoes and put everything on the fire, stirring occasionally. Once you see the sauce thickening to the consistency of a runny cream, pass it through a sieve, and it is ready to use.

This sauce lends itself to innumerable uses, as I shall indicate in due course; it is good with boiled meat, and excellent when served with cheese and butter on pasta, as well as when used to make risotto.

XXIV: The Macaroni

'Spaghetti can be eaten most successfully if you inhale it
like a vacuum cleaner'

Sophia Loren

One day in the 1960s Sophia Loren was asked about
the secret of her looks. 'Everything you see,' said the
world's most admired beauty and best-loved paragon of
Italian-ness, 'I owe to spaghetti.' In a career spanning seven
decades she starred in nearly a hundred films and wrote a
heart-warming cookbook called *In Cucina con Amore* (*In the
Kitchen with Love*). In this she explained how one of her aims
in life was to pass on the great Italian food-making traditions with which she had grown up. As renowned for her
warmth as her radiance, Loren was no diva. On movie sets
she made a point of cooking huge pasta dishes for everyone,
including technicians, cast and extras. Could anything be
more typically Italian than that?

A similar point about the centrality of pasta to Italian
identity is evident in the love for comedy actor and director
Alberto Sordi. When he died in 2003, TV presenters wore
black and Sordi's body lay in state. His funeral at the San
Giovanni Basilica drew most of Italy's political leaders, the

cream of the entertainment industry and half a million ordinary Romans. That's almost 10 per cent of the population, and comparable to the number of *cittadini* who mourned John Paul II two years later when most of the people in the crowds were foreigners. (By contrast, when Sordi's contemporary Eric Morecambe, England's best-loved comic, died suddenly in 1984, only about 1,000 fans attended the funeral.) One reason Sordi was loved was that he represented his city so well, playing characters in his films with a thick Roman accent. Another was that he captured something deep about food. A block-length graffiti in northern Rome still reads: 'Alberto we miss you'. Then again, he's never really gone away. Sordi's old house near the Baths of Caracalla is a museum to him, Rome's most elegant shopping arcade, on Via del Corso, bears his name and his face can be seen on the walls of almost every tourist restaurant in the city. It's a very particular image, too: the nation's most popular entertainer doing his best-loved summing up of the essence of the nation. Looking both dopey and half-crazed, Sordi is stuffing an impossibly large amount of pasta into his mouth.

The still is taken from the most revered moment of a career that spanned sixty-five years and nearly two hundred films. Sordi's macaroni-eating scene from *An American in Rome* sums up how Italians like to picture themselves in relation to their national dish. Made in 1954, the film mocks Italy's post-war rush to embrace all things American. Sordi plays a Roman teenager obsessed with baseball and Marilyn Monroe. He wears jeans and T-shirts, tries to model himself on James Dean and talks to himself continually in what he imagines to be English (though he doesn't speak a word). After an evening in Rome pretending to be a cowboy, he comes home and finds the dinner his mum has left for him on the table. Naturally, the food is Italian – a heaped plate of macaroni and a bottle of red wine. He is appalled: '*Macaroni*!? That's for cart-drivers! I don't eat macaroni! I'm *American*!' Contemptuously, he pushes away his mother's offering, gives it dark looks, insults it, threatens to slap the pasta with the back of his hand. He proudly assembles the ingredients for what he takes to be a proper American meal: milk, jam, yogurt, mustard and marmalade. 'That's why Americans beat the Indians!' he says. 'Americans don't drink red wine. They drink milk! That's why they never get drunk. Have you ever seen a drunk American? Americans are strong!' All the while, he continues to belittle the plate of macaroni. From his absurd 'American' ingredients he constructs a truly silly sandwich and begins to chew. After a few seconds, the taste overwhelms him. He gags. Disgusted, he spits out the 'American' food, turns to the macaroni, utters the famous line: '*Macaroni, m'hai provocato e io ti distruggo adesso, io me te magno!*' ('Macaroni, you've provoked me and now I'm going to destroy you, I'm going to eat you!') Suddenly he is stuffing himself with proper Italian pasta, compulsively cramming it into his face. The scene is still funny and evocative. Despite his superficial transatlantic passion this Italian boy is clearly in the grip of something irresistible. By returning to the pasta, the deepest part of his being, as one Italian newspaper obituary put it, has risen up and expressed his 'profoundly Mediterranean and Italian soul'. The scene works because everyone knows that pasta is the supreme, ultimate and defining Italian foodstuff, as old as the mountains and the sea. Pasta is to Italians what snow is to the Inuit: ancient and primal, as integral to the nation as the landscape. Only it isn't. Until remarkably recently few people in the peninsula even ate pasta (or indeed spoke Italian). For Italians pasta-eating is like tartan-wearing for the Scots: a tradition largely invented in the late nineteenth century.

Up until the Risorgimento (the movement of unification) Italy was a confusing patchwork of different regions and nationalities. The new nation created in 1861 was something of a Frankenstein monster: some ill-fitting parts had been bolted together by force and theory. The country was overwhelmingly agricultural. Education levels and incomes were low, and the land was divided by a bewildering variety of dialects, customs and even weights and measures. Some regions, especially the South and the mountains, were isolated and poor. In 1860, barely 2.5 per cent of the population spoke Italian as a first language. Furthermore, there was no such thing as a national cuisine. Italians in all corners of the country ate different things.

In 1878 an official report into conditions recorded that peasants in Mantua lived almost mainly on polenta 'augmented in the evening by onions and bad cheese'. When work was available, bread and *minestra* might be eaten once a week, but in winter it was 'polenta morning noon and night and often even the three meals are rotten because there are no drying ovens or ventilators; so it ferments, and sometimes even germinates in storage'. Pasta was 'rarely used' in Gaeta, and eaten 'only on festive occasions' in Trapani. In *The Magic Harvest* Camporesi tells us how peasants survived in Emilia and Romagna in the mid-nineteenth century: 'men and women of emaciated appearance venture forth from [. . .] villages and climb the muddy dykes, braving the menace of snakes and swamp miasma to fish, to hunt, to gather marsh grasses'. When they could, these people lived on game and fish, made their bread from maize or bran and sometimes ate rice. Pumpkin, frog and fish soups were also popular (at least when pumpkins, frogs and fish could be found). In the forests around Ravenna, the poor foraged for mushrooms, wild asparagus, blackberries and pine nuts. For protein, they boiled porcupines or land turtles and ate them with potatoes. The local uplands had their own alimentary culture, too, which was dominated by chestnuts. Very few places ate wheat, the essential ingredient of pasta. For centuries, Italian peasants ate porridge ('eternal whitish or greyish') made from inferior cereals such as buckwheat. In the eighteenth century maize and yellow polenta took over as staples. In seventeenth-century Bologna, vetch, 'three-month barley' and millet (the 'great relief' of peasants) were used but peasants and their animals alike mostly ate broad beans. In most parts of the peninsula, the poor made bread from whatever grains or fodders were at hand (at best, for many, this was barely, vetch, rye or oats). Sorghum helped 'rustics drive away hunger in winter'. The most important exception to this pattern was the south. By the late nineteenth century the peasants there were poorer than those of the north, yet they were less hungry. This was because Sicilian peasants ate wheat bread while those in Lombardy ate maize, though, because it had relatively recently arrived from America they didn't how to make the best use of it. Wheat was more nutritious. And Sicily had traditions that would prove important for the whole country, including Rome.

Fresh pasta is remarkably ancient. Apicius describes a flat sort called, in Latin, *lagana*, which was good for covering pies. It seems to have been the forerunner of modern lasagne. If we search for an alimentary clue to modern Italian identity, however, we will not find it in fresh pasta. Dried pasta, on the other hand ... Well that's an entirely different kettle of bubbling carbohydrates.

Pasta secca (the dried stuff) was not invented by Italians but by Arabs. It first entered the peninsula from Arab-controlled Sicily, probably in the twelfth century. The long-cherished notion that Italy first tasted pasta when Marco Polo brought some back from China to Venice in 1295 was disproved some years ago. In a will dated 1279, a Genoese soldier called Ponzio Bastone left a box of *macaronis* to his family. The bequest is the earliest known reference to the food in Italian. Rather, it seems, Sicilian-Arab pasta was brought by Genoese merchants to two main places on the mainland. It came first to Genoa and neighbouring districts in Liguria, and later to Naples. Of these, Naples proved the more significant. From the twelfth century onwards there is evidence of vermicelli and other types of dried pasta produced in Liguria and northern Tuscany. By the sixteenth century it was common enough in Naples for Giordano Bruno to write: 'the macaroni fell, as the proverb goes in Naples, into the cheese'. But pasta was still a luxury item. 'For a long time, pasta was only one food among many,' write Capatti and Montanari in *Italian Cuisine*. 'Even in the sixteenth century it was perceived as a delicacy that could be, or should be, abandoned in times of difficulty.' In Naples a law of 1509 forbade making *taralli, susamelli, ceppule, maccarune, trii vermicelli* and all other 'things made with dough' in times when the cost of flour was raised by war, famine, or bad harvest. Generally, the population lived on bread, soup, vegetables, and meat. Even in Sicily, pasta was expensive. In the mid-sixteenth century macaroni and lasagne still cost three times as much as bread. Only around 1630 did the use of dried pasta become normal in the city.

By this time it was common for the people of different regions to insult each other on the basis of the foods they ate. Lombards were known as 'turnip eaters', the people of the central Appennines were (chestnut bashers); those of Cremona 'bean eaters'. Florentines were *cacafagioli* (bean-shitters) and Neapolitans either *mangiafoglie* (leaf-eaters) or *cacafoglie* (leaf-shitters). The staple Neapolitan foods were meat and greens. According to cultural historian Massimo Montanari's history of alimentation in Europe, this pattern was common throughout the continent. But around 1600, as the population rose and the effect of forests clearances were felt, meat became scarcer. It was in Naples that a crucial innovation was made.

The process was revealed in the 1950s by a Communist-resistance hero turned post-war government minister. In an essay called 'Neapolitans from Leaf-eaters to macaroni-eaters' Emilio Sereni used literary sources and scientific analysis to show how a seventeenth-century economic crisis transformed the eating habits of the city, and eventually the peninsula. Naples was a big city with a population of 300,000 when a series of political and economic upheavals made the old diet prohibitively expensive. At this point, said Sereni, the Neapolitans revealed their genius by solving complex problems of logistics, economics, and food distribution. It didn't happen overnight, but evolved over the course of a century. Rather than invest in ever-more expensive perishable vegetables from distant places, the city began to import a richer dry commodity: grain. With this they began to produce a food which they could store more easily and for longer. By adding water, which cost nothing, they turned the new product into a nutritious 'alimentary mass' – *pastasciutta*, or 'pasta soup'. Another breakthrough came when the Neapolitans realized they could replace meat protein by sprinklings of cheese: macaroni cheese was born. As Sereni explains:

> Apart from the energy-giving hydrocarbons that they contained, macaroni provided (at a level noticeably higher than bread) fibre in the form of vegetable protein, which cannot totally replace meat protein. Sprinkling pasta with cheese – which became the rule in the latter part of the 1600s – gave a supplement of animal protein and fats that came close to making a plate of macaroni a complete meal capable of providing (although at a much lower level than a meat diet) the alimentary mass and the energy-giving materials and fibre necessary to maintain even a famished populace above the level of physiological starvation.

Technological developments meant that macaroni and other types of pasta could be made more cheaply. Pasta became essential to the diet of the city's poor. This, says Montanari, was a rare instance of the changing of the 'grammar' of an entire alimentary system. Even when famine and plague hit in the late eighteenth century, Neapolitans didn't die in large numbers, as others did elsewhere. Macaroni had saved the city. When Goethe visited in 1789 he observed that 'macaroni of all kinds [. . .] are found everywhere at a low price'. Much of the population now lived off macaroni sold cheaply by street sellers who used charcoal-fuelled stoves. By 1785 there were 280 pasta shops in Naples and the city appeared laced with pasta hung over balconies and from frames in the streets to dry. The image of the Neapolitan pasta-eater, holding the spaghetti in his hands over his mouth, became a stock figure all over Europe.

The next impact was both political and cultural: Naples and the rest of Italy were about to overrun one another.

In 1860 Camillo Benso, Count Cavour, the Piedmontese prime minister and chief architect of the military and political campaign to unite Italy, wrote in code to his ambassador in Paris: 'the macaroni are not yet cooked, but as for the oranges, which are already on our table, we have every intention of eating them'. What he meant was: Garibaldi's Risorgimento forces are not yet ready to take Naples (the macaroni) but they are poised to take Sicily (the oranges). Politically the Risorgimento would mean takeover of the south by the north. Alimentarily, it would be the other way around. Garibaldi was crucial in both transitions. His army, the so-called One Thousand red shirts, soon enough took Naples as well as Sicily. His soldiers were drawn from the rice-eating north, mainly Piedmont, Lombardy and the Veneto. Now they came into contact with the Naples street pasta-sellers and were astonished. A few months later, soldiers from the new Italian army led by Cialdini had the same experience. The Italian diet would never be the same again. When the soldiers went home, they took pasta and its accompanying tomato sauce with them.

Franco Cecla in his book *Pasta and Pizza* argues that the new Italian kingdom needed a unifying image and identity, and found one by 'pulling the Mediterranean bedclothes more to the north'. Pasta became symbolically important. There had long been a distinction between the French-influenced cooking of the aristocracy of northern Italy and the 'rowdy' and 'robust' cuisine of the south. Pasta now 'begins to unwind like a ball of yarn and wrap itself around the Italian identity'. In the past, pasta had to be dried laboriously on racks in the sun, which was fine for hot and breezy Naples, but hopeless for other parts of Italy. Now new machines made it easy and cheap to manufacture. As part of the modernizing of Italy, food production became industrialized. In 1877 Pietro Barilla established his first pasta factory in Parma. Now pasta could be produced in a bewildering variety of shapes and colours. It was a wonder food, cheap, nutritious and with a remarkably long shelf life. The new industry was not centred on Rome, but the city did have a few medium-sized dry-pasta factories, including that of the Cerere company, which opened in 1905 on the corner of Via Tiburtina and Via degli Ausoni in San Lorenzo. Brochures from its heyday show the six-storey *pastificio* advertising more than eighty types of pasta, from the thread-like *sópracapellini* to great tubes of *coccapieller*, all made with 'perfected and modern machinery'. The factory closed in 1960, when new machinery was required and transporting products from the residential area was no longer permitted. In 2004 the building, which had become dilapidated, became the Cerere Foundation art centre, home to a hip gallery and gourmet restaurant.

Another key figure in this Italian food revolution was a pet-loving Florentine bachelor with 'enormous side whiskers' called Pellegrino Artusi. He had made his fortune as a silk merchant, and, on retirement, devoted himself to his principal passion, which was food. In 1891, at the age of seventy-one, he finished a cookbook which he called *La scienza in cucina e l'arte di mangiare bene (Science in the Kitchen and the Art of Eating Well)*. Unable to find a publisher, he used his own money to print it and dedicated the first edition to his cats: 'to two of my best friends, with their white fur, Biancani and Sibillone, I dedicate this book, to you, innocent of envy and rancour, you have never tired of keeping me constant company [. . .] to you who with your concord teach men fraternal love'. By the time Artusi died in 1911, his book had sold more than 200,000 copies and transformed the nation. The book fused Artusi's encyclopaedic knowledge with gentle humour and practical values and wisdom. Taking recipes from all corners of the country, he produced a new stereotype of 'national cuisine' that the middle class of the entire country took to its heart. The book includes dozens of pasta dishes, including a *maccheroni alla Napoletana* recipe especially appealing to 'people who like their pasta swimming in sauce'. Garibaldi had said: 'It will be macaroni, I swear to you, that will unite Italy'; but, as Camporesi observed in the introduction to his famous 1971 edition of *Science in the Kitchen*, Artusi provided the recipe. He had used a culinary system 'that recommends itself by its temperate good taste, its basic principle of eating no more than necessary – a system that knows no waste, unusual splendours or extravagances [. . .] nutrition, guided by science, serves the purpose of generation by satisfying needs and sweetening the bitterness of life a little, in accord with the spirit and ideals of nineteenth-century scientific philanthropy'. Artusi is said to have done more for unification than anyone else.

Meanwhile, however, the Risorgimento had disrupted the old feudal systems of the south and triggered mass poverty on a scale that forced emigration. Millions of Italians fled the new country, mostly for America. Ironically, on the far side of the ocean, Italian immigrants created a new 'authentic Italian cuisine', which became a proud badge of their Italian identity and which was eventually exported back to Italy.

The American food writer Corby Kummer has pointed out that pasta actually first came to the Anglosphere in the eighteenth century via aristocratic English travellers who had visited Naples as part of the Grand Tour. Such Englishmen were even known as 'macaronis' for their Italian affectations. English colonists later brought macaroni to America. Eventually, local factories opened and prices fell, ending macaroni's upper-class social cachet. By the time of the American Civil War macaroni was eaten by the working classes, usually baked with cheese and cream. The more than five million Italians who fled to America in the decades after unification brought a different approach. At first, American experts were appalled by immigrant pasta, hard cheeses, vegetables, fruit and garlic. It was too expensive to get the vegetables they liked, so American-Italians started eating more meat, because it was cheap, and developed a taste for cakes and rich desserts. They also ate more pasta and a new cuisine came into being: Italian-American, whose signature dish was spaghetti and meatballs, a thing unknown in Italy. According to the food historians Levenstein and Conlin Italian-Americans even began to think this was the stuff they had eaten back home. La Cecla argues that this new 'Italian' food rapidly became homogenized and standardized. At first this excited only contempt. Italian immigrants in the USA were looked down upon as 'spaghetti-eaters'. But later their 'Mediterranean cuisine', made available to the American middle classes via Italian restaurants, became popular and as much a signifier of Italian-ness as Coca-Cola was for American-ness.

*   *   *

In Italy, in the space of a few decades, a food once reserved for the middle and upper classes, and eaten by the poor only on feast days, had become ubiquitous. Hundreds of *pastifici*, pasta-making factories, opened all over Italy and new kinds of presses and extrusion techniques made hundreds of new pasta shapes and varieties possible. Not everyone was charmed. In his *Manifesto of Futurist Cuisine* of 1930 the Futurist poet and provocateur F. T. Marinetti called for pasta to be banned because it caused 'weakness, pessimism, inactivity, nostalgia, and neutralism'. If Italians must eat starch, they should stick to rice. Macaroni, was a 'symbol of oppressive dullness, plodding deliberation, and fat-bellied conceit'. Marinetti slightly undermined his case by being caught eating an enormous plate of spaghetti in a restaurant. In any case, the nation wasn't interested. Pasta had unified the country and carried a new image of Italy around the world. It continues to be crucial, says La Cecla: 'What Italians eat in order to *feel themselves Italian* has been as important as, if not more than, the Renaissance, Michelangelo, Donatello, Leopardi and Manzoni.' Indeed, the late-nineteenth-century invention of Italian-ness was so profound and comprehensively successful that modern Italians have almost forgotten it happened. The country's 'unique and collective capacity to invent and present themselves by means of odd-shaped edible objects that may be long, short, round, solid, tubular, and even flat' has been one of the most successful propaganda operations by any people in recent world history.

XXV: The Fig and the Anchovy

'You are my older brother'
John Paul II symbolically greets Chief Rabbi
Elio Toaff on the first visit by a pope to
the Great Synagogue of Rome, 1986

'If you fry it, even a shoe will taste good,' says Ghetto tour guide Micaela Pavoncello, revealing the secret behind not only *carciofi alla giudea* but also the survival of the Jewish people. Over the millennia Rome's Jews learned to make the best of any nourishment or warmth that came their way. The Jewish-style artichoke, eaten whole and deep-fried to make the thick leaves edible, has become the signature dish of the city's tiny community. 'All over the world Jewish cooking has the same concept,' Micaela explains. 'Poor ingredients but a lot of love. We always make food with what's to hand.' And why did the Jews have to make do with the poorest ingredients? We'll get to that.

I'm tagging along as Micaela leads a small group of American tourists around the Ghetto. The once dank and immiserated sliver of land by the Tiber, where the city's Jews were imprisoned for 300 years, has become one of the most fashionable spots in the city. It's a sunny Friday lunchtime, just before the Sabbath, and, beneath the watchful eyes of security men guarding against terrorist attack, a festive mood reigns on the Ghetto's main drag. Here in Via del Portico d'Ottavia, Romans and tourists alike flock to nibble at history. In the shade of a side-alley sits an old lady who commutes in every day from the suburbs to be with her friends. Around the tables of outdoor cafés children from the Jewish school swarm happily, their lessons over for the week. Rome's Jews are Orthodox, but their observances are relaxed. One bakery near the school has two sections: one kosher, the other selling mortadella, ham and salami. Nearby, the Pasticceria Boccione is famous for its macaroons, sweet pizza, cheesecake with chocolate, and biscuits coated with cinnamon and almonds. There's a three-month waiting list for its cakes. 'You should see this place on Sundays!' says Micaela. 'Jewishness has become cool. Really, you're nothing in Rome unless you buy your cookies from the Jewish baker. Christian groups go to Mass, then come to see the *shul*, then they go and eat fried *carciofi*. Everybody wants to have Jewish friends, study the kabbalah. Everyone is looking for their Jewish roots.'

This is the Western world's oldest diaspora community, Roman Jews pre-dating the categories of Ashkenazi and Sephardi because they arrived in 146 BC direct from Jerusalem, seeking an alliance with Republican Rome against the Greeks. And they never left. Not only are Rome's Jews the most ancient of all current Romans, but they are also the founders of the city's popular cuisine. Micaela explains: 'Roman food is Jewish food, so people come to the Ghetto and eat 'typical Roman food' because the only intact Roman cuisine is what we have. And the funny thing is that the kosher restaurants are now very fashionable. Wealthy non-Jewish people come here and order chopped-liver pâté, heart, lungs, tongue, tail, all the things that were poor dishes from our tradition.' We sample one of the famous artichokes at one of the Ghetto's many kosher restaurants. At the next table is a group of Israeli cardiologists, in town for a conference. Joining us is Fred, a psychoanalyst from California. Micaela turns out to be right about frying: it rather magically renders the woody, chewy, thick outer leaves surprisingly light, crispy, nutty-flavoured and Twiglet-brown. The inner bits are soft, hot and tasty in the usual artichoke way. Squeeze lemon on the thing and it's really rather good.

Throughout the Christian era the fortunes of Rome's Jews depended on the personalities of individual popes. Benign ones such as Nicholas IV and Martin V were warm and decent. While some popes ordered the Talmud to be burned, the humanist Leo X asked for a copy and even set up a short-lived Jewish printing press. Borgia Pope Alexander VI welcomed Jews expelled from Spain. Clement VII was known as 'the favourer of Israel'. Doctrinaire oppressors such as Eugenius IV and Boniface VIII were memorable in different ways. Despite being second-class citizens, until the thirteenth century, Roman Jews were allowed to own property and live where they wanted. Trastevere was the main Jewish district and Jews worked as fish-sellers, bankers, silk merchants and doctors. Some even held public office. Under Innocent III, however, the most powerful and bloodstained of popes, the Jews' position worsened sharply. Roman rituals ensured the Jews knew their lowly place. When a pope was elected, the rabbis of the city had to present him with a Torah scroll, which the pontiff might hurl to the ground. The Jews were obliged to swear loyalty beside the Arch of Titus, which celebrates the Roman sack of Jerusalem. The carnival (*carne vale*: 'farewell to meat') marking the beginning of Lent was often a time of fear. Jews were obliged to race through the streets, sometimes naked, sometimes fed rich food to make the race more difficult for them and more amusing for the spectators. During the Counter-Reformation, Rome's rabbis had to dress in clown-like costumes and walk through the streets to be pelted with mud. Later, this indignity was replaced by tax, forcing the Jews to pay for carnival. Jewish fish-traders were obliged to sell big fish to Christians, and keep only anchovies for themselves.

The Ghetto itself was the creation of Paul IV who, on 26 July 1555, ordered all Rome's Jews into a single street and walled them in. It was, he explained, 'completely senseless and inappropriate to be in a situation where Christian piety allows the Jews (whose guilt – all of their own doing – has condemned them to eternal slavery) access to our society and even to live among us'. Jews had to sell their property at knock-down prices and were no longer allowed to marry or employ Christians. Jews were also banned from trading in grain, barley 'or any other commodity essential to human welfare' and were permitted work only as 'rag-pickers'. By day Jews might enter other districts, but at night their Ghetto gates slammed shut. The Church was obsessed with trying to convert Jews for Christ, so the Ghetto was ringed with little churches where they were forced to attend conversion sermons. Nearly 300 years later the American writer William Wetmore Story described the weekly humiliations:

> Every Sunday came the *sbirri* [cops] into the Ghetto, and drove the wretched inhabitants with the crack of their whips, like veritable overseers of a slave plantation, into

the precincts of the church. Guards stood at the door to make sure that the appointed number were there; and the *sbirri* within, if they caught a poor devil of a Jew asleep or inattentive, brought him to his bearings at once by a lash of the whip over his shoulders. The sermon was delivered by a Dominican priest, upon the very text which had formed the theme of Jewish discourse the previous day in the synagogue. The effect does not seem to have been very satisfactory for very few of the Jews were ever whipped into Christianity, though the lashes were laid on with an unsparing hand.

By the same token, even in the darkest times, there were always plenty of Romans willing to support the Jews, and sometimes they showed prodigious wit and courage. Gian Lorenzo Bernini, the greatest sculptor and architect in Rome's history, created his Fountain of the Turtles in the Ghetto as a tribute to Jews. According to Benjamin Blech and Roy Doliner's book *The Sistine Secrets*, Michelangelo's Sistine Chapel Ceiling is really a subversive, pro-Jewish plea for brotherhood and freedom of thought. (Michelangelo came from tolerant, more secular Florence and had studied the kabbalah.) At the darkest moment of all, during the Nazi round-ups of 1943, the Roman doctor Giovanni Borromeo, head of the Fatebenefratelli Hospital on Tiber Island, saved the lives of dozens of Jews by locking them in an isolation ward and claiming they suffered from the mysterious 'K Syndrome', a deadly, contagious and entirely fictitious disease named after the Wehrmacht and SS commanders in Rome, Kesselring and Kappler.

Dante Aligheri's best friend was the Roman Jewish poet Immanuel ben Solomon, but these days the Jews of Rome are better known for their clothes shops than their intellectual giants. Micaela's dad, however, is a mathematician who writes comedies in Giudeo Romanesco, the unique dialect which blends Roman slang, Hebrew and Spanish. In his version of *Fiddler on the Roof*, Tevye the Milkman becomes Davide, Second Hand Clothes Seller, a Jewish archetype from the time of the Ghetto, when selling rags and money-lending were the only jobs allowed to Jewish men. Micaela's mother, meanwhile, came to Rome from Libya, one of the thousands of Jews forced to flee Muslim countries after the 1967 Six Day War. Oddly enough, Micaela's own job began when she lived for a year in Buenos Aires. Missing home, she started a website about Jewish Rome. When someone asked her for a tour, she sent them an itinerary. Requests kept coming. By the time she got home she had a new vocation: passing on Roman Jewish history and culture in her inimitable and passionate style.

She's feisty, funny, speaks five languages and has some nice lines. 'There are 16,000 Jews in a city of five million,' she explains, 'so you have to be very unlucky to get hit by a Jewish car.' She is fiercely proud of her community's resilience and achievements. But mention any of the countless historical injustices visited on the Jews of Rome and Micaela flashes with unrehearsed feeling. At the old Ghetto boundary she points out the mocking, cajoling Hebrew words written on the Santa Maria della Pietà church, part of the Church's unstinting efforts to get Jews to convert: 'All day long I have stretched out my hands to a disobedient and faithless nation'. The line is from Isaiah and Micaela snorts her contempt: 'How do you like that? They use the words of *our own prophet* against us!' She shows us the piazza named after Stefano Taché, the two-year-old boy murdered in front of the synagogue by Palestinian terrorists in 1982. (The little girl who pushed Stefano's pram that day and was covered with his blood happens to be with us: she is now learning to be a tour guide.) Then there's the Piazza 16 Ottobre 1943, named to commemorate the victims of the Nazi round-up of 1,092 Jews. Only sixteen survived, and one of the last of these happens to amble by. Micaela greets him warmly and compliments him on his panama hat. Later, she tells the story of her great-grandmother. When Jews went into hiding after the round-up (many into Church institutions, including the Vatican), the Nazis set up a system of rewards. For information leading to the capture of an adult male Jew the going rate was 5,000 lire. For a woman it was 3,000 lire. Jewish children were worth just 1,000 lire. As the Allied armies drew near, the rate fell. Two months before liberation a Fascist policeman decided to cash in on Micaela's great-grandmother, and received 400 lire. She was murdered in Birkenau; the policeman was later jailed. A year or so later, Micaela's grandfather got a call: 'Mr Pavoncello you must come to the police station, we have news concerning your mother.' On arrival he learned that an amnesty had been declared; the Fascist policeman was about to be released and the police therefore needed Mr Pavoncello's help. 'The man is coming out and he has a family with small children,' they explained. 'Nobody will feed them unless he can get a job. But he can't get a job with this bad mark on his career unless you sign a letter. The war is over. Your mother is gone. Forget her! Let's look to the future! We've prepared this letter for you to sign [. . .]'

Despite the widespread and genuine warmth towards Rome's little Jewish community, such wounds are not fully healed, and events have a way of picking at the scar tissue.

Evidence of this isn't hard to find. Just look at the city's walls where, for decades, far left and far right have continued the Civil War of 1943–44 through the medium of graffiti. In the 1970s and 1980s, the left won, with the slogan *la lotta continua* ('the struggle continues') seen everywhere. Now the far right is doing better. In my old district near Via Latina, a Fascist social centre seemed to be the source of posters for the neo-Nazi Forza Nuova party, and a short walk from my apartment took me past swastikas aplenty, tributes to Hitler and daubings denying the Holocaust. No one in the district seemed bothered by any of this. Leftist enclaves, where support for the Palestinians is *de rigueur*, can also bring you up sharp. In January 2009, in San Lorenzo, the old workers' and students' neighbourhood, which prides itself on its anti-Fascist traditions, a poster of a Jew as hook-nosed, rabbinically bearded, yarmulke-wearing demon appeared in a prominent position on a wall over a bank in the main street. As the graffiti artist explained to me later, he had not meant to be anti-Semitic. A speech bubble declares 'Fuck the War!' and the face in the poster was meant to show a 'typical Jew' protesting the Hamas–Israel war in Gaza. Unfortunately, the artist had no clue what a 'typical Jew' looked like, so he consulted an old school history textbook and, in a chapter about the Second World War, found just what he needed. Only one problem: the image was a 'typical Jew' as imagined by the Nazi hate-sheet *Der Stürmer*. And when the artist put up his version of it no one in San Lorenzo noticed anything amiss. Not only did the *Stürmer* poster remain undisturbed for months, by Liberation Day a further twist had been added. Alongside the anti-Semitic poster no one noticed was anti-Semitic, new posters had been posted, without apparent irony, calling on the populace to remember and resist the horrors of Fascism.

My head spinning, I called the historian David Cesarani at the United States Holocaust Museum in Washington and asked why such things might be happening. Historical research over the last decade or so, he explained, has demolished the comforting old image of Italy under Fascism. Until the late 1990s, the consensus was that anti-Semitism in Italy had been a purely German import and that Italian Fascism, bad though it was, was not intrinsically anti-Semitic except during the Salò Republic. Now, however, it was clear that anti-Semitism pervaded Italian Fascism from the beginning, and that many Italians had collaborated in the plunder and murder of Jews. 'Mussolini made anti-Semitic comments from the time of the First World War and when his regime passed anti-Jewish laws and began expropriating Jewish property, Italians were as eager to steal Jewish businesses as people in other countries. It's a myth that Italians boycotted anti-Semitism. Italy's anti-Fascist left now, in fighting Fascism, should be fighting anti-Semitism as well. You can't separate the two. It is outmoded and simply historically wrong to hold that Italian Fascism was in some way different from Fascism in Germany.' So why are Roman leftists, who think of themselves as *anti*-anti-Semitic, blind to an image as disturbing as the one in San Lorenzo? 'Because they don't know this. What they read in their history is that the struggle against Fascism is a struggle against monopoly capitalism, against imperialism. They don't read about anti-Semitism or the fate of Italian Jews, except in the context of German atrocities. And after the war the left simply expunged anti-Semitism. It wasn't deliberate blindness. It was just that the Marxism–Leninism of the time had no time for religion, the Jews and so on. It included the Jews as victims of Fascism – not as Jews, but as citizens. So there is no tradition of acknowledging the specific fate of Jews.'

Anti-Semitism is once more shaping daily life in the Ghetto. Armed men again stand guard around the Jewish buildings, now to protect against terrorism. We are obliged to divert for a few pages to try to explain the historical background.

The first thing to stress is that since the liberal reforms of Vatican II Catholic attitudes to Jews have improved to a degree once inconceivable. In the aftermath of the Holocaust, the 1965 edict of *Nostra Aetate* reversed a policy going back nearly 2,000 years and finally absolved the Jews of the deadly ancient charge of deicide. Furthermore, 'all hatreds, persecutions, displays of anti-Semitism levelled at any time or from any source against the Jews' were condemned. This inaugurated an unprecedented golden age in Christian–Jewish relations. Later, Pope John Paul II improved things still further. As warm towards Jews as any pope ever has been, he revealed a deep understanding of their suffering during the Holocaust, some of which he had seen for himself in Nazi-occupied Poland. John Paul went well beyond Vatican II, breaking ancient taboos and building bridges of friendship between the faiths. He visited, prayed and spoke movingly at Auschwitz. He visited Israel and pushed a prayer into the Western Wall. And in Rome, in 1986, he visited and prayed in the Great Synagogue, something no pope would previously have dreamed of doing. The change this wrought was so great that by the time Benedict XVI followed in his footsteps in 2010 years later such a visit seemed almost routine. And when, later that year, Silvio Berlusconi made a bad-taste joke about the Holocaust, the

Vatican newspaper *L'Osservatore Romano*, which once fever-
ishly promoted anti-Semitism, thundered that the prime
minister had 'offended the sentiment of believers and the
sacred memory of six million Holocaust victims'.

In recent decades, Christian and Jewish scholars have
been doing fine work together trying to understand the
root cause of the problem: the complex history of how the
followers of Jesus (all Jewish to begin with) came to split
from Judaism over the first three centuries. There is no
firm consensus on precisely why Christianity, supposedly
a religion of love based on the teachings of a Jewish teacher
and healer, came to depict all Jews as evil 'Christ killers'.
Were the seeds of anti-Semitism sown by the bitter arguments between St Paul and James, brother of Jesus, about
the status of Mosaic law? Or was the damage done by the
idea that Christians had superseded Jews in God's scheme?
Was the anti-Jewish tone of the Gospel of John decisive? Or
was it that deadly line inserted into the Gospel of Matthew
which has the Jews asking for the blood of Jesus to 'be upon
us and on our children'? How much harm was done by
the mutual hostility and occasional violence between Jews
and Christians in the first and second centuries when Jews
initially had the upper hand? Or by the revolutions of the
fourth, when Christianity became the religion of empire?

In any event, seeds were planted, terrible fruit grew and
after 2,000 years of Christian anti-Semitism came the Nazi
Holocaust. What was the relationship between these two
phenomena? There's no consensus here either. The Church
still cannot bring itself to admit that its past teachings and
policies made the Holocaust possible. The Vatican's 1998
document *We Remember: A Reflection on the Shoah* insisted that
the Church only ever objected to Judaism on *theological*

grounds, and was therefore not to blame for Nazi ideas on race. Nazism, the report said, was 'based on theories contrary to the constant teaching of the Church on the unity of the human race and on the equal dignity of all races and peoples, and the long-standing sentiments of mistrust and hostility that we call anti-Judaism, of which, unfortunately, Christians also have been guilty'. Non-Vatican experts on the subject were not impressed by this line of argument. As Yehuda Bauer, doyen of Holocaust historians, put it:

The Church, as such, actively persecuted Jews, not only Judaism; it never planned a genocide of the Jews, but since the time of the Church Fathers it permitted, and very often encouraged, beatings, torture, humiliation, dispossession, exile and forced conversions, and occasionally massacres. Its princes then often had to try and defend the Jews from their own incitement against them. It is true that Nazi anti-Semitism was different from the Christian variety, and that Nazism opposed the Christian churches, often violently. But Christian anti-Semitism was a necessary, though not a sufficient source of the Nazi ideology. All Nazi ideas about Jews have their source in Christianity; even Nazi racism has a precedent in the racism of the Spanish Church after the expulsion of the Jews from Spain. To deny that can be interpreted as a 'soft' form of Holocaust denial.

In Rome, under imperial and mediaeval Christianity, Jews certainly fared better than pagans and heretics, who were wiped out. Then again, the Jew's allotted role of cursed outsider was always perilous. And the uniquely Christian idea that the Jews were a cosmically evil people who had rejected and killed God still underlies and drives all forms of anti-Semitism, making it different to other prejudices. While common-or-garden racism tends to depict the 'other' as dirty, lazy or stupid, the Jews were imagined to be powerful and cunning. Any wickedness, however absurd or fantastical, could be ascribed to them. Behind this idea, as Sartre suggested, murder always lurked. Thus, in the Middle Ages Jews were massacred for poisoning wells, torturing consecrated wafers and making matzos with the blood of Christian children. Closer to our own time, Jews were slaughtered for being (simultaneously) capitalists and Bolsheviks, and for polluting Aryan blood. Expressions of anti-Semitism may change, but it retains this essential element, these days focused on Israel more than on individual Jews. On the internet and in mainstream media in the Muslim world, we read that Jews variously cause AIDS, perpetrated the Holocaust (which did not take place) and steal Palestinians' body parts. Cut adrift from its Christian origins, the idea has mutated freely. After 9/11, old tropes took on new form. The US government blew up the World Trade Center and invaded Iraq and Afghanistan on behalf of 'the neocons', and anti-Americanism fused with anti-Semitism: now it was the innately evil USA (controlled by 'the Israel lobby') that cared only about money and sought global domination.

Bizarrely, Christianity's worst idea has been enthusiastically adopted by Muslim *anti*-Christians. The pathological Jew-hatred now expressed by the likes of Hamas, al-Qaida and the President of Iran directly echoes that of Hitler and is as central to the radical Islamist threat to the world as it used to be to the Nazi threat to the world. The parallel is no accident. Until the mid-twentieth century, Islamic attitudes to Jews were quite different. But Nazi anti-Jewish propaganda, especially in the form of radio broadcasts to the Middle East, proved hugely effective. Later, Islamists like Hajj Amin al-Husseini, the Mufti of Jerusalem who spent the war in Berlin urging the Nazis to conquer Palestine and exterminate its Jews, helped fuse Nazi ideas with Islamic religious language to create a new form. Among Islamists, slaughtering Jews is now presented as a religious duty of resistance to the 'corrupters of the world'. As Christopher Hitchens says: 'It is a moral idiot who thinks that anti-Semitism is a threat only to Jews. The history of civilization demonstrates something rather different: Judaeophobia is an unfailing prognosis of barbarism and collapse.' It hardly seems fair to blame the modern Church for the ravings of a bin Laden or Ahmadinejad, but traces of the original source code lead all the way back to Rome and its Ghetto.

It is hard now to picture the Ghetto as it was. After liberation in 1870, most of its ramshackle slums were replaced by spacious new buildings. In 1905, the grand new synagogue replaced the five earlier ones that had to be squashed into the single permitted building. But in 1836 a study had reported that nearly half the Ghetto's Jews 'languish in the clutches of untold misery. Tiny, fetid rooms house eight or twelve people, built in such a way that they lack any air, and light shines in only from the door [. . .] and only a little fireplace allows those miserable souls a glimmer of light at night'. Cholera struck frequently. As James Carroll says in *Constantine's Sword*, a history of Christian anti-Semitism: 'For three hundred years, the keeper of the keys of the Jews' first and, until modern times, last and most squalid concentration camp was the keeper of the keys of St Peter.'

Controversy has swirled around the question of whether Pope Pius XII did enough to protect Jews during the Holocaust. Historian David Kertzer argues that this is not the key question, because by the time the Second World War started the die was already cast and there was little any pope could have done. He looked instead at the role of earlier popes who helped promote Jew hatred in the preceding decades. When the Church sought to absolve itself with *We Remember*, Kertzer plunged into the Vatican archives to find the other side of the story. He emerged with a damning verdict in his book *The Popes Against the Jews*: 'physical elimination of the Jews of Europe came at the end of a long road [. . .] a road that the Catholic Church did a great deal to help build.' The book shows how high-level Church officials, including popes, promoted fear and hatred of Jews in large part as a reaction to what had happened to Rome's Jews. Throughout the nineteenth century the Roman Ghetto became symbolic of the struggle for and against modernity. Brief moments of revolution (in 1798, 1809, 1848) would be followed by long periods of reaction. Every time secularists, democrats or radicals deposed the Pope, they immediately tore down the Ghetto walls and freed the Jews. And each time the Pope returned to power, he immediately locked the Jews up again. When papal temporal power was swept away forever in 1870 by the new Italian state, the popes blamed the Jews for their defeat. Vatican officials supported blood-libel allegations and backed the campaign against Dreyfus in France. The Vatican's newspaper *L'Osservatore Romano* and the Jesuit paper *La Civiltà Cattolica* played particularly ugly roles. At the height of the Dreyfus case, *L'Osservatore* was denouncing 'the Jewish race [. . .] the deicide people, wandering throughout the world, [which] brings with it everywhere the pestiferous breath of treason'. In the fourteenth century, notes Kertzer, popes had protected the Jews from accusations of the Black Death. By the late nineteenth, the Vatican itself was the source of such wild conspiracy theories. The deadliest of these, *The Protocols of the Elders of Zion*, the 'warrant for genocide' fabricated by the tsarist secret police, received top-level Church support, with popes honouring their Italian and French publishers.

The Church is now committed to good relations with the Jews, but things can still get tricky. For all the gains of the last fifty years, the Church sends mixed messages, like deciding to make a saint of an anti-Semitic pope, reviving a prayer calling for Jewish conversion, or readmitting a previously excommunicated far-right sect whose members include a Holocaust-denying bishop. This sort of thing makes Jews nervous, as does the ongoing battle between liberal and conservative Catholics. Might mainstream Catholicism one day want to turn its back on Vatican II? 'There are days when I'm more optimistic and some days when I'm more pessimistic,' says the liberal Catholic theologian John Pawlikowski. He notes that the leadership of the Church has become more conservative and liberal interpretations of Vatican II are increasingly disputed. The Church gives the impression of 'praying out of two sides of its mouth'. Ed Kessler, who runs an institute promoting dialogue between Muslims, Christians and Jews, is more optimistic: 'I don't think Vatican II is in danger of being overturned at all. There's been a profound and absolute revolution. If you look at the last ten years you can say there are bumps in the road; but judged over 1,500 years Catholic–Jewish relations are remarkably positive. There is a clear acknowledgement that anti-Semitism is a sin. There's no question about that now. A generation or two ago even the idea that Jesus was Jewish would have caused consternation in the churches. Now it's accepted.'

The papal knight and Jewish philanthropist Sir Sigmund Sternberg, who has done as much as any living person to improve relations, takes a nuanced view: 'Yes, there are setbacks, but the progress from Vatican II has been remarkable and there's no going back. Many Catholics still think the Jews "killed Christ". Of course no cardinal will say it now but it's there among ordinary people. It's a lack of education and this is changing slowly. Things are going forwards.'

Sometimes even the worst stereotypes can be deployed in a good cause. In the early nineties Sternberg helped defuse the toxic Christian–Jewish dispute over Carmelite nuns who had set up a convent at Auschwitz. At the crucial point only one man was blocking a settlement: Cardinal Józef Glemp, head of the Catholic Church in Poland. 'Cardinal Glemp didn't like the Jews very much,' Sternberg recalls. 'And the Jews wouldn't meet him because of that. But I went to meet him. He thought Jews control the media and run the world, so I said to him: "You're absolutely right. The Jews are very important people. We run the world. It's very tiring, you know, but someone has to do it." I said this to him. And we became friends.' Sternberg assured Glemp he could get him favourable press coverage if the convent were moved. He then frantically phoned the religious affairs editor of *The Times* in London, who happened to be an old mate, and managed to persuade him to ditch a hostile piece about Glemp and write something nice instead. Later, Sternberg invited Glemp to lunch at a Jewish religious and cultural centre in an old school. 'He said, "Nice Jewish home, this is." He thought we lived there! Why should I tell him otherwise?

So now he thinks I'm really one of the people who run the world. And we're still friends. We're friends to this day. We send each other Christmas cards.' Sternberg was also instrumental in persuading John Paul II to visit the main synagogue in Rome. 'I was talking to a cardinal who told me the Pope often asked his driver to stop his car outside the synagogue so he could say a prayer to bless the Jews. I said: "There's no need for the Pope to bless the Jews from the outside. He should come and visit. It will be much better." Then came the great day itself. 'The Pope gave a good speech and called the Jews "our elder brother". He hugged the Chief Rabbi. Afterwards the Pope asked me what I thought of it. I said: "You are 2,000 years too late. You should have come 2,000 years ago and it would have saved a lot of life." '

XXVI: The Artichoke

Everyone has their particular way of cooking them, each enriched by family lore and nostalgia. According to the writer Bruna Tedeschi, the best time for *cimaroli*, the most authentic of Roman artichokes, is March and April. The vegetables are cleaned with water and lemon, then cut with a special round knife to keep their roundness. They are then dressed with salt and pepper and subjected to two rounds of frying: first on its side, then upright. The aim is to get the artichoke to open like a sunflower. As soon as the heart is soft enough to insert a wooden toothpick you know the artichoke is done. Tedeschi recalls life as a child just after the war when Rome's surviving Jews came out of hiding and resumed life in the impoverished city. Her mother was a fine cook and their house in Trastevere was always full of friends and relatives. Her mother had a special way of preparing the artichoke. 'We cut them with a very sharp knife into a "rose". Nowadays there's a special little knife you use only for artichokes but at that time there wasn't a special artichoke knife. It was a proper art to get rid of the hardest parts.' Her mother used to go every day to the market at Piazza San Cosimato. After the war it sold potatoes, chestnuts and powdered egg. Gradually it came back to life and became what it had been before the war – one of the main markets selling a big choice of products coming from the roman countryside. The family had no fridge but an 'ice box', cooled by ice bought each day from a man who came every morning. 'When I could I would go with mum to the market, so I learned to recognize the freshest produce and their quality and also learned to pick the right quantity of food. My dad was quite demanding at table. He knew fish very well, often coming back with lots of nice fresh things to prepare. And mum liked cooking very much, having inherited the passion from her family. Which was then handed down to us daughters.'

XXVII: The Spiral

'How kind you are, Mr Winner'

Pope John Paul II

As my Uncle Paul can attest, Pope John Paul II's many qualities included a gift for the deadly one-liner. Paul has a lovable artistic habit. Wherever he is and whatever the occasion, he takes out his drawing pad and records the scene in little pen-and-ink sketches. Over the years this has earned him compliments, friends, and even a few exhibitions. But it didn't entirely impress the Holy Father. A few years back, Paul found himself part of a delegation of the Council of Christians and Jews granted an audience at the Vatican. Naturally, Paul sat at the back of the room drawing and, when time came for his personal introduction, he offered his little sketch. The Pope regarded Paul for a moment, studied the drawing briefly, then, with a twinkle, gestured around the magnificently decorated room. 'How kind you are, Mr Winner,' he said slowly. 'But, as you see, we already have art in the Vatican.'

Yes, Vatican City does have a bit of art. So much of the stuff, and of such importance that UNESCO designated every inch of the place a World Heritage site. And if you spend a day walking round the city-in-itself Vatican Museums you'll likely be so overwhelmed by marbles, paintings and ancient religious artefacts that by the time you stagger to the spiral exit staircase you'll be in no mood to appreciate one of the very best bits: the spiral exit staircase.

This strange and fabulous sweeping, ramp-like double helix was built in 1932 by the Turin architect Giuseppe Momo. It mediates, as they say. One swirl goes up, the other goes down. (It used to be both entrance *and* exit but the in part is now out of action.) Physically, the stairway stands between the museum, the street and the giant walls around the Vatican. Conceptually, modernity and tradition meet here, as do sacred and profane. More obscurely, it evokes an era of technological change, when swirly pasta shapes and ice cream symbolized all that was sparkly and new. Perhaps most intriguingly, although the reputation of the staircase is surprisingly slight, it may have inspired the most important building in America.

Momo rose to fame in his native Turin either side of the First World War, building villas, factories and workshops. These combined classicism with new technology. The Vatican noticed him when he won a competition for a seminary in Umbria and, after that, employed him to design seminaries all round Italy. By the late twenties he was Pope Pius XI's favourite architect and, after the signing of the Concordat, was handed the plumb job of designing Vatican City. On the down side, Momo cooperated with Marcello Piacentini, Mussolini's favourite architect, on the Via della Conciliazione, the triumphal avenue bulldozed through a mediaeval district from the edge of the Tiber to St Peter's Square. This rather mucked up and diminished Bernini's original concept whereby the impact of the huge square was enhanced by approaching it through narrow little streets. But never mind. Momo also created the governor's palace, the Lateran University, the railway station, and the Palazzo delle Sacre Congregazioni. But it's the stunning entrance and exit to the Vatican Museums that reverberated.

When Momo built his stairs the bitter conflict between modernism and traditional values had scarcely abated since the late nineteenth century. The Vatican still regarded itself, in architecture as everything else, as the guardian of tradition. And the Pope had insisted that the new buildings of the Vatican should reflect traditional classical values. Yet they could hardly fail to be influenced by modernity. Industrialization had come later to Italy than it had to Britain, Germany and France, but now all Rome was affected. New refrigeration technology made possible the ice-cream marvels of Giovanni Fassi's Palazzo del Freddo. The new pasta factories, such as the Pastificio Cerere in San Lorenzo, employed impressive modern machinery to extrude and cut pasta into a bewildering variety of new shapes: stars, teardrops, saws, tubes, circles, butterflies, spirals. And in and around the Holy See, Giuseppe Momo, who was an engineer as much as an architect, deployed cutting-edge methods and materials such as reinforced concrete.

As architecture historian Guido Montanari explains, Momo's stairs fused history with his own originality and ended up as a potent Italian example of modernity. Looking back, Momo clearly drew heavily on the double-spiral stairs (one going up, one going down) of the famous St Patrick's Well built in Orvieto by Antonio da Sangallo for the sixteenth-century Pope Clement VII. More intriguingly, with its spiral walkway, great glass skylight and museum setting, Momo's staircase anticipated Frank Lloyd Wright's Guggenheim Museum in New York, built twenty-seven years later, in 1959. Of course the spiral is a naturally occurring shape. And the Guggenheim is a bigger, more developed and better building. Even so, the similarities do seem astonishing.

The Guggenheim isn't just renowned as one of the great architectural works of the twentieth century. It's a *modernist* masterpiece. And this may explain why the connection is not better known. The Guggenheim's revolutionary design changed architecture. And when Wright was asked about his inspiration he said the idea came to him from study-ing the shape of ancient Assyrian ziggurats. Some scholars, however, have argued Wright must owe some sort of debt to the Vatican. In obscure corners of the internet, Wright has even been accused of plagiarism. In 1992, Peter Blake, the American architect, critic and former editor of *Architectural Forum* who admired Wright, had interviewed him and writ-ten a book about him, wrote an article recalling the shock he experienced when he visited the Vatican in the early 1960s. 'When I walked into Giuseppe Momo's Entrance Hall that day,' wrote Blake, 'I nearly fainted – and not only because I thought it was a stunning space. For what [Momo] had designed, some thirty years before Frank Lloyd Wright built the Guggenheim, was the prototype of the Museum we all know so well – a tall, cylindrical space, lined with a spiral coil of ramps, and topped by a huge, octagonal skylight divided by radial mullions. In short, he had, for all intents and purposes, designed the Guggenheim!'

There were of course 'some differences'. Momo's space is only half as large as the volume of the Guggenheim spiral; the Momo ramp is actually an ingeniously coiled double helix rather than the Guggenheim's single spiral. Moreover, the Momo ramps are stepped. Its parapets are faced with bronze. The skylights are slightly different, too. The Guggenheim's skylight is twelve-sided; Momo's octagonal. Wright cleverly reversed the spiral curve in the Guggenheim to accommodate elevators, giving visitors a point of reference at every level. Still, said Blake,

> the Momo Spiral Hall is a brilliant job, and deserves much more credit than it has ever received. After I saw it some thirty years ago, I wrote a paragraph or two for the Architectural Forum describing Momo's remarkable prototype; but my academic betters, who tend to read only their own profundities, apparently failed to take notice [. . .] No one would suggest that Wright was a plagiarist. But the fact is that he spent much time in Rome between the two World Wars, usually with assorted lady friends, and he certainly visited the Museums of the Vatican on numerous occasions. All of us know that architects tend to stash away images and impressions in their private memory vaults, and trot them out if and when the occasion arises – often not at all aware of where and when they encountered the original image. Still, the details of the Guggenheim skylight, for example (and some of the Guggenheim's other details), are so obviously derived from the Vatican Spiral that Signor Momo deserves equal billing – or almost equal billing.

One may search in vain at the Vatican Museum for a reference to the Guggenheim. And when the Guggenheim celebrated its fiftieth birthday, in 2009, with an exhibition about its creator, there was no reference to Giuseppe Momo either. So why is the connection not better known? The reason may be simple embarrassment. Neither side were keen to claim the link – for ideological reasons. The Vatican never wanted to claim credit because the Guggenheim Museum was a controversial (almost aggressive) symbol of an aggressively secular spirituality and modernism. And in New York, Wright and his champions weren't too keen to develop theories of a link either because they preferred to see Wright as a self-made American modernist genius. And Romans have so many other architectural and artistic treasures to boast about, the wider significance of Momo's creation has never been more than a blip on their radar. Yet the fact appears to remain: the architectural masterpiece hailed as one of the greatest, most important and most original ever built in America looks as if it was based on a Vatican original.

XXVIII: The Coffee Cup

'Not in the healthy oyster, but rather in the sick, does the
fisherman seek for pearls'

Stendhal, *Rome, Naples and Florence*, 1817

It was touch and go as to whether coffee would be allowed
in Italy. By the late sixteenth century the dark brew with
strangely stimulating properties had reached the peninsula
from Turkey and Catholic scholars were getting worried.
When vendors started selling the stuff on the streets in
Venice officials of the Inquisition referred the matter to
the Vatican. Coffee, they feared, was 'the bitter invention
of Satan' and 'Satan's latest trap to catch Christian souls'.
Some even argued that the ritualized drinking of a hot black
liquid amounted to an infidel-derived perversion of the
Eucharist. Pope Clement VIII was vigorously urged to ban
coffee. Before issuing his ruling, however, he asked to taste
the controversial cup. To everyone's surprise, he liked it.
'This Satan's drink is delicious!' he declared. 'It would be a
pity to let the infidels have exclusive use of it. We shall fool
Satan by baptizing it.' Clement's moral judgement was not
always *impeccabile*. He was, after all, the man who had the
great philosopher Giordano Bruno burned alive for heresy.

But for the correct functioning of his taste buds we should all be grateful. Without Clement we would never have had the Antico Caffè Greco. And that would have been a pity.

The Via Condotti is famous now for its clothing brands. But Caffè Greco at number 86 has become a national monument. Along with the Florian in Venice and the Procope in Paris, the Greco is one of the oldest cafés in Europe. Named for its Greek founder, Nicola della Maddalena, it opened some time before 1750 and can claim as many famous patrons over a longer period as any literary café anywhere. The artist Giorgio de Chirico used to come here every morning to drink cappuccino. The Greco, he said, was 'the only place where you can sit and wait until the end of the world'. Other regulars included Goethe, Casanova, Tennyson, Tsar Paul I, the future Pope Leo XIII, King Ludwig of Bavaria, Hans Christian Andersen, Ralph Waldo Emerson, Nathaniel Hawthorne ... (pause and gulp for breath) ... Marconi, Toscanini, Schopenhauer, Liszt, Wagner, Shelley, Thackeray, Twain, Heine, Byron, Bizet, Berlioz ... and Buffalo Bill. To think of the chat this place must have witnessed on almost any subject ever makes me giddy. And from his expression I see that Orson Welles agrees with me. He too was once a star attraction. Young bearded and majestic, he's been staring at me for a while now from near the back of a group photograph taken in the late 1940s. Others in the picture include Carlo Levi and Alberto Moravia.

In the late eighteenth and nineteenth centuries, the French, English and Germans all had their own meeting rooms here, and took turns to dominate the place. At first the Germans were pre-eminent with a literary circle centred on Goethe, who lived not far away on the Via del Corso. In the early eighteen hundreds, the English took over after they switched allegiance from the old English Coffee House in Piazza di Spagna. Byron had a room on one side of the square and Keats lived his last three months in a little room on the other, beside the Spanish Steps. Both were barely 100 metres from the Caffè. In the 1830s it was the turn of the French, the Greco being handy for the Academie Française. Mid-century, the Germans came again. Not everyone has always been charmed. French historian Hippolyte Taine called the Greco 'a long rather low room in no way elegant or resplendent'. Mendelssohn damned it as 'a dark little room'. And the view of Hector Berlioz barely rose above insult: 'ghastly tavern', he called it, 'the most odious place imaginable'. In his time the tiny wooden tables were covered in grease and the air was thick with cheap cigar smoke. Greco was known for being dark, dirty, crowded and noisy, especially in winter. Yet it was indispensable as both *poste restante* and an expat meeting point. A century later, by the late 1940s, the place was still dingy but Edmund Wilson found the manner in which the owners had begun to play up the past glories of the place 'cloying'.

These days the café is a tad decorous and expensive for my taste. It is long, thin and divided into a series of elegant little rooms, each decorated with faded gilt mirrors, eight-eenth-century landscapes, and portraits of famous patrons. In its heyday this was a raucous, chaotic place. Now it is unduly quiet, full of slightly overawed tourists and wait-ers in waistcoats and black ties. In fact, with its great age and random accretion of resonances the Antico Caffè has become quite a good metaphor for the entire city: a charm-ing old museum in which one drinks coffee. Curiously, the café is also noted for having invented one of the essential accoutrements of espresso. In 1806, during the Napoleonic

Wars, imports from the East were cut off by the British so the price of coffee rocketed. Other *botteghe del caffè* stayed in business using cheap substitutes like chestnuts, barley and chickpeas. But Salvioni, owner of the Greco, had a better idea. He continued to serve top-grade coffee, but in tiny cups of his own design, and charged his customers double. Thus was invented the espresso cup.

On my first visit to the Greco, much as I was sugared and stirred by the literary ghosts, I was also frustrated by the impossibility of communing with any of them. Isn't the fantasy of indulging in imaginative time-slippage the whole point of such a place? On my second visit I got a little luckier and found myself in the company of Marie-Henry, a leathery old Frenchman with a strangely intimate knowledge of the city in the old days.

I return to the room with the Orson Welles photo and pick a table under the big mirror. I know it's not really done in mid-afternoon, but I order a cappuccino and a double macchiato for my friend. Marie-Henry seems strikingly intelligent, displays a piercing curiosity about everything and has an appealingly old-fashioned way with words. It's a little fusty in here, but I'd almost say he looks old enough to be yellowing around the edges. He doesn't look old or battered enough but he insists he was in Russia during the war with the Man himself. Got cold, made it all the way to Moscow. But he doesn't want to talk about that today. No. He'd much rather chat about Rome. Suits me. He's pompous and snobbish, and not the least interested in answering questions, but no one could accuse him of being dull. In the spirit of the café I decide to just lean back on the velvet sofa and let him tell me stuff, which he does, unstoppably. Exquisitely formed sentences cascade from his elegant frame. His monologue becomes so interesting I start taking notes. Every now and then I glance up, adjust my position and look into his kind, round face for clues to his personality, but I find none. He's wearing a dark, old-fashioned suit and has a curious comb-over hairstyle to cover his bald patch. At the peripheries of his face the hair on his head merges with that of his moustache-free beard to give the effect of a furry balloon. He says he's been travelling around Italy and Caffè Greco has always been one of his haunts; though frankly he preferred the Caffè Nuovo, but it's not here any more. I fancy he looks sad when I tell him that other old favourites like the Cracas bookshop and Trattoria Armellino have closed as well. He used to get a magnificent dinner at Armellino's for three francs, he says. 'That must have been quite a while ago?' I venture. He seems not to hear.

What emerges immediately is that Marie-Henry is not a big fan of the Church. He also likes to observe and pass judgement on all layers of Roman society. He is intrigued, for example, by the rivalries between various Catholic orders. At the moment Capuchins and Dominicans hate the Jesuits, apparently. He wonders why so much energy is wasted on snobbery and petty rivalries. And while we're on the subject, have I noticed how many young men around the city are fat? And all the aristocrats are morons? And how music and love are the staple topics of conversation? Actually I hadn't noticed any of these things. But on he plunges, waspish, opinionated and generous all at the same time. Ordinary Romans are the finest people in Italy. They have the greatest 'strength of character', 'deepest simplicity' and the most intelligence. He loves their appreciation of wit and humour too. 'I doubt there is any race in Europe with a greater fondness for the bite and ingenuity of satire.'

His greatest passion seems to be for performance art of all kinds, whether on stage or in a church. And he's quite the expert on the history of opera and theatre. The only problem in Rome is that the opera is second-rate, not just compared to Naples, Venice or Milan, but everywhere, especially in the north. I mean, he was thrilled to get a box at the Teatro Argentina for the Rossini season. But when he finally saw their *Tancredi* it was *nauseating*! 'As a performance it would have been *hunted off the stage* in Brescia or Bologna!' The orchestra was more dismal than the singers and the dancing had to be seen to be believed. Yet all the Romans in the audience thought it was brilliant. Why was that? 'Here, all is decadence, all is memory, all is dead!' At least there was no mistreatment of the audience, though. Come again? Well, when he went to the Teatro Valle he arrived early and found himself studying the old police regulations and you can't imagine how draconian they were. It seems that audiences were behaving badly and were very rude. So the Governor of Rome threatened 100 strokes of the cane for taking another person's seat, five years in the galleys for raising your voice to an usher. Such punishments were to be carried out in accordance with the procedures of the Inquisition. You know what, Marie-Henry? I think you're making that up. No, he says, it's perfectly true. He promises to get hold of a copy to prove it.

Meanwhile, he tells me, in the early nineteenth century, papal censorship was so suffocating that the conventional live theatre in Rome became unwatchable. But interesting stuff happened in improvised marionette shows performed in tiny theatres such as the old Fiano, not far from here. The audiences were so quick and the puppeteers so skilful, they could get away with mockery that would land less sophisticated performers in jail. One staple character was a ludicrous old bachelor called Cassandrino. Nothing about his clothes or name suggested he was connected to the Church, yet the audience clearly understood him to be a cardinal. To see such a man humiliated, say, in his romantic pursuit of a girl forty years his junior, would have an audience whooping and crying with laughter and delight. While Marie-Henry usually mocks the Church, he quite likes seeing it up close. Thanks to a couple of artist friends from Bologna, he recently wangled a prime seat at the traditional papal Mass at the Sistine Chapel, sitting in the middle of a group of cardinals. Even more remarkably, he saw and heard the fabled *castrati* of the Sistine choir. I'm jealous! That must have fantastic. 'Excruciating.' Really? 'Never in all my days did I endure so demonic a caterwauling!' The choir was so bad, he says, he tried distract himself from the noise by looking up at Michelangelo's *Last Judgement* on the ceiling, and studying the faces of the cardinals around him. What did you make of them? His verdict: 'Simple-souled.' And most of them looked ill. Which is not the impression you get of cardinals from TV. On the other hand, he spent two surprisingly pleasurable hours at a service at the Jesuit church near the Piazza Venezia. It sounded hair-raising to me. The congregation was so rough-looking that soldiers with fixed bayonets guarded the side chapels while others patrolled the nave. The music, though – with organs in different parts of the church responding to one another – was 'decidedly agreeable'. As I take all this in tourists chatter and clatter around us. Black-clad waiters hover. I feel I should order another coffee.

Even so, continues my new friend, there's no denying the power of Church spectacle. For example, he was impressed in August by a ceremony at St Peter's. The Pope, wearing all-white silk, came out and distributed blessings among the crowd. 'This was one of the most impressive spectacles I have ever seen.' A few days later it was even better. The streets around the Vatican were specially cleaned and buildings draped with banners. In the Square itself stands had been set up for paying spectators in front of the colonnades and my new friend looked out over a sea of faces of people who all believed the Pontiff could decide their eternal happiness or damnation. Then the procession started. First up were the monks in brown, black and white habits, carrying 'monstrous' flaming torches. They were obviously trying to impress the crowd through their sheer 'abject humility'. But the humble way they cast down their eyes down while braying hymns was rather undermined by the expressions of contempt flashing from their eyes. Then the clergy of Rome's seven great basilicas appeared, each group carrying scarlet-and-yellow banners and with little bells rung at one minute intervals. Then came the cardinals, all wearing high-pointed hats, and the crowd genuflected. Finally the Pope himself appeared, a pale, inanimate, proud figure swathed in draperies of the richest, rarest stuff. Marie-Henry heard a child nearby complaining to his mother: 'You never told me that the Pope was dead.' This conveyed perfectly 'the utter and motionless fixity of this unearthly apparition'. Yet at that very moment there wasn't a single unbeliever in the great crowd –including himself. Really? 'If beauty may be counted a religion.' Ha ha. Yes, I see what you mean.

Look, I say, your audience might be rude, and the authorities a bit mad. But at least they all *care*. Does anyone care now? I wrote a piece a couple of years ago about how opera in Italy was basically dying. Once upon a time it was as raucously popular as football. Every town of note used to have an opera house. Now just the biggest thirteen are left. The standard of education is very low. Berlusconi has been incredibly hostile. Funding has been cut. Television and radio don't even support opera much any more. Several experts told me that opera can survive only by appealing to a rich elite. Luciano Berio said Italians used to listen to Rossini or Verdi and it was as if they were 'holding hands in the darkness' but that was all gone. And he was speaking in 1989. Then again, there are some optimists. Do you know Mario Martone? Terrific young director, I explain. Lots of social theatre here at Ostiense. From Naples originally. Part of the group around Paolo Sorrentino and Toni Servillo who did *Il Divo* and *Consequences of Love* together. Marie-Henry doesn't really keep up with such things. Well, anyway, Martone is more optimistic. He says Italian opera must go back to its 'true path', its roots. I've got the quote somewhere. Shall I read it to you? He said:

Our idea of opera is a bit false. Before we can talk about economic, political or structural problems, we must first deal with this confusion. Opera is theatre with music. But above all it is *theatre*. Mozart and Verdi knew nothing about recordings. They never imagined people would only *listen*. For them, the life of their operas was on stage. We lost this and it was a very serious break. Opera is our national theatre. The British have Shakespeare. We have Verdi and Puccini. The operas of Mozart and Verdi were simpler than we imagine. So I want to return opera to its true path. Opera is something of life, for the people. We need to work a long time in this way, but it is not impossible to revive opera. Opera is not dead.

Interesting, no?

But Marie-Henry doesn't seem to have heard a word I've said. He's gazing past the front counter of the café, through the window at the bustling shapes in the street. 'You really love Rome, don't you?' I say. He gets wistful. Yes, when he's in a nostalgic mood part of him just wants to be here forever. Then he remembers how the atmosphere of the city steals away strength of spirit and plunges the mind into a sort of languid torpor. In Rome, he says, energy is without purpose. Anyway, he doesn't like the architecture. 'With the solitary exception of St Peter's, nothing could be drearier than the architecture of modern Rome.' He doesn't even like St Peter's, because it's vain. He reckons the money it cost to build would have been better spent on reclaiming marsh-land or giving land to the poor. So something isn't good just because it looks good? 'Not in the healthy oyster, but rather in the sick, does the fisherman seek for pearls,' he declares. 'I have learned to despair of art.' He suddenly looks old, distant. Abruptly he says he has to leave. I tell him I've really enjoyed his company. What's your name again? 'Marie-Henry Beyle,' he says. Well, it was lovely to meet you. I'll be here again tomorrow. Will you be here? 'I never leave.'

XXIX: Not the End

'Sprinkle my ashes with pure wine and fragrant oil of spikenard: Bring balsam, too, Stranger, with crimson roses. Tearless, my urn enjoys unending spring. I have not died, but changed my state.'

Ausonius. *Epitaph from the Tomb of a Happy Man*

Beneath the streets the car parks lurk, and sometimes they open the way to mysteries. Over the last few years, in a futile attempt to solve Rome's chronic traffic congestion, cavernous underground concrete chambers have been carved all over the city, especially in the suburbs. Not even the Vatican has been immune. In the year of the Jubilee, the Pope blessed a new five-storey, 900-space car park under the Gianicolo Hill; but 'God's Garage', as it was called, did not solve the Vatican's parking problems. In 2003, therefore, construction work began on yet another car park, this time under the walls of Vatican City itself. This yielded a remarkable discovery. Some time during the reign of the emperor Nero a landslide had covered part of a necropolis, one of the many that ringed the ancient city. Long forgotten, the place had escaped looting by tomb-robbers. Archaeologists were amazed by what they found. It was, said Giandomenico

Spinola, head of the Vatican Museums' classical-antiquities department, the equivalent of 'a little Pompeii'. Never before had the physical evidence of Ancient Rome's relationship with its dead been preserved in such vivid detail.

Plans for the car park were ditched and work began to turn the place into a museum instead. The unearthed necropolis had been part of a much larger city of the dead laid out beside the ancient Via Triumphalis. Not only were tombs of the wealthy preserved, but also simpler burial places of middle- and lower-class Romans. Some tombs contained ornate altars. One sarcophagus was of a young knight depicted in a statue with his hands stretched in prayer. Dionysus appeared in a black-and-white floor mosaic. Among numerous intact skeletons was that of a young boy buried beside a hen's egg. Most intriguing of all were the terracotta pipes found attached to graves and urns. Evidence of such pipes has been found at other Ancient Roman grave sites as far apart as Tunisia and Britain. In and near Rome such tubes, sometimes also made of lead, were remains at Ostia and even near the 'tomb of St Peter' under the Vatican. The modern technical term ascribed to these objects provides the clue to their function. They are called 'libation tubes'. Grieving relatives would once have used them to pour honey, milk and wine directly to the corpse or ashes of their loved ones. Or, to put it another way, these tubes fed the dead.

And just why did dead people need to eat? Franz Cumont, the great Belgian historian and archaeologist of the early twentieth century, touched on the answer in his *After Life in Roman Paganism*. Romans, he said, shared the belief of other ancient peoples that the dead continued to remain somehow alive in the tomb. 'The primitive man, disconcerted by death, cannot persuade himself that the being who moved, felt, willed, as he does, can be suddenly deprived of all his faculties [. . .] The most ancient and the crudest idea is that the corpse itself keeps some obscure sensitiveness which it cannot manifest. It is imagined to be in a state like sleep. The vital energy which animated the body is still attached to it and cannot exist without it.' A complex web of ritual evolved to make sure the living and the less living could stay in touch with one another. 'The dead were not then cut off from the society of the living; the connection between them and their surroundings was not broken; the continuity between the hour which preceded and that which followed their decease was not interrupted.'

Around Rome, cities of the dead were set beside busy roads. This helped to stop the dead from feeling too lonely. Cumont suggests something even stranger: the dead were put close to the bustle of daily life in order that they might no longer think themselves *as dead*. He cites numerous inscriptions carved on tombs in which the departed call out to the living, and even chat with them. 'I see and I gaze upon all who go and come from and to the city' says the inscription of a man called Lollius. Lollius hopes strangers will stop by his tomb and say, 'Good day, Lollius.' In some inscriptions the dead one-sidedly console loved ones or pass on wisdom. Others are written as dialogue. 'May the earth be light on you!' says one to a passer-by (the dead were said to feel the weight of the grave), to which the dead man, Fabianus, replies: 'Fare you well in the upper world [. . .] and may the gods be propitious to you, travellers, and to you who stop by Fabianus! Go and come safe and sound! May you who crown me with garlands or throw me flowers live for many years!' Borrowing from the Etruscans, Romans imagined tombs as houses where the dead lived. Such monuments were designed to be as elegant and comfy as possible. The tombs of the rich had frescoes, stucco and mosaics and stone beds for eternal sleep. Objects the deceased had used in life were placed alongside the remains. Soldiers would be buried with weapons and pieces of armour, women with toiletries, children with favourite toys.

By far the most important connection with life, however, was food. Tombs came equipped with utensils for cooking, and vessels for eating and drinking. In her classic study *Death and Burial in the Roman World*, Jocelyn Toynbee tells us that the rich left money in their wills to provide for 'bread, wine and grapes, cakes, sausages, ceremonial meals thought of as shared by the living with the dead'. Indeed, eating at the grave became the key act in the cult of the dead. All through the year, funerary banquets, often noisy and cheerful, were consumed in the tomb by friends and family. Big tombs had dining rooms and kitchens, while in smaller ones the top of the sarcophagus might be used as a dining table. Such feasting began on the day of the funeral with the *Silicernium* meal, after which food might also be left at the tomb for the dead – though it was often eaten by the hungry poor. Nine days after the funeral came another feast: the *cena novendialis*, which marked the formal end of mourning. But grave meals continued through the years. Birthdays of the dead were particularly important, as was the *Parentalia* festival in February. On such occasions mourners were expected to share food with the departed by dripping milk, honey and wine down the libation tubes.

Nourishing the dead had a dark side. After all, if spirits could feel the same emotions as the living might they not be prone to anger and cruelty? Cumont takes the point to its logical end-point: 'Those whose humours have dried, whose mouths have withered, are tortured by the need to refresh their parched lips. It therefore is not enough to place in the tombs the drinks and dishes [...] by periodic sacrifices the *Manes* must be supplied with fresh food also.' You can already guess what kind of food they liked best. The dead sometimes asked for water to quench their thirst, but above all they were 'eager for the warm blood of victims'. Sacrifices were most often of animals, but sometimes they were human. When future-emperor Augustus captured Perugia from Mark Antony's brother in the year 40 BC he had 300 men of the city slaughtered at an altar to Julius Caesar on the anniversary of Caesar's assassination. Such murders were linked to old religious tradition: gladiator-fighting, designed to drench the soil in blood, began as part funeral of ceremonies for the rich and powerful. Food could also be used in exorcism-like ceremonies against troublesome ghosts. Toynbee describes how hungry and unpleasant spirits called *Lemures* were driven off with black beans: 'At midnight the worshipper made a sign with his thumb in the middle of his forehead, washed his hands in clean spring water, turned, took black beans and threw them away with averted face, saying nine times "These I cast, with these I redeem me and mine." The ghosts were thought to gather the beans and follow unseen behind the worshipper, who then touched water, clashed bronze, and asked the ghosts to leave the house.'

Banquets with the dead, however, were genial affairs, held at night with tombs lit by torches and decorated with roses and violets. These feasts were intended to be jolly, even boisterous, not unlike a modern Irish wake. One dead man, via his will, urges his friends to refresh themselves at his tomb 'without quarrelling'. Another tells his relatives: 'Come in good health for the feast and rejoice together.' A third leaves instructions for his burial vault to be equipped with a bed with fine coverings and cushions for his guests. Nothing, comments Cumont, could be further from modern ideas about the importance of quiet holiness in modern graveyards than the conviviality of the Roman cult of the departed: 'among the guests crowned with flowers, the drinks went round and soon produced a noisy intoxication'. The fact that diners knew they would one day take part as the corpse gave the event an extra piquancy. According to the American historian Regina Gee, dining with the dead 'was a dynamic performance enacted to articulate and fix proper relationships between the living and the dead' and part of the process of 'separation, transition, and transformation'. Until the Church put a stop to funeral feasts, they were hugely popular. On festival days, the *necropolei* swelled with the living as Romans travelled out of the city necropolises to eat in or near their beloved dead. These banquets were 'the key ritual action for the transformation of the dead from polluted body to sanctified ancestor'. Not everyone, though, was convinced that eating and drinking was possible in the afterlife. 'I shall not drink when I am dead,' says one epitaph. 'By wetting my ashes with wine you will make mud.'

Acknowledgements

Writing this book would have been impossible without the help and encouragement of everyone quoted in the text. My particular gratitude goes to: Valeria Vallucci, my agent Jane Judd, my editor Mike Jones and everyone else at Simon and Schuster, especially Monica O' Connell, Will Webb, Rory Scarfe, Liane Payne and Colin Midson, Liberato Vallucci, Nadia Iafrate, Anna Avona, Giuseppe Aliprandi, Andrea Piccoli, Alessia Piovanello, Maddalena Del Re, Pier Andrea Canei, Fulvio Abbate, Maurya Simon, Domenica Villa, Ezio Iafrate, Lina Unali, Èlena Mortara, John Heine, Boris Lauser, Ian Rosenfeld, Jonathan Stamp, Simon Martin, Alessia Tuzio, Jennifer Rupp, Alex Gordon, Margaret Brearley, Jennifer Unter, Jan Michael, Fiona Campbell, Paul Winner, Sean Kelly and the staffs at the Libary of the British School at Rome, the British Library, and the Library of the University of Tor Vergata, Rome.